Praise for Griffith REVIEW

'Griffith REVIEW represents "the best game" in journalism, providing quality analysis in an age of diminishing journalistic integrity.' *Walkley Magazine*

'Griffith REVIEW, under the editorship of Julianne Schultz, just keeps getting better and better.'
Australian Book Review

'Griffith REVIEW is a wonderful journal. It's pretty much setting the agenda in Australia and fighting way above its weight…You're mad if you don't subscribe.'
Phillip Adams

'A stalwart of best essays in recent years…arguably the best of all the Australian literary magazines.'
Sydney Morning Herald

'Rigorously intelligent and far from self-satisfied.'
Peter Pierce

'Griffith REVIEW takes academic journalism out of the ivory tower onto the street and into the countryside… a refreshing and invigorating move.' *Courier-Mail*

'The indispensable read for literate Australians.'
Geraldine Brooks

'Absorbing…powerful.' *Weekend Australian*

'One of the few places in Australian media where arguments can be developed and complexity teased out.'
Margaret Simons

SIR SAMUEL GRIFFITH was one of Australia's great early achievers. Twice the premier of Queensland, that state's chief justice and the author of its criminal code, he was best known for his pivotal role in drafting agreements that led to Federation, and as the new nation's first chief justice. He was also an important reformer and legislator, a practical and cautious man of words.

Griffith died in 1920 and is now best remembered in his namesakes: an electorate, a society, a suburb and a university. Ninety-six years after he first proposed establishing a university in Brisbane, Griffith University, the city's second, was created. His commitment to public debate and ideas, his delight in words and art, and his attachment to active citizenship is recognised by the publication that bears his name.

Like Sir Samuel Griffith, Griffith REVIEW is iconoclastic and non-partisan, with a sceptical eye and a pragmatically reforming heart and a commitment to public discussion. Personal, political and unpredictable, it is Australia's best conversation.

GriffithREVIEW25

AFTER THE CRISIS

Edited by Julianne Schultz

GriffithREVIEW25

Cover: *Zero Dollar Bill* by Brian Romero. Brian is a illustrator and photographer based in Los Angeles, California. His work can be viewed at brianromero.com

Griffith REVIEW gratefully acknowledges the support and generosity of founding patron Margaret Mittelheuser.

GriffithREVIEW25 SPRING 2009
GriffithREVIEW is published four times a year by Griffith University
in conjunction with Text Publishing. ISBN 1448-2924

Publisher	Marilyn McMeniman AM
Editor	Julianne Schultz AM
Deputy Editor	Erica Sontheimer
Picture Editor & Production Manager	Paul Thwaites
Associate Editor	David Winter, Text Publishing
Publication & Cover Design	WH Chong & Susan Miller, Text Publishing
Text Publishing	Michael Heyward, Emily Booth, Sarina Gale, Kirsty Wilson, Ed Austin
Proofreader	Sue Jarvis
Administration	Andrea Huynh
Typesetting	Midland Typesetters
Printing	Ligare Book Printers
Distribution	Penguin Australia

GRIFFITH REVIEW
South Bank Campus, Griffith University
PO Box 3370, South Brisbane QLD 4101 Australia
Ph +617 3735 3071 Fax +617 3735 3272
griffithreview@griffith.edu.au www.griffithreview.com

TEXT PUBLISHING
Swann House, 22 William St, Melbourne VIC 3000 Australia
Ph +613 8610 4500 Fax +613 9629 8621
books@textpublishing.com.au www.textpublishing.com.au

SUBSCRIPTIONS
Within Australia: 1 year (4 editions) $99.80 RRP, inc. P&H and GST
Outside Australia: 1 year (4 editions) A$149.80 RRP, inc. P&H
Institutional and bulk rates available on application.

LETTERS TO THE EDITOR
The Editor, Griffith REVIEW, PO Box 3370, South Brisbane QLD 4101 Australia
or email Griffith REVIEW: griffithreview@griffith.edu.au
The Editor reserves the right to edit letters for publication online.

ADVERTISING
Each issue of Griffith REVIEW has a circulation of at least 4,000 copies.
Full-page adverts are available to selected advertisers. To book your advert,
in the first instance please email Griffith REVIEW: griffithreview@griffith.edu.au

CAL | Cultural Fund Griffith REVIEW recieves project sponsorship from Copyright Agency Limited.

Australian Government

Australia | **Council** for the Arts

This project has been assisted by the Australian Government through the Australia Council, its principal arts funding and advisory body.

End of another era

The journey to a sustainable knowledge economy

Julianne Schultz

WHEN thousands of unemployed miners, steel, clothing and textile workers, their friends, families and organisers pushed through the glass doors of Old Parliament House and into Kings Hall on 26 October 1982 shouting 'We want jobs,' it was the end of an era. The protestors were at the sharp end and their anxiety, pain and anger were palpable. Placards demanded the 'right to work'.

At the same time thirty-one of their colleagues were five kilometres underground, occupying a BHP coalmine near Wollongong where 206 men, two-thirds of the workforce, had been made redundant ten days earlier. The well-organised miners broke the routines of traditional industrial action: rather than staying out, the Kemira miners stayed in.

For thirteen days they had made do in the crib room deep underground, journeying to the surface to collect meals and supplies, hug their wives and kids, and then returning to the cramped underground space – a makeshift home, hammocks slung between poles, electricity and ventilation maintained at the order of the Premier. Meanwhile, an inquiry into their future and that of the underground coal industry proceeded above ground.

The miners were the latest to be told that their services were no longer required; a swathe of redundancies had left thousands of people without work, unemployment climbed to postwar highs, gross domestic product fell 4 per cent, trade ground to a standstill. Steel and coal were at the heart of the domestic industrial economy, so they were hit first and hardest – 15,000 people lost their jobs with BHP in the Illawarra alone – but it did not take long for the freeze to chill the whole economy.

This provoked raw, desperate politics, fuelled by class-driven anger. Individuals and their worried families were pitched against company executives who were mystified and governments that seemed helpless. The market deteriorated with unprecedented speed: 'It just came from nowhere, one day we had full order books, the next the orders just stopped, no one was buying here, and no one was buying abroad,' one executive after another told me as I researched the recession and its impact for *Steel City Blues* (Penguin, 1985).

There was great concern about the future, and for all the tentative talk of a service economy, jobs in McDonald's didn't seem to compare with the hard yakka these men and their families had known for generations. The new industries based on education, finance, tourism and hospitality felt intangible and insubstantial. Electronic technology was beginning to transform work processes, but automating mining and steel seemed more like a job destroyer than the creator of interesting new work; uncertainty was widespread.

Few were surprised when a Labor government was elected five months after the storming of Parliament; Bob Hawke's last rally was at the Bulli Showground near Wollongong. Three days after the Canberra protest the miners returned home: they had spent a record sixteen days underground. The action had not got their jobs back, but had tripled their redundancy pay from one week for each year of service to three. It was a victory of sorts. It also marked the end of the dominance of underground mining, and the end of a national economy defined by manufacturing staffed by a unionised workforce.

Just as it took a long time before the legacy of the Great Depression revealed the end of an agricultural economy, the import of the early 1980s transformation, dramatically played out in the Illawarra coalmines and steelworks, took time to crystallise as the end of the industrial era. Yet a year after the Kemira stay-in strike, the reality of the new economic order was there in microcosm: eight of the men were still unemployed, sixteen had travelled to the new open-cut mines in Central Queensland and the Hunter Valley, five were working in the service industry and one was studying.

WITH THIS IN mind, it should scarcely be surprising that until this year, 1982 held the record as the year when Australian shares lost the most value. The link between the share market and the 'real economy' is inextricable. There have been days with more spectacular losses and gains, but 1982 was a watershed in the way that 2009 is likely to become.

The globally connected, technologically enabled economy was born in the ashes of the recession of 1982–83. The pattern was repeated throughout the developed world – technology transformed old industries, squeezing undreamt-of productivity from them, replacing antiquated mills and workplaces with new factories and offices; unionisation plummeted; deregulation reduced costs and increased organisational flexibility; women joined the workforce in unprecedented numbers; and multinational companies explored economies of scale and comparative advantages (resources, labour costs, market size, infrastructure, educational levels) wherever they operated. For Australia it meant services and resources.

That era was captured in Oliver Stone's Oscar-winning *Wall Street,* most often remembered for Gordon Gekko's defining credo: 'Greed is good.' Yet at the heart of the movie was a battle that now seems impossibly old-fashioned – between local enterprises that rewarded workers with secure reasonably paid jobs and clever schemers who could make a quick buck from mergers and acquisitions.

The schemers won. It did not take long before Sydney became one of the global beneficiaries of the new era. The New South Wales government was profoundly shaken by the collapse of manufacturing in 1982, and escalated the exploration of economic alternatives for the state which had already begun in a less urgent, almost ad hoc way.

With the election of the Hawke government and the deregulation of the economy that followed, Sydney, the capital of the Premier State, was well placed to take advantage of the new global order. Within a decade it had been transformed from a raffish, provincial industrial city – where small factories lined the roads to the airport – to a regional financial capital with dark-windowed hire cars zipping along sleek tunnels from the airport. Sydneysiders became accustomed to the income disparities that characterise these cities everywhere.

The process of remaking Sydney, of wresting the crown of business leadership from Melbourne, was incremental. It was not without social cost, but it was a product of a deliberate political strategy informed by shrewd information – especially from advocates of the new global order. Those wanting to create an investment-banking sector in Australia recall with wry amusement how gambling legislation had to be changed before Sydney could become a financial capital – the new financial products looked like wagers.

It was a bet that paid off. The city was transformed. For many years its growth and activity fuelled the nation. Trickle-down economics took on real meaning, as the divide between the wealthy harbourside suburbs and the west widened, and then narrowed as the good times rolled on year after year.

Sydney has now lost that crown – it has stalled, and even as the growth in the resource-rich states slows New South Wales is falling behind. There is little evidence of the urgency that characterised the debates of the 1980s.

IT IS LIKELY that in another twenty-seven years we will look back at the global financial crisis as another watershed. The precise shape of the new economy that will emerge is of course impossible to predict, but there are some early pointers. It is likely to be knowledge intensive, to value sustainability, to be less tolerant of global inequality and, in a sea of instant communication, to demand greater regulation.

This era has been marked by complexity. It is one of the rules of 'complexity science' that as systems become more labyrinthine and interconnected, they also become more fragile. The unravelling of the global economy in the past year is proof of this principle.

Within days of the collapse of Lehman Brothers on 15 September 2008, companies all around the globe evaporated, national economies dissolved, the first of millions lost their jobs, governments were spooked into implementing unprecedented policies – taking over banks, guaranteeing deposits, regulating the share market and dispensing vast amounts of money to keep the system working. It is estimated that something like sixty trillion dollars disappeared from the global economy – an unimaginable number until it is broken down into the countless jobs and activities that will cease to exist.

The Ponzi scheme that sent Bernie Madoff to jail for 150 years depended on perpetual growth, repaying investors with the capital of future investors. It depended on ever more money coming in and rising prices. But when the market crashed, like the child who misses out on a chair when the music stops, there was simply not enough to go around.

If Madoff did not exist it would have been necessary to invent him – his extraordinarily complex scheme was a metaphor for the times. Like Madoff's 'investors' the global system is simply not sustainable if it depends on robbing the future.

Each of the major recessions of the past century has resulted in a profound economic restructure: from agriculture to industry, from industry to services, from local to global. Other lessons from past recessions have been applied to the costly, short-term rescue packages, keeping money flowing, creating jobs, expanding education – but there is less evidence that the thinking that drove these big transformations has similar traction. To prevent a global dystopia, sustainable energy, knowledge and productivity-enhancing communications will be central if we are to look back and see how the future was created from the ashes of this crisis.

THIS IS THE first edition of Griffith REVIEW with our new partner, Text Publishing. We are excited that this new partnership will enable Griffith REVIEW to build on its strengths and reach new heights. The elegant new design signals this; we hope you enjoy it and welcome your feedback at www.griffithreview.com. If you enjoy *After the Crisis* tell your friends and subscribe now, to be one of the first to receive our special summer fiction edition.

3 July 2009

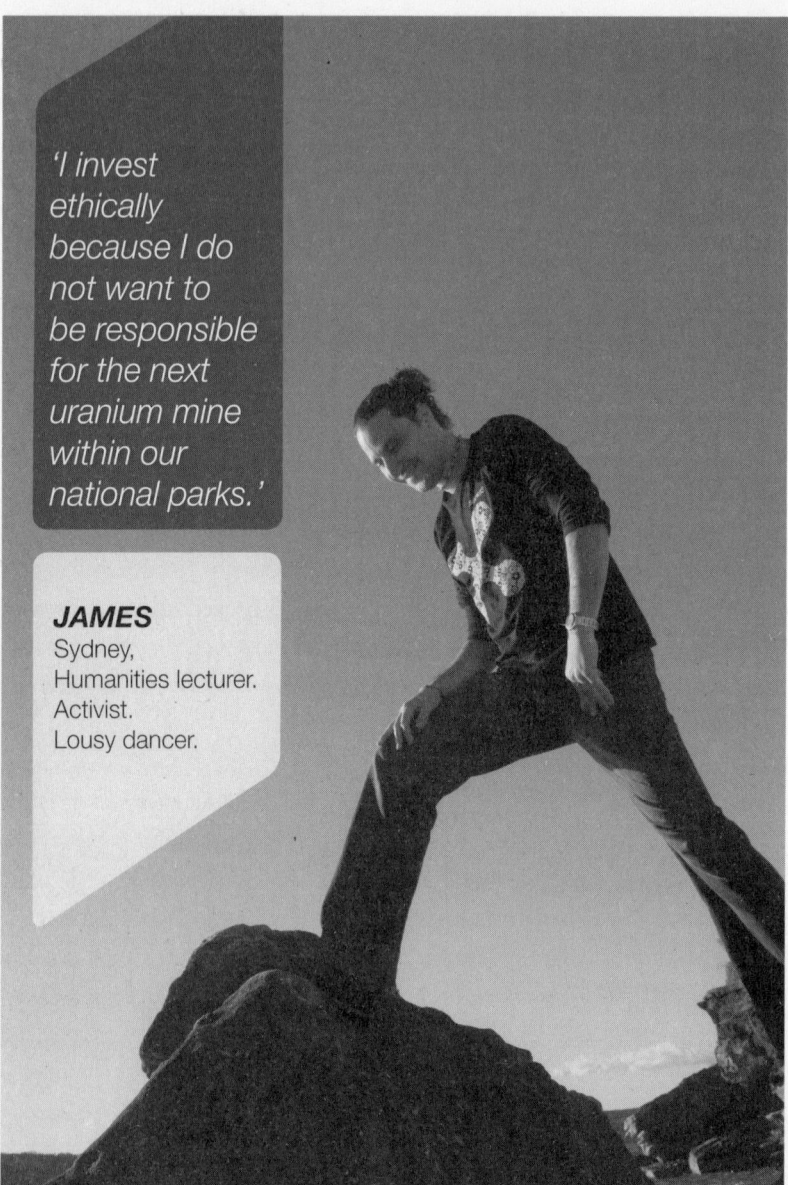

ESSAY

Stupid money

The tortuous path to a real-economy crisis

Gideon Haigh

At particular times a great deal of stupid people have a
great deal of stupid money...At intervals...the money
of these people is particularly large and craving; it seeks for
someone to devour it, and there is a 'plethora';
it finds someone, and there is 'speculation';
it is devoured, and there is 'panic'.
— Walter Bagehot, 'Essay on Edward Gibbon', 1856

IN the late 1990s, when I was busily employed writing the history of a bank, one of the choicest vantage points was the foyer of its skyscraper each morning. This would begin filling with employees around seven, while remaining strangely devoid of hurry or flurry; there was a sense of deep solitary deliberation, of people already at work in their minds long before they arrived at their desks. Although the suits were smart and the outfits expensive, there was little ostentation. The standard accessory was not a slimline briefcase but a gym bag: lunch was for wimps; running and pumping iron were preferred.

Business had such a buttoned-down air that the outside world was easy to forget. One morning, late in August 1998, my first appointment was with a veteran fixed-income executive. It happened that, overnight, the Dow had swooned almost a fifth in response to Russia's decision to suspend coupon payments on its rouble bonds; even as we spoke, the default was wreaking havoc on local equity markets. Not that you would have known it. Only occasionally, as he fielded questions about note and bond issues from days of yore, did my interviewee turn to one of his screens and check prices, remarking lightly at the money being lost by everyone, including himself. His sangfroid was impressive; in the span of our conversation, his wealth must have been lightened by a million dollars or so. But, as I learned, he wasn't unusual. Even as stocks plunged, yield curves contorted and interest-rate spreads blew out through the afternoon, the difference in the trading room from a normal day was difficult to discern. Save for a few more chagrined glances and amused asides, the hum of quiet industry was hardly disturbed.

PREVIOUS PAGE: Alan Greenspan testifies before the House Budget Committee. Photographer: Brendan Smialowski. *Source: gettyimages.com.*

Eleven years earlier, I had watched foam-flecked operators roaring themselves hoarse on the floor of the Melbourne Stock Exchange during the share-market crash; now, it seemed, crisis could be bridged by recalibrating a few models – a hedge here, a haircut there, a little restructuring everywhere.

Perhaps it was different elsewhere – I'm sure it was. Yet it also felt like a motif of an era in which financial upheaval was a routine, while remaining oddly distant and unreal, like an occasional disconcerting thud in another room heard through the wall. Capitalism decorated itself with a daisy chain of disasters: the Tequila crisis, the Asian meltdown, the defaults of Russia and then Argentina, the rout of the dotcoms and then the telcos; the disgracing of Enron, WorldCom, Tyco and even Martha Stewart; Australia filled its own corporate pillory with the likes of FAI, HIH and One.Tel.

Yet, somehow, these misfortunes always seemed to befall *other* people. Sooner or later, central bankers stepped in, poured money on troubled markets, and the moment passed – until, one unexpected day, 15 September 2008, it didn't. On that day, the 158-year-old Wall Street investment bank Lehman Brothers, driving force behind RCA and the birth of television, patron of enterprises from Pan Am and TWA to Sears, Roebuck & Co. and Macy's, slid into bankruptcy under a burden of debt rendered insuperable by the collapse of the American housing market.

That day, a day we are still living through, and will be living through for some years to come, an old saw was varied. Owe the bank a million and you have a problem, it used to be said; but owe the bank a hundred million and the bank has a problem. To this now add: when millions owe trillions they have no hope of paying back, the government has a problem.

THE CREDIT CRISIS is already quantitatively and qualitatively different to those earlier misadventures, to which we grew so inured. Trading rooms are again subdued, but it is the quiet of paralysis, apprehension about what else might lie in wait on battered balance sheets, anxiety at mushrooming deficits that imperil national credit ratings. Industry is straining to adjust to a world of scarcity, both of credit and of consumption, and global trade is more circumspect for the apparently long-term economic realignments ahead.

Politicians and central bankers have stepped in but their monetary-policy party tricks have so far failed to rekindle confidence, while one bank bailout has followed another and a succession of stimulus packages has been unable to revive demand. Indeed, it's partly the central bankers' solutions to prior problems, their repeated irrigations of illiquid securities markets that precipitated such a promiscuous wastage of credit, in particular the incomplete resolution of the currency collapses twelve years ago in Indonesia, Thailand and Malaysia. Bulwarking themselves against a repeat of events, Asian economies between 2001 and 2007 poured US$5 trillion in savings into funding a yawning American current-account deficit. This allowed the central banks of the OECD to keep interest rates artificially low, and spenders to surfeit themselves.

Booms, too, are usually associated with mirages, speculations, peculations. But the boom we are doomed to repent was as solid as bricks and mortar, involving the satisfaction of that most familiar of yearnings, home ownership, and driven by that uniquely human quality, optimism – the belief, fundamentally, in a perpetually brightening future. The bust, meanwhile, has prostrated an industry, finance, that had prided itself on consciousness and control of risk, on non-stop growth and innovation. The giants of Wall Street have already been humbled; for Europe's banks, which have recognised just a fraction of an estimated US$1.1 trillion in losses, that day is coming. Australia's better-capitalised banking sector has so far absorbed the shocks from abroad, but perhaps a decade's deleveraging lies ahead: according to the Asian Development Bank, global financial assets depreciated last year by roughly $50 trillion – equal to the world's economic output for a year. The interconnectedness of the global economy has for years been a matter of marvel; it has in fact proven more far- and deep-reaching than anyone acknowledged, with Iceland near-ruined by the carelessness of its banks in Britain, the Congo slowed almost to a standstill by Chinese investors repatriating capital, and bank collapses from Spain to the Caribbean.

THE RISE OF finance had earlier seemed irresistible. As recently as the early 1990s the financial sector provided only about a fifth of American corporate profits. By the peak of the boom, however, that proportion had doubled, and the sector was generating almost a tenth of GDP. As the proportion of American workers in manufacturing shrank from a third in 1950 to a tenth today, finance appeared to be taking up the slack, rewarding itself according to that improved station: mean compensation grew from about the average of all domestic private industries to almost twice that, and the top seven American banks dispersed US$95 billion among employees between 2005 and 2007. Increasingly, finance offered the keys to the kingdom. More than a fifth of American CEOs were once chief financial officers, according to a survey last year by *CFO* magazine – twice the proportion of a decade earlier. Even in Australia, a resources economy, balance-sheet legerdemain was regarded as a *passé-partout* to success. Heroes of equity investors have been the financial cosmeticians of Macquarie Bank, Babcock & Brown and Allco, whose makeovers have wrung sexy returns from the dourest infrastructure.

Finance, moreover, seemed welcome everywhere it went. In the past quarter of a century almost every advanced economy touted for banking and asset-management business, in order that it might claim to be a 'financial centre'. Some have been old centres rejuvenated. The City grew to provide a tenth of Britain's GDP, and a quarter of total corporation-tax receipts; at an industry dinner just two years ago, Gordon Brown congratulated bosses for 'an era that history will record as the beginning of a new golden age for the City of London'. Some have been new. Fostered by huge tax breaks and regulatory incentives, Dublin's International Financial Services Centre transformed a stretch of the Liffey formerly sprawling with dormant docks and shuttered warehouses into a vertical principality of glass and steel. The IFSC is the setting for Ava McCarthy's new thriller, *The Insider* (HarperCollins, 2009), where it is savoured as 'the place where rich people come to get richer'.

For twenty years, Sydney has promoted itself in competition with Singapore, Hong Kong and Tokyo as a regional financial centre. As recently as last year, the then Assistant Treasurer Chris Bowen was leading an 'Olympics-style push' for business, abetted by tax incentives, short cuts through bureaucracy and the attention of a dedicated financial-services advisory council within Treasury. Prime Minister Kevin Rudd hosted events for the financial-services industry while visiting the US, China and Japan, while committing Australia to mutual recognition of securities regulation with the US – presumably before discovering he was the dupe of a horrid neo-liberal plot.

For government, the enticements of finance were not far to seek. The regular profit outperformance of financial-services companies in an era of low interest rates tended to disguise slower economic growth elsewhere. Finance does not require major infrastructure development or lengthy lead-times to begin operating, while its apologists argued that competition imposed disciplines which regulators could not. Its assets, meanwhile, as the famous saying has it, go down in the lift every night. That was fundamental: finance provided nice, clean, respectable jobs for graduates, who voted, and whose parents did as well. By 2007, for instance, finance was absorbing more Harvard graduates than any other industry: a fifth of males and a tenth of females. One of the stated objectives of Australia's Bradley Review of Higher Education was to find how universities could produce more finance graduates for local and international consumption.

There were, of course, always refuseniks. Financial services often appeared as the vanguard of globalisation, an incitement to rage on both the left and right of politics. Paranoia about the encroachments of modernity also made it the object of violent expression: when al-Qaeda plotted 9/11, it chose as its target not an old-economy bastion, like the headquarters of General Motors in Detroit, or a new economy symbol, like the Googleplex in Mountain View, but the gleaming spires of New York's World Trade Center, putting them on hegemonic par with the Pentagon and White House. Public ire during the G20's London Summit in April was directed at, among other locations, the headquarters of the profligate Royal Bank of Scotland, sacked by demonstrators in emulation of the anarchists who tried to bomb the venerable House of Morgan in September 1920.

Except that ninety years ago, hatred of 'Morgan the financial gorgon' sprang from the *idée fixe* that it concentrated wealth for an unelected elite; anger springs now after a period in which wealth was spread to the edges and borrowers were lent money on almost any terms, for almost any object of their hearts' desire. And while financial calamities are traditionally and proverbially larcenous, with the standard complaint that the big guy made a clean getaway and the little guy was fleeced, the top of town has here taken unexampled hits: *l'affaire Madoff*, perhaps the greatest fraud ever committed by a single person, was perpetrated at the expense of rich professionals, not poor suckers. Bernie Madoff aside, this has not been a crash accompanied by evidence of widespread malfeasance. Rather, it seems to have occurred in the ordinary course of business, to be a crisis of the system not in spite of it – which is precisely what has made it so intractable. That being so, it is useful to consider the origins of that system, the genesis of the core banking function of credit creation.

IN BILLY WILDER'S delirious Cold War comedy *One, Two, Three* (1961), Otto Piffl, the headstrong young communist whom the Coca-Cola executive CR MacNamara is trying to convert to capitalism, is surprised to learn that his wedding in the West has already buried him in debt. 'I've been a capitalist for three hours and already I owe $10,000?' he exclaims. MacNamara, played with sardonic relish by James Cagney, thinks he's finally got it. 'That's how the system works!' he explains. 'Everybody owes everybody else!' Quite – and it is this apparent paradox that underpins what JK Galbraith called simply 'the miracle of banking'.

This year marks the four-hundredth anniversary of the dawn of modern banking, the foundation of Amsterdam's Wisselbank. Established in response to the hundreds of different denominations of gold and silver coins then in European circulation, it issued credit notes based on the weight and assay value of currency presented. But, as the bank kept the physical currency on the premises to cover the paper it issued, this was only half a revolution. The other half came fifty years later, with the establishment of Stockholm's Banco, which took deposits for a fee and issued loans secured against property, a task previously the preserve of moneylenders.

Initially, the acceptance of deposits and the making of loans were separate operations, and the idea of merging them was a stroke of genius for which Banco founder Johan Palmstruch almost paid with his life, being not the last banker to discover that short-term deposits do not always coexist harmoniously with long-term loans: the bank collapsed and Palmstruch's death sentence was commuted only at the last minute. But it was an idea whose time had come, and it is appropriate that banking's emergence coincides with alchemy's last efflorescence: credit creation has about it a touch of the philosopher's stone, even today, for where business prefers martial allusions, from 'captains of industry' to 'guerrilla marketing', financiers are still routinely 'wizards'.

The original banking model has since been stretched numberless ways. Banks began taking deposits from and lending to companies and among themselves, and dealing in every conceivable security of every possible maturity – with a certain amount of creative destruction along the way. The first great 'banker's bank' devoted to trading bills of exchange, Overend, Gurney & Co., collapsed in ruins; the first great 'commercial bank' designed for lending to industry, Crédit Mobilier de Paris, collapsed amid scandal. And, sooner or later, everyone is reminded that 'credit' comes from the Latin *credo*: I believe. There is faith at every level of banking: in the value of collateral, in the enforceability of contracts, in the solvency of customers and counterparties, in the abiding liquidity of markets. It is a faith that fissures readily, as Walter Bagehot noted in surveying the City of London 136 years ago: 'Every banker knows that if he has to prove he is worthy of credit, however good may be his arguments, his credit is gone.'

It is a faith that central banks were granted monopolies of issuance over currency to counteract. Yet, if anything, that basis in faith has grown, as markets have grown global and electronic, and finance more reified. The taunt that finance is mere 'paper shuffling' is nowadays obsolete; it hardly involves even that level of substantiality. Thus the scene in Po Bronson's droll *Bombardiers* (Penguin, 1996), where the wunderkind trader Eggs Igino causes consternation by asking to see a bond: 'I've sold billions of dollars worth of bonds,' he explains. 'I think it's time I got to know what I was selling…I would sleep better at night knowing I wasn't part of some big hoax.' The search that turns the bank upside down to produce a modest certificate is anti-climatic, but when a spontaneous auction breaks out, Igino sells at a profit. 'You're a fucking genius, Igino,' says his boss. 'You could sell venom to a snake.' And while reporting of the world of money sticks loyally with the fortunes of stocks, currencies and commodities, it is the bond that is the financial instrument of greatest ubiquity and versatility – again, in name, operating at a level of faith. Any debt with a payment stream can underpin a bond – and, in our lifetime, almost every debt has come to.

WITH THEIR DOLLAR'S giant slalom in the 1980s, Australians fixated on the foreign-exchange trader as their financial cowboy of choice. But the bawling, brawling, braces-wearing blowhards of Tom Wolfe's *Bonfire of the Vanities* (Picador, 1988) and Michael Lewis's *Liar's Poker* (Hodder & Stoughton, 1989) were trading bonds: at that stage mainly government securities, US treasuries, UK gilts, with what was politely called 'emerging market debt' for bigger swinging dicks, and what were unambiguously called 'junk bonds' for investors with the biggest cojones of all. It was an age of big deficits, big corporate borrowings, and also greater personal indebtedness, for alongside these traditional instruments were soon to be seen other collaterals: bonds backed by auto loans, student loans, credit-card debt and royalty streams, bundled up and rendered fungible by a process called securitisation.

In parallel, there emerged a market for derivatives – again, traditional instruments finding modern applications. Options are known to have been traded in Holland in the 1630s, and futures to have been offered in rice on Osaka's Dōjima Exchange in the 1730s; swaps, more recent, were first initiated in currencies in 1980 (between the World Bank and IBM), in interest rates in 1982 (between the Student Loan Marketing Association and ITT), and in equities in 1989 (arranged by Bankers Trust). Most people know little more than that derivatives are designed to mitigate risk and are often, if not always, very complex, governed by esoteric concepts like 'convexity' and 'duration', and relying for evaluation on 'zero curves' and 'coupon curves'. But what matters most is who developed these parallel and gradually intersecting concepts, and why.

The Great Depression left a schism in American banking, the Glass-Steagall Act, which split commercial banking, the acts of making loans and taking deposits, from investment banking, the art of underwriting securities for corporates and trading stocks and bonds for private clients and pension funds. Where the anarchists had failed, Senator Carter Glass and Congressman Henry Steagall succeeded. In September 1935, the House of Morgan was rent asunder: most of it became the blue-chip commercial bank JP Morgan & Co., clustered eventually with peers like Citibank, Chase Manhattan and the Bank of America, and guaranteed by the Federal Deposit Insurance Corporation (FDIC); the residue moved a few doors down to constitute the fledgling investment-banking partnership Morgan Stanley, ranking then alongside the likes of Dillon, Read & Co. and Kuhn, Loeb & Co., then later with Goldman Sachs, Merrill Lynch, Bear Stearns, Salomon Brothers, Lehman Brothers – the loose agglomeration of names that collectively and popularly constitute Wall Street.

For the next forty years, both groups enjoyed relatively cosy and discrete franchises. Then, on 1 May 1975, the Securities and Exchange Commission, the Depression's other regulatory outcome, abolished Wall Street's system of fixed commissions for securities trading. Many commentators on present discontents, such as Australia's Prime Minister, deem deregulation to be part of a neo-liberal agenda. Yet the scrapping of the commission structure on Wall Street, widely lauded as busting up its cloistered cartel, is every bit as significant as the eventual repeal of Glass-Steagall, through the Gramm-Leach-Bliley Act, ten years ago.

Investment banks did not enjoy low-cost funds from deposits; they depended on the resources of their partners and, increasingly, on wholesale markets. Consequently they were compelled to earn fees from competing and innovating, pioneering new markets and exploiting volatilities, pushing tolerances of risk. Opportunities duly materialised. With the steady disintegration of the last vestiges of the Bretton Woods system of fixed exchange rates, in the early 1970s, they developed trading expertises; with the vogue for hostile takeovers, they expanded their advisory capabilities in mergers and acquisitions; with the deregulation of finance in foreign climes, they cultivated subsidiaries and joint ventures abroad. Investment banking, in its new varieties and global extent, steadily outstripped the wherewithal of the old partnership structures: competitors needed big balance sheets on which to park securitised assets, and to act as credible counterparties in derivatives transactions. Salomons was the first to go public, and a succession of huge paydays followed: when Morgan Stanley's partners sold out, in March 1986, some reaped as much as US$50 million. The last to go that route, Goldman Sachs, did so ten years ago, by which time the apparent shilly-shallying of the partners had become a talking point; in hindsight, their circumspection was understandable.

With the end of the partnership, Wall Street firms acknowledged that they had lost something – that elusive collegial binding, that sense of loyalty to the franchise. They sought to replicate it by pampering their star earners with increasingly lavish equity-based incentives: options and preferred stock, on hugely advantageous terms where it was not free. By the peak of the boom, American financial institutions were paying their employees sums equivalent to more than half their annual revenues. Their explanation? They deserved it. Wall Street's frat-boy ascendancy passed almost as soon as it was immortalised by Tom Wolfe and Michael Lewis. By the early 1990s, investment banks were plundering universities of their nimblest mathematical minds and most creative computer modellers. When everyone had balance-sheet grunt, the selling differential became structuring capabilities – sheer, unadulterated brainpower. As Lewis puts it in his new book, *Panic* (Penguin, 2009): 'A gap opened up between high and low finance. It was the end of anti-intellectualism in American financial life.'

Although derivatives had been devised as a means of reducing or at least redistributing risk, they had also become part of finance's profit-making armoury, and the more complicated the instrument, the greater the fee – although, no less often, the greater the concealed risk to the holder. In his memoir of derivatives trading, *F.I.A.S.C.O.* (Norton, 1996), Frank Partnoy describes popularising an apparently innocent structured note called PERLS, Principal Exchange Rate Linked Securities, whose marketing documents contained the soothing advice that 'downside was limited to the size of the initial investment': 'These words appeared as boilerplate throughout Morgan Stanley's marketing documents and almost always generated snickers from the salesmen...The most a buyer could lose was everything. Morgan Stanley, in contrast, had nothing to lose.' The other appeal of trading securities and originating derivatives was that the activities were unrestricted by the now-antiquated Glass-Steagall Act, so investment banks and commercial banks alike could profit. This was a game everyone could play and, apparently, win.

BUSINESS'S TENDENCY TO migrate to environments of least supervision, however, had a more perverse outcome: a dangerous knowledge gap began to open, between those who ran banks and those who…well, *really* ran banks. Financial institutions were still ostensibly governed by chairmen, directors, chief executives and chief financial officers, all in their forties and fifties. Yet they were increasingly dependent for the heft of their earnings on the ingenuity and industry of younger executives exploiting market opportunities that were usually fleeting, and using devices generally new and untested. JP Morgan himself was proud to say he could do the job of any man in his firm: 'I can sit down at any clerk's desk, take up his work where he left off and gone with it…I don't like being at any man's mercy.' A possibly apocryphal story of the early days of swaps is that the chief executive of the firm bearing Morgan's name, Lewis Preston, rounded on his derivatives pioneer, Connie Volstadt, convinced that the US$400 million profit he was claiming should be a US$400 million loss – he had to be painstakingly proven wrong. Mind you, at least Preston had the nerve to issue the challenge; his peers were happy enough to fall further behind with each passing year. For innovation in the financial markets is unlike that in medicine or science. There is no copyright protection, no notion of intellectual property, and little semblance of peer review, except as a means to imitation. If one competitor has success with a zero-coupon structured note or a covenant light bond, the market is soon flooded with lookalikes; unless either very complex or exceedingly risky, products are instantly perishable, and knowledge grows rapidly obsolete.

Some tried to point this out. In a January 1992 speech to the New York State Bankers Association, the lugubrious president of the New York Federal Reserve, Gerald Corrigan, urged bankers to take a 'very, very hard look' at derivatives: 'Off-balance-sheet activities have a role, but they must be managed and controlled carefully, and they must be understood by top management, as well as by traders and rocket scientists. I hope this sounds like a warning, because it is.' A wave of derivatives shocks all over the world – Procter & Gamble, Orange County, Metalgesellschaft, Daiwa Bank, Sumitomo – duly culminated in a scandal shocking to bankers everywhere.

Eighteen months after Corrigan's speech, the chairman of Barings Bank, Peter Baring, visited the supervision department of the Bank of England. It was a regular visit, and a cordial one, because Barings, one of the City's most venerable names, had lately reported an impressively robust profit. Minutes of the meeting recorded Peter Baring's honeyed words: 'The recovery in profitability has been amazing…leaving Barings to conclude that it is not actually terribly difficult to make money in the securities business.' When this transcript was published, a young Barings employee stood on the floor of Singapore's SIMEX futures exchange enunciating the quote in the poshest sneer he could summon. 'This was a conversation between two experienced bankers who were smugly congratulating themselves on this secret way of making money. And they would have shaken hands in farewell and gone their separate ways thinking what a super chap the other was. They should have known better.'

That they didn't left them acutely vulnerable to the depredations of the speaker, Nick Leeson, who was piling his derivatives losses into an electronic bottom drawer called Error Account 88888, while eluding the lunges of incompetent and half-hearted investigators: 'The only good thing about hiding losses from these people was that it was so easy. They were always too busy and too self-important, and were always on the telephone. They had the attention span of a gnat. They could not make the time to work through a sheet of numbers and spot that it didn't add up.'

WHEN BARINGS VAPOURISED in January 1995, bankers everywhere felt a pang of simpatico with its management and resolved to do a better job, although they did not linger long over its implications, perhaps because a rogue trader could be made a scapegoat. Yet, in some respects, the collapse of Barings was even more a harbinger than the subsequent and far larger collapses of Long-Term Capital Management and Enron. For what has been gruesomely fascinating about finance's recent travails is how little top management was aware of how their banks made money, and therefore of the risks they were running. Some of the strangers in banking's strange land were never hard to pick, like the former retailer Andy Hornby, who ran Britain's HBOS. But there were others, better camouflaged yet just as ill-adapted to the altered landscape. As Gillian Tett notes in *Fool's Gold* (Little, Brown, 2009), her new account of the false promise of financial innovation, 'By 2005, very few men running investment banks had extensive experience in structuring and trading derivatives. The field was just too young to have produced many high-level leaders, and many derivatives experts were too cerebral to play the type of internal corporate political games needed to rise to the top at most banks...Citigroup, Merrill Lynch, UBS and numerous others were run by former bond and equity salesmen, lawyers, wealth managers and commercial bankers. Such men had little instinctive understanding of the technical details of managing risk. Moreover, the wider competitive climate provided an overwhelming incentive for them to focus on revenues above all else.'

As the mortgage market deteriorated in late 2007, for example, Citigroup fell victim to an instrument of its own design that allowed investors to return $25 billion of the deteriorating financial products they had been sold. Neither chairman Chuck Prince, a lawyer, nor his successor Robert Rubin, an economist, had heard of the 'liquidity put', despite having skimmed hundreds of millions of dollars in annual compensation. 'How did this happen?' asked JP Morgan boss Jamie Dimon of a Citigroup peer. 'We are not entirely sure ourselves,' came the reply.

Similarly, when AIG began unravelling, chief executive Martin Sullivan was completely dependent on his heavily implicated financial-products group chief Joseph Cassano – the company had for six months failed to fill vacancies for a chief financial officer and chief risk-assessment officer, and Sullivan's background was property. As Matt Taibbi reported in *Rolling Stone*: 'That meant that the eighteenth-largest company in the world had no one checking to make sure its balance sheet was safe and no one keeping track of how much cash and assets the firm had on hand. The situation was so bad that when outside consultants were called in a few weeks before the bailout, senior executives were unable to answer even the most basic questions about their company – like, for instance, how much exposure the firm had to the residential-mortgage market. When the growing credit crunch prompted senior AIG executives to re-examine its liabilities, a company accountant named Joseph St Denis became "gravely concerned"…Cassano responded by personally forcing the poor sap out of the firm, telling him he was "deliberately excluded" from the financial review for fear that he might "pollute the process".'

Bosses at Bear Stearns – 2006 Financial Institution of the Year, according to the prestigious *Euromoney* – appeared to personify Wall Street at its most practical and unostentatious: chairman and CEO Jimmy Cayne was a stockbroker, co-CEO Alan Schwartz a corporate adviser, CFO Sam Molinaro an accountant, asset-management chief Rich Marin an experienced portfolio manager, elder statesman Ace Greenberg a sixty-year industry veteran. But in the most thorough exposition of the crisis so far, William Cohan's *House of Cards* (Allen Lane, 2009), they are recalled by colleagues as barely able to ask questions, let alone provide answers. At a speakerphone Q&A with banking analysts at which Bear was coming under pressure, for example, the storied Cayne was baffled by the only question posed him: 'All heads in the room swivelled to Jimmy, who was sitting in the room with Sam, and Jimmy went blank like a deer in the headlights. Sam jumped in to save him and said Jimmy had to leave the room. Our vaunted CEO was incapable of answering a single question…it was pretty much a softball question, too, like "What do you see in the markets?"…It was a nothing question. Jimmy couldn't open his mouth, so he didn't.'

When Cayne fired his senior fixed-income executive, Warren Spector, mainly because he didn't like him, the situation became even more confused. 'It was clear when Warren left, Jimmy had no idea what we did in fixed income. Unlike Alan, who didn't get it and knew he didn't get it and tried, Jimmy had no clue. He would now come up to the fixed-income floor and wander round and try to find some common ground: "How you doing?" And: "What's going on?" He'd have heard of some customer name – Thornburg, for example, was falling apart at that point – and he'd go: "How's Thornburg going?" It's like, "Fine. Nothing's changed since yesterday"…There was no way he could learn it unless he experienced it. It was sort of hopeless.'

Schwartz was little better: 'It was like Bonds 101. You're starting with, "prices go up, yields go down. And how do you calculate duration?"…It's not what he did for a living, and he picked up on it faster than most humans could. But he never really got it…It would take you fifteen years to get up to speed on the funky shit that we owned.'

Nobody had fifteen minutes, let alone fifteen years. Here was an industry that had lost its head, so segregated in its complex specialisations as to have become a mystery to itself. A fashionable phrase is that banking institutions had been allowed to become 'too big to fail'; it is just as arguable that they had become 'too big to run'.

WHAT EXACTLY DID these top executives fail to grasp? In one sense, the origins of the crisis are disarmingly prosaic. It has become popular to trace it to Bill Clinton's National Homeownership Strategy, launched in August 1994 with a clarion call for 'new financing strategies, fuelled by the creativity and resources of the public and private sectors', to extend home ownership to more low-income families. But Clinton's was an ancient preoccupation made new. Americans had already embarked on a love affair with home and hearth by the time of their first Federal Income Tax Act, which in 1913 permitted full tax deductibility of mortgage repayments, while their politicians have repeatedly espoused the social efficacy of property ownership, in terms reprising those of Herbert Hoover nearly ninety years ago: 'The home owner has a constructive aim in life. He works harder outside his home, he spends his leisure hours more profitably, and he and his family live a finer life and enjoy more of the comforts and cultivating influences of our modern civilization.' Hoover's Own Your Home Scheme, an elaborate array of incentives for marginal mortgagees, was the first of any number of well-meant and ill-starred initiatives aimed at encouraging Americans' real-estate dreams; by encouraging dreams at odds with reality, it was also integral to a sizeable proportion of the thousand foreclosures a day at the height of the Great Depression.

Other developed nations, notably Australia, have also fetishised home ownership. But only in the US has the state carved out such a colossal role. The Depression, in fact, fostered both the Federal Housing Administration

(FHA) to insure mortgages, and the Federal National Mortgage Association (FNMA, usually called Fannie Mae) to purchase those insured mortgages. Had Roosevelt helped draft the Declaration of Independence, he would almost certainly have dedicated the country to freedom of borrowing in addition to life, liberty and the pursuit of happiness. To the tough-minded Al Stephenson (Frederic March) in William Wyler's *The Best Years of Our Lives* (1946), it was worth a war to defend. Irked when the Cornbelt Loan and Trust Company, to which he's returned from active service, turns away a poor but industrious borrower who lacks 'sufficient collateral', and emboldened by a few drinks, he gives a stirring speech at his homecoming banquet: 'One day in Okinawa, a Major comes up to me and he says, "Stephenson, you see that hill?" "Yes sir, I see it." "All right," he said. "You and your platoon will attack said hill and take it." So I said to the Major, "But that operation involves considerable risk. We haven't sufficient collateral." "I'm aware of that," said the Major, "but the fact remains that there's the hill and you are the guys who are going to take it." So I said to him, "I'm sorry, Major…no collateral, no hill." So we didn't take the hill and we lost the war. I think that little story has considerable significance, but I've forgotten what it is…I love the Cornbelt Loan and Trust Company. There are some who say that the old bank is suffering from hardening of the arteries and of the heart. I refuse to listen to such radical talk. I say that our bank is alive, it's generous, it's human, and we're going to have such a line of customers seeking and getting small loans that people will think we're gambling with the depositors' money. And we will be. We will be gambling on the future of this country. I thank you.'

With the GI Bill of 1944 and the Housing Act of 1949, this promise of future largesse and liberality was steadily fulfilled: over the past fifty years, total mortgage debt in the US grew seventy-fold, with owner-occupiers finally owing a sum greater than the country's GDP. This was despite the curtailment of direct government assistance for low-income borrowers – casualties of the Reagan years. Lately, it was the work instead of a massive, integrated and hugely efficient private-sector machine, albeit with the continued implied support of Fannie Mae and its consort Freddie Mac (the Federal Home Loan Mortgage Corporation), not to mention bipartisan backing from Capitol Hill.

ACCOUNTS OF THE credit crisis seldom do justice to the intricacy of that machine. At the front end was generally a loan broker acting in cahoots with one or more mortgage originators, with the assistance of a valuer. Then there was either an investment bank or a commercial bank to scoop those mortgages up, securitise and sell them to other financial institutions, with the endorsement of a credit-ratings agency, accountants and lawyers, especially after an August 1996 policy change announced by Alan Greenspan, the US Federal Reserve's gnomic chairman. Henceforward, Greenspan decreed, a mortgage-backed security could be held by a bank with less than half the capital required for the equivalent quantum of mortgages. With a quasi-government guarantee from Fannie Mae or Freddie Mac available, it was an invitation to start securitising with both hands; banks did not miss it.

In that machine, however, only the front end, and then fleetingly, had any contact with the borrower and the asset – each step placed a greater distance between the individual who had taken out the mortgage and its eventual holder, which could be anyone from a bank in Scotland or a money-market fund in California to a public-service pension provider in Iceland or a hedge fund registered in Bermuda. Yet each step was also vitally interested in the business taking place; it was how they extracted their fee or obtained their return. So, as homebuyers were pitched in at ever greater extremities of gearing, bankers began performing ever greater stretches to accommodate them, while articulating ever greater self-deceptions to explain them. In October 1997, the first securitisation took place of what came to be called 'sub-prime' mortgages, those taken out by low-income borrowers, with payments guaranteed by Freddie Mac, and underwritten by Bear Stearns and First Union Capital Markets; Fannie Mae then also agreed to begin purchasing loans made to 'borrowers with slightly impaired credit'. To assuage investor anxiety, Bear insisted that low-income borrowers regarded owning a home as 'a near-sacred obligation' and that 'a family will do almost anything to meet that monthly mortgage payment' – cod sociology *and* wishful thinking.

In truth, as the economic historian Robert Shiller learned while researching his *Irrational Exuberance* (Scribe, 2000), nobody knew very much about how housing markets behaved at all. 'To my surprise,' Shiller wrote, 'everyone I asked said that there were no data on the long-term performance of home prices – not for the US, nor for any country…Stop and think about that. If the housing boom is such a spectacular economic event, wouldn't you imagine that someone would care if this kind of thing had happened before, and what the outcome had been?…This is at once a lesson in human behaviour and a reminder that human attention is capricious. Clearly *no one* was carefully evaluating the real estate market and its potential for speculative excess.'

EXEGESES OF THE credit crisis quickly proliferate with acronyms, from ABS and ABCP to SIVs and SPVs; familiar words in unfamiliar settings, like conduit, mezzanine, synthetic and repo; and just occasionally a cross between the two, such as BISTRO (Broad Index Secured Trust Offering, if you must know). But only two pieces of jargon are genuinely consequential: collateralised debt obligation (CDO) and credit-default swap (CDS).

A mortgage-backed CDO derives its value and payments from a portfolio of home loans, which it borrows money to acquire from an originator. These portfolios are sliced into bonds in different tranches of risk, from super-senior to junior: the super-senior, based on securities of ostensibly higher quality, pay a lower coupon; the junior pay more, in return for the investor accepting greater default risk. At first, because relatively few lenders dared tarry with 'sub-prime' borrowers, CDOs were constructed only of high-quality 'conforming' credits. Then that taboo relaxed and, as Gillian Tett reports, everyone got rich: 'Precisely because sub-prime loans were risky, the homeowners who took out such debt typically paid a higher rate of interest than prime borrowers did, and that meant the "raw material" of sub-prime loans produced higher-returning CDOs than those built of "prime" mortgages. For returns-hungry investors, sub-prime mortgage-based CDOs were gold dust.' With sub-prime lending underpinned by this reassuringly tailored and focused security, lending to low-income borrowers grew 500 per cent over the next eight years. Hedge funds accumulating these CDOs on margin to further juice up their returns, moreover, were often funded by the same investment banks that underwrote the securities.

The CDS, meanwhile, was a credit derivative devised by JP Morgan that allowed investors to bet on, and thus hedge against, the risks of a bond defaulting. After successfully marketing CDSs on European government debt, the so-called Morgan mafia started offering them to banks as a means of 'cleaning up' their balance sheets: by selling tranches of bonds based on the securitised default risk, a bank could now effectively insure against a corporate loan or an emerging market economy defaulting. This market, too, exploded: by mid-2005, it had a nominal value equivalent to that of the entire American economy. Mind you, CDS protection continued to look like the acme of prudence. When the Morgan mafia sought a way to deal with the super-senior CDO risk that was always hardest to sell, they even wheeled in the world's mightiest insurer, AIG – the ultimate endorsement.

Some side effects were always obvious. If nobody was holding mortgages through to maturity, what incentive existed to make them robust? If risk was to be moved off balance sheets in such quantities, who would end up watching it? And at what point did securitisation shift from being a means of reducing risk, thereby rendering the economy more susceptible even to minor shocks? They were questions without answers. A CDO was a leveraged bet on lever-aged bets, destined to flourish only in an environment of low interest rates. A CDS relied on assumptions about liquidity and stability never hitherto tested – indeed, AIG seems to have regarded mortgage risk as like the self-contained risk of house fires or car accidents, which do not affect the probability of other similar events; while banking panics are spontaneous, contagious and *sauve qui peut*. An old folk-wisdom of the financial market runs: shouting 'Fire!' in a crowded theatre is a bad strategy – unless you happen to be near the door.

The cumulative and complementary impacts of CDOs and CDSs, then, were to encourage bankers to recycle the capital on their unburdened balance sheets for even further adventures, while also feeling that appropri-ate precautions had been taken – an effect exacerbated by the industry's involuted incentives. For the assumption on Wall Street had always been that, somehow, the stupendous rewards available to elite workers would protect the industry from mishap; after all, who would willingly imperil an institution on which their future wealth depended? Equally, however, who wanted to retard a machine that in 2006 spun off US$6 billion in investment-banking fees? Lucrative equity-based remuneration packages turned out not to engender prudence; if anything, they exacerbated a predisposition to cut corners and relax credit standards, in order to maximise quarterly revenues, thereby enhancing stock prices and remuneration. In this world, what counted was not deal quality but 'deal flow' – the number of transactions that could be executed, and thus the number of tickets that could be clipped on the way through. What counted for CDOs and CDSs, indeed, counted every bit as much – in the Australian setting – for the securitised infrastructure in which Macquarie Bank specialised, or the leveraged property schemes of Centro.

Rather than a personal evaluation of worth or even a market certification of value, rewards had become something more like casino winnings – in the gaming vernacular, 'house money'. Almost twenty years ago, the behavioural economist Richard Thaler demonstrated what had long been thought, that gamblers are far more inclined to stake house money on possible further gains. Because limited liability protected personal downsides, moreover, the costs of failure were vastly incommensurate with the rewards for success. Wall Street had actually never been making its inhabitants richer than at the point it blew itself to smithereens.

SO FAR, SO bad, and so familiar. But from here on, the standard narrative of financial collapse begins breaking down – because, as observed earlier, a striking feature of the crisis was the emphatic flourish with which Wall Street signed its own death warrant, hanging guilelessly on to souring sub-prime securities, gripped by the widespread delusion that house prices could only rise, despite them already having doubled between 1997 and 2005, and that the economy could only grow, even in an environment of trillion-dollar deficits. While the dotcom boom was underpinned by the proverbial 'bigger fool' syndrome – the belief that there will always be a bigger fool to relieve you of overpriced stock – the biggest fools last year were banks themselves.

For all the rapacity and recklessness on show, furthermore, the ethical standards of Wall Street do not seem to have been more than averagely dubious. Bernie Madoff is like one of those bug-eyed, big-mouthed deep-sea grotesques occasionally dragged to the surface in a trawler's net: a freak of nature, satisfyingly symbolic but not truly representative. For connoisseurs of colourful villainy, in fact, this bust has been a squib, containing nothing like the pleasing perp walks that followed the collapses of Enron or World-Com, or the satisfying Spitzer settlements. Bear Stearns' terminal error was choosing to protect its reputation with clients and counterparties by standing behind its own disintegrating hedge funds. CEO Jimmy Cayne wanted to let the funds go under: 'Fuck them,' he told his fellow executives. 'It's not our money.' But his executive-committee colleagues outvoted him. Ironically, it was Cayne's one correct call of the crisis: when an orderly liquidation proved impossible, the securities turned out to be worth a fraction of their book value, and recapitalising the funds was like emptying the bank's coffers down a capacious drain.

For once, too, it seems, Wall Street more than met its ethical match. While there was certainly predatory lending among mortgage originators, there also appears to have been at least as much 'predatory borrowing'. Perhaps the most telling research to have emerged from the mortgage markets has been a study by BasePoint Analytics, a Californian consultancy, evaluating more than three million loans from 1997 and 2006 with an emphasis on the most recent. Reporting the findings, the economist Tyler Cowen explained: 'As much as 70 per cent of recent early payment defaults had fraudulent misrepresentations on their original loan applications...Many of the frauds were simple rather than ingenious. In some cases, borrowers who were asked to state their incomes just lied, sometimes reporting five times actual income; other borrowers falsified income documents.'

Worse still, lenders actually expected their customers to dissemble – even exhorted them to do so. In 2006, more than two-thirds of funds dispersed to sub-prime borrowers were through 'liar loans', where borrowers were able simply to state their income without providing verification. Borrowers on teaser rates that required virtually no repayments in the first year, further-more, could afford indifference to the prospect of losing equity in their houses because, as Cowen's colleague Russell Roberts observes, 'they didn't have any equity in these houses to start with'. This is not necessarily indicative only of ethical elasticities. For all the borrowers trying to game the system, there were probably always more counting on refinancing on more advantageous terms – something seemingly straightforward in the environment of abundant credit. But considered together, the behaviour of financial institutions and borrowers implies a subtle but unusually egalitarian shift in attitudes to risk in the past decade.

IN THIS THEY weren't alone. In June 2001, the five-month-old Bush administration pushed through the first of three personal tax cuts of unexampled extent, leaving the president with less money to work with than any of the previous eight incumbents, just months before he opted to bankroll an ill-defined and illimitable war. But the cuts mimicked, too, the behaviour of an electorate that had – barely – chosen him. Americans' savings rates, which neared a tenth of disposable income in the 1980s, had dipped suddenly in the 1990s and recently tailed off to an average of nothing, while for the first time since such records were kept household debt actually exceeded Americans' ability to pay, even though interest rates were at forty-year lows. Mortgages formed only part of this: credit-card debt alone soared trillionwards, with auto loans and student loans not far behind. Americans, in other words, had settled on a president perfectly in tune with their latter-day thriftlessness; they then carried right on. There had been hand-wringing in the early 1980s when American private debt reached 123 per cent of GDP; by 2008, it had reached 290 per cent without causing anything like the same public discomfort.

Australians were hardly more frugal, household indebtedness spiralling to more than $700 billion, and domestic spending outpacing annual earnings, as against traditional savings rates of about a tenth of earnings. There was not quite the same profligacy in government, the Costello Treasury treating the size of the surplus almost as a measure of manhood: one of the exquisite ironies of budget time, in fact, became the boastings of fiscal rectitude to an electorate fast losing such habits. Yet Canberra also developed a direct interest in high levels of personal spending, the goods and services tax contributing an ever-growing proportion of total tax rake-off. And for all the grumblings about income tax, it is at least levied on money has been earned, while tax based on outlays reflects money that hasn't – and that became increasingly likely to have been borrowed.

A HOST OF explanations have been advanced for twenty-first century squandermania, from a collective hankering to live in the present due to apprehensions about the future, to sluggish growth in real wages inciting increased reliance on borrowings. Property prices certainly acquired a palliative quality. While worldwide wage growth in 2006 was puny thanks to generally high levels of employment, inflation in house prices made everyone feel wealthier. Indeed, the accent on home ownership in developed nations in the past fifteen years has been, at least in part, a concession of weakness: if true financial security derives from anything, it is from a steady income, which the industrial economies of the West have been faltering in their capacity to guarantee. But exactly why former habits of thrift were abandoned so thoroughly will probably never be known; it may be as simple as individuals, like the CEOs of the banks funding them, no longer fully grasping what they were dealing with.

Surprisingly little is understood about human behaviour with credit. Experiments have demonstrated what stands to reason: that, for instance, people keep better account of cash than credit-card debt, because the experience of acquisition and payments is decoupled and distanced in the latter. What we do know, however, is that between the decoupling and distancing exists a continent of incomprehension. According to a 2007 survey, nearly a third of American credit-card holders were unaware of the interest rate they were paying – and of them a third thought it was less than 10 per cent, when it was usually two to three times that. According to a 2008 survey, two-thirds of Americans had no grasp of compound interest. In a recent episode of *The Simpsons*, Homer is irrepressibly enthusiastic about his home-equity loan. 'I borrow as much as I want,' he explains, 'and the house gets left with the bill!' When the bank forecloses, he is baffled: 'When I borrowed this money, you said I wouldn't have to pay it back until the future. This isn't the future! It's the lousy stinking now!' Among many borrowers, unconsciousness of indebtedness extended to indifference to insolvency; indeed, among those with no assets to confiscate or wages to garnishee, such indifference was entirely rational.

For while a foundation of credit is the borrower's promise to repay, we have always known that such promises are not invariably met, and that this does not always play out as personal disaster. In the classical depiction of debt and its dangers, Shakespeare's *The Merchant of Venice*, the dishonouring has dire consequences not for the debtor but for the creditor. This being so, as Niall Ferguson comments in *The Ascent of Money* (Penguin, 2008), one of the world of money's most intriguing questions is, 'Why don't debtors always default on their creditors?' The obvious answer would be that credit is usually scarce, and not a commodity to be abused, because one is never sure of needing it again; but when credit becomes as superabundant and debauched as in the past ten years, the temptation is to think of it as permanent, bottomless, blind and even, perhaps, a potential relief from monotony. 'Could it be that some people get into debt because, like speeding on a motorcycle, it adds an adrenaline hit to their otherwise humdrum lives?' wonders Margaret Atwood in her recent primer, *Payback: Debt and the Shadow Side of Wealth* (House of Anansi, 2008). 'When the bailiffs are knocking at the door and the lights go off because you didn't pay the hydro and the bank's threatening to foreclose, at least you can't complain of ennui.'

Whatever the case, nobody seemed to much care: although their economy and they themselves had never been more financially gaseous and distended, investors behaved increasingly as though risk had simply been abolished. Crisis had become normalised, and induced not caution but recklessness: with a widespread belief in America that the Fed would simply douse any financial conflagrations with liquidity, there was a steady narrowing of risk premiums – the extra yield that investors demand for riskier securities like mortgage bonds or low-rated corporate debt. Even as the Fed made seventeen consecutive upward adjustments of interest rates, from the start of 2004 to the middle of 2006, increasing short-term rates from 1 per cent to 5.25 per cent, premiums continued diminishing, hitting record minimums in February 2007. Investors, in other words, were treating tranches of bonds based on sub-prime mortgages as being as secure as a ten-year US Treasury. Alan Greenspan called this 'a conundrum'. Yet the anomaly points straight back at him as the chief personification of the regulatory apparatus.

SINCE THE ABOLITION of fixed commissions coaxed investment banks into diversifying their businesses, Wall Street has straddled ever wider and deeper conflicts of interest. Investment banks sell stock, issue bonds, execute mergers, perform research. Client companies want high prices and low interest rates; client investors want low prices and high rates; the bank, between them, extracts fees from both, at any time potentially working at odds with one or the other. Perhaps because of this comfort with conflict, the role of ratings agencies passed without comment. For ratings agencies certified CDOs and other mortgage-backed securities allegedly on the basis of disinterested analysis, while actually earning their fees from issuers with a vested interest in the risk being priced as cheaply as possible.

Illusions flourished about the nature of the work these agencies performed. Agencies never read individual loan files: by the time loans reached Moody's, Standard & Poor's or Fitch, having probably been made on the advice of a loan broker through a mortgage originator, then sold to a bank that blurred them into an amorphous mass to be parcelled up as bonds, they had long since been pulverised, concentrated and flattened out into aggregates of data. What the agency did instead was work on the basis of averages, such as of borrowers' asserted incomes, and concentrations, like the geographic distribution of loans, adjusted for other factors, including the proportion of primary homes involved, because of a general rule of thumb that primary homes are less often abandoned. Such modelling as the agencies did, furthermore, was mainly static: Moody's, for instance, did not update the default-rate assumptions of its CDOROM model between 2002 and 2007, despite steepling increases in delinquencies and foreclosures in the last couple of those years. Based on its analysis, the agency might make a positive rating conditional on an 'enhancement' – usually a thin additional sliver of equity. Or, especially if the client looked like they might 'ratings shop' and take their business elsewhere, they would not, the standard fee for rating a CDO being in the region of $100,000, and for rating a complex CDO, like those called a CDO-squared and a CDO-cubed, sometimes double or treble that: by 2005, in fact, Moody's was drawing half its revenue from such work.

Evidence presented to the US House Oversight Committee Hearings on Ratings Agencies in October 2008 suggests that raters knew full well the increasingly suspect nature of their work – and were ignoring it. A December 2006 email from senior S&P executive Chris Meyer to colleagues Nicole Billick and Belinda Ghetti ends with a sigh: 'Rating agencies continue to create and [sic] even bigger monster – the CDO market. Let's hope we are all wealthy and retired by the time this house of cards falters. :o)' A droll email exchange between S&P analysts Rahul Dilip Shah and Shannon Mooney in April 2007 might almost have been lifted from *Dilbert*:

Shah: By the way, that deal was ridiculous.

Mooney: I know, right – model def does not capture half the risk.

Shah: We should not be rating it.

Mooney: We rate every deal.

Shah: It could be structured by cows and we would rate it.

In a *Portfolio* magazine profile of the maverick investor Steve Eisman, who picked the housing market as overinflated long before most, Michael Lewis recounts an August 2007 conference call where Eisman asked an S&P analyst why he was downgrading CDOs now rather than many, many months earlier. 'It's a good question,' said the analyst. 'You need to have a better answer,' replied Eisman. The answer was obvious: fees for rating a CDO were three times as great as the fees on conventional bond ratings, although, because these fees were paid by the seller rather than the buyer, agencies were always essentially granting licences rather than issuing opinions. Why anyone believed in the ratings is more difficult to answer. At the peak of the boom, there were 64,000 issued securities with AAA ratings, compared to only a dozen public companies with the same rating on all the world's stock exchanges – which even then was one too many, because AIG was among them. At its simplest, perhaps, it was the ancient story: *Mundus vult decipi, ergo decipiatur.* The world wants to be deceived, therefore let it be deceived.

FUTURE HISTORIANS STUDYING this crisis will likewise search in vain for cautionary words or actions from law makers and enforcers. They will see instead 1999 legislation which allowed AIG to choose to be regulated by the complaisant Office of Thrift Supervision alongside other forthcoming disasters like Washington Mutual and IndyMac Bancorp, 2000 legislation which largely exempted CDSs from regulation even as they swelled to a market worth a notional $45 trillion, and 2004 reforms of the Securities and Exchange Commission relaxing net-capital rules on securities firms to increase permissible leverage to forty times equity. Ironically, the consequences of the much-abused Gramm-Leach-Bliley Act have been mainly positive, allowing JP Morgan to bail out Bear Stearns, Bank of America to acquire Merrill Lynch, and Wachovia to kick the tyres of Morgan Stanley before the intercession of Mitsubishi UFJ Financial Group. Lots else, however, in the US and elsewhere, was wilfully wrong-headed.

Above all, those future historians will note the continuance of interest rates at historic lows. The Fed's autonomy is guaranteed by the Banking Act of 1935; it is self-funding and self-governing. Greenspan's dour precursor, Paul Volcker, once received a note from Ronald Reagan asking if the president could pay him a visit; Volcker replied tersely that this was 'inappropriate'. Yet no governor was so freely and successfully courted by the White House as Greenspan, charmed by the administrations both of Clinton and Bush, whose interests were generally best served by an environment of easy credit and false prosperity. The historians will also note that even while raising interest rates, successive Fed governors remained obdurately bullish, issuing soothing communiqués about the capabilities of the banks they were meant to be regulating, and in doing so sounding more like spruikers than supervisors. Both Alan Greenspan and Ben Bernanke, for example, acted as boosters for the bushwah that credit derivatives like CDSs answered all potential ills. Thus Greenspan in May 2005: 'The development of credit derivatives has contributed to the stability of the banking system by allowing banks, especially the largest, systemically important banks, to measure and manage their credit risks more effectively.' Thus Bernanke in March 2006: 'The management of market risk and credit risk has become increasingly sophisticated...Banking organisations of all sizes have made substantial strides over the past two decades in their ability to measure and manage risks.' In this they were echoed by the International Monetary Fund, in its 2006 annual report: 'The dispersion of credit risk by banks to a broader and more diverse set of investors, rather than warehousing such risk on their balance sheets, has helped make the banking and overall financial system more resilient.'

At the time, it was actually popular to argue that there was no compelling rationale for the continued existence of the IMF – to which the G20 has now pledged a fighting fund of $1.1 trillion. But, then, the crisis is presenting many ironic saviours. While at the New York Fed, and in collaboration with the fourteen biggest originators of credit derivatives, Tim Geithner, now US Treasury Secretary, oversaw the creation of an electronic network that hugely simplified and accelerated the trading of these instruments. In February 2007, at which time American sub-prime mortgage debt had grown to US$1.3 trillion, a review of risk management at large banks under Geithner's watch concluded that the quality of loans and investments remained 'strong', and that there were 'no substantial issues of supervisory concern'.

Remember the cosy chat between Peter Baring and his affable Bank of England interlocutor? Here was an initiative of similar character, the regulator acting as friend, familiar and ally to those it was empowered to police. Some of this can be ascribed to Greenspan's personal philosophies, as perhaps the world's most public and adamantine apostle of Ayn Rand; indeed, one could hardly have a more counterintuitive candidate for a senior regulatory role than a libertarian implacably hostile to regulation. Some can also be sheeted home to the freedom with which bankers in the US move between their industry and its bureaucratic mandarinate, whether that be Hank Paulson and Jon Corzine leaving Goldman Sachs to become the Treasury Secretary and the New Jersey governor respectively, or the journeys of Rubin from the Treasury to Citigroup and Greenspan from the Fed to PIMCO. When AIG came to discuss a bailout with the Fed last September, for example, who should be sitting alongside Geithner but the CEO of Goldman Sachs, Lloyd Blankfein? Why? Not for reasons of expertise or authority, but because no institution was more exposed to AIG's CDSs than Goldman Sachs.

Regulation, being almost invariably in arrears of market developments, can only achieve so much; bad judgement persists in any age. 'A strong case can be made for stricter regulations and supervision of banks to forestall euphoric lending that may end in a financial crisis,' observed the great dean of financial turmoil, Charles P Kindleberger, in his classic *Crashes, Manias and Panics* (John Wiley, 2005). 'Historical fact suggests that such a case rests on a counsel of perfection.' But here, perhaps, was the worst of all possible worlds: ratings agencies reduced simply to endorsement, regulators dedicated chiefly to encouragement, as intent in their own way as the brokers, valuers, mortgage lenders and bankers on the business getting through, yet who by their very visible existence instilled a sense that everything was under close control.

AUSTRALIA HAS BEEN fortunate in its banks. Unlike the fragmented and dispersed American banking sector, the 'four pillars' were able to spread their risks around markets and geographies; they have run high capital ratios, enjoy low-cost retail funds and, after heavy losses there in the 1980s, have gradually disinvested overseas. Casualties have accumulated in the realm of asset-backed securities, whether property or infrastructure, and the days when Macquarie Bank was referred to as the 'millionaires' factory' suddenly seem the stuff of nostalgia. But the regulatory system, chiefly the Reserve Bank of Australia, the Australian Prudential Regulation Authority and the Australian Securities and Investment Commission, seems largely to have avoided the phenomenon, famously delineated by the economist George Stigler, of 'regulatory capture', where market participants coerce regulators into serving primarily their own interests.

America offers a demonstration of what Australia avoided. Simon Johnson, former chief economist at the IMF, has argued persuasively in *The Atlantic* that the crisis in the US is 'shockingly reminiscent' of crises of crony capitalism in Russia and Argentina. In the US, as in emerging markets, Johnson contends, 'elite business interests...played a central role in creating the crisis, making ever larger gambles, with the implicit backing of the government, until the inevitable collapse.' In their deliberations on the crisis, regulators ended up speaking to people exactly like themselves, often old friends too senior to have a sophisticated sense of market conditions and credit quality, but willing participants in mutual disorientation; between them, they then did everything possible to protect their industry's interests, staving off insurrectionary talk of nationalisation. Ironically, American financiers and economists have scourged developing nations for just such coalitions of interests. In the aftermath of the Asian crisis a decade ago, for example, the much-admired economist Rudi Dornbusch deplored the mentality of 'Dial 1-800-BAILOUT for reckless businessmen, greedy bankers and corrupt politicians'. He told the Davos World Economic Forum: 'It's important that some people lose a lot of money, important that they be punished for their stupidity and greed.' But nobody enjoys the taste of medicine, least of all their own.

Bankers, regulators and politicians alike have resolved instead to gamble that theirs is a crisis of liquidity rather than of solvency, like those hostages in mass kidnappings who insist that if everyone just sits tight and keeps calm then no one need get hurt. Bankers have rediscovered how important they are to the 'real economy', reminding whoever will listen that credit creation is integral to all industry; regulators and legislators have taken them at their word, trusting that stability will rekindle optimism. The agreed solution has been to perpetuate the banking system with repeated infusions of taxpayers' money, and indeed to take certain parts of it over: British taxpayers are already majority owners of Royal Bank of Scotland and Lloyds Banking Group; American taxpayers will soon own the largest stake in Citigroup; German taxpayers look like controlling Hypo Real Estate. This has been done, so far at least, without actual formal representation, or the setting of limits and targets, thanks partly to a dread of the repeat of the panic glimpsed last September, but mainly because of an engrained ideological antipathy to such state controls. Barack Obama's modest regulatory proposals of June came with a resigned sigh about 'the speed, scope and sophistication of a twenty-first-century global economy' – a formulation that could have come directly from the pitch documents of the banking industry lobbyists who have besieged the Beltway these last six months. One area of risk management in which American financial institutions have continued to excel is the area involving risk to their own freedom of opportunity. If asset and securities repricings since last year reflect fundamentals rather than a temporary discount for illiquidity, however, those lobbyists have a great deal more work in front of them.

IF THERE WAS a point at which this crisis metastasised from one of finance into what is sometimes euphemised as 'the real economy', it was with the demolition of Lehman Brothers, which had had the misfortune to seek regulatory clemency at the same time as AIG and after Bear Stearns. Lehman had a concentrated version of what would soon be identified as a widespread problem: a balance sheet fat with assets that weren't worth their ascribed values, and that were therefore too injurious to sell.

Unlike at Bear Stearns, where investors had some warning, nobody had seen it coming, and there was fright at the tyranny of mark-to-market accounting, which requires more or less instant recognition of fluctuation in asset values, thereby seeming to bankers the acme of common sense in boom times and a diabolical imposition in busts. A colossal broad-based liquidity crisis ensued: banks doubled the reserves they held at the Fed, inter-bank lending ceased almost altogether, and the market for short-term and asset-backed commercial paper froze as if flooded by liquid nitrogen. The panic was so pervasive and paralysing that you half-expected tales of ATMs refusing to disgorge depositors' cash.

In the preceding years, the relationship between finance and business had appeared an increasingly distant one, reflected in the media's topsy-turvy preferences, reporting the fluctuations of stocks, commodities and curren-cies as news, while treating the manufacture of physical goods as something arcane and esoteric. Market turmoil after Lehmans' collapse threw everyone into turmoil together, credit creation being next to impossible in an environ-ment where nobody quite knows what anything is worth.

Corporates singed by recession in the early 1990s, and by periodic reckonings in the equity and property markets since, have actually only been averagely wasteful in recent years. Some leveraged buyout funds and venture capitalists have tended their reputations for daredevilry – in KKR's $26 billion acquisition of First Data in April 2007, interest payments were set to absorb the target's entire cash flow – but business conditions had not been so buoyant as to cajole companies into over-borrowing. General Motors perished of pre-existing wounds, decades in the seeping.

The calamity in private consumption, however, reverberated. Flush with credit, American consumers have accounted for more than two-thirds of the country's economic growth since 2000, and more than a third of world-wide growth in private consumption since 1990. Now, like a deep-sea diver hurriedly yanked to the surface, they were decompressing dangerously, and in intensifying anguish. Certainly they were too busy dealing with existing borrowings to incur more, which hurt the economy at every level: retail sales, corporate profitability, capital investment, dividends and distributions, consumption and personal-tax revenues.

Goldman Sachs' balance sheet stress test is famously known as 'the WOW', standing for 'worst of the worst'. The WOW is designed to inter-rogate whether the bank could survive the worst conditions encountered in the preceding decade in each market simultaneously, worsened by a further 30 per cent – and it was here made to appear optimistic. As American consumption slackened month by month, cruelling worldwide demand, forecasts became unremittingly bleak, whether it was the International Labour Organisation estimating that fifty million jobs would be lost, or the World Bank's prophecy that between 200,000 and 400,000 more children will die annually between now and 2015 than had earlier been predicted. Of course, there is something deeply ironic about trusting the prophecies of many of the same economists whose predictions were so rosy so recently.

The coping mechanisms agreed on are risky, involving the continuance of institutions of dubious solvency. The crisis has already been marked by several intemperate acquisitions, such as Wachovia's of Golden West and Lloyds TSB's of HBOS: governments are placing themselves in similar positions. The burden of salvage on the state almost beggars belief. In renais-sance Florence, keepers of the exchequer distinguished between the Monte Vecchio (Old Mountain), debt sustained in fighting Genoa, and the Monte Nuovo (New Mountain), debt sustained in fighting the Turks. The American economy now bears similar twin burdens: the toll of the initial damage and the cost of the repair. Barack Obama's budget digest, ironically entitled

A New Era of Responsibility (Office of Management and Budget, 2009), forecasts his government taking on more than US$9 trillion in new debt in the decade to come, and deficits averaging almost 5 per cent in each of the five years after the recession's forecast end. An auction of British government debt failed in March; the Australian budget in May was a sobering reflection of the layers of cost lying ahead. With levels of risk aversity as pusillanimously high as they were casually low two and a half years ago, the state's capacity to spend will be severely constrained.

In other words, crisis is again worth the name, rather than being the stuff of passing headlines, short-term corrections and token recalibrations; indeed, it has embedded itself with a vengeance. For even after its economic impacts have faded, the collapse of credit and the end of stupid money will leave a social and cultural imprint, in the form of fears, taboos, superstitions, cautionary tales, diminished expectations – indeed, in some respects, perhaps this is to be hoped for, lest it be repeated sooner rather than later. Last time I was in Sydney, I happened to pass through the foyer of the same tower in which I'd worked a decade ago, although the bank itself is no longer there, swallowed by another, franchise destroyed, personnel scattered. The intents, the expressions, the atmosphere – all brought back old memories. But experientially, the people could not have been other than different.

Gideon Haigh is a Melbourne-based author and journalist. His most recent book is *The Racket: How Abortion Became Legal in Australia* (MUP, 2008). His essays have been published in *Griffith REVIEW: Addicted to Celebrity, The Lure of Fundamentalism* and *Getting Smart*.

MEMOIR

Windows on Lehman

Confronting the inevitable destruction

Erica Sontheimer

EMERGING from the subway I joined the crowds of Lower Manhattan, anxious about my first day on the job. The older buildings of the financial district were squat, tarnished sandstones puckered with sooty recessed windows. I walked towards a sense of openness and, turning a corner, saw the World Trade Center towers rising before me.

Like pewter-skinned jewels, the twin towers sipped sunlight from the source, illuminating all of Wall Street, both a beacon and a boast. The North Tower held aloft antennae which slipped under the sheath of firmament, like a hypodermic needle, poking bubbles of Babel into the stratosphere. The steel columns channelled gusts of wind and I imagined cloud particles swirling in the dust around me.

I passed through the plaza on my way to Lehman Brothers, next door, where I took up a temp job that lasted for four years. It was 1999; I was twenty-five years old and wearing a cheap polyester suit from my small home town. The echoes of hard-heeled shoes clattered off the marble walls and cancelled out my own footsteps. The lobby's revolving doors were a banal fortification against Trojan Horses.

For my first two weeks I answered line two when line one was busy, assigned to a pool of assistants supporting a vice chairman who spent most of his time in Israel brokering mergers between pharmaceutical companies. Line two only rang once or twice a day. I sharpened a box of pencils and arranged them neatly in a cup on the vice chairman's desk. I read the *New York Times*, and then filled in all the O's with one of the pencils.

In between these tasks, I stared past the glass wall, out to my patch of eighteenth-storey view: a swatch of sky, a stitch of Staten Island and a swathe of Tower One. I pictured myself as a co-ordinate on a three-dimensional grid. I imagined a transparent New York, all structures clear and colourless. I would walk along streets squinting up at clusters of bodies standing self-consciously rigid in imperceptible elevators, rising and falling along thermal shafts. My vision − a city disrobed and vulnerable − was a perversion of New York's collective consciousness and its tough, cool persona.

PREVIOUS PAGE: A mannequin dressed as a banker is hanged from a traffic light. Photographer: Rosie Greenway. *Source: gettyimages.com*

After that first assignment I was promoted to an ongoing temporary position in the recruiting department. The market was strong and Lehman Brothers spared no expense to attract the best talent from the Ivy League universities and business schools. We offered signing bonuses, stock options and moving allowances, plus all-expenses-paid outings to Yankee games, No Doubt concerts and catered evenings at the trendiest bars and clubs. The four of us in the recruiting department – all young, single women – co-ordinated these events and tagged along to help the recruits break the ice. We were also there to step in when a 'situation' arose, like the time one of our candidates pissed on his seat at the No Doubt concert and had to be escorted away from the open bar by the security guards.

During this time I also spent two months in Windows on the World, where Lehman had hired space to train the new recruits. The express elevator ride to the 110th floor took ten minutes. The elevator operator chewed gum to pop his ears. There was no running out for a breath of fresh air: once you arrived at Windows you were there for the day.

The restaurant and conference centre were panelled in dark wood and burgundy fabric, with a low ceiling that hid a network of ducts, wires and pipes. Closer to the windows, sunlight streamed in unobstructed by anything save the clouds and the curve of the earth. New York and New Jersey lay flattened out below, extending into a smoggy haze, the Empire State Building twinkling like a toy.

The view, elevating us above the community of eight million below, was designed to stun and brought to mind the archaic sense of *real estate*: that the king possessed all within view from his royal seat. Within a week I was fatigued of the ride and the rise, the sensation of feeling the earth fall away beneath me. The proximity to the clouds, sky and sun unravelled no myths or poetry in this tomb of trade. I remained a temp in my corporate masquerade, earning a regular pay cheque and biding my time until something better came along.

Secluded high in the recesses of this cloud-cave, I felt mummified. Everything had to be piped in or wired up to us: air, water, food, electricity, information. The panorama distorted eye-level details, and my mind grasped for something fundamental, something which would rein the world back to direct sensation. My mind wandered: What would it be like to fall? How many people collected the trash and brought it back to ground level? Where did these buildings cast their shadows?

BY THE SUMMER of 2001 the market was softening as the dotcom bubble burst. There was no budget for temp workers but I hadn't lined up anything else, so I agreed to take on a permanent position as an executive assistant to a managing director. He had a reputation for tyranny, but I was up to the challenge and was able to name my salary in addition to negotiating a three-month leave of absence shortly after I began working for him.

I spent those three months at a yoga ashram in California, happily exchanging my hard-earned money for the privilege of washing dishes and yanking weeds, with clover and dirt poking up between my toes. The first day I climbed 108 steep wooden steps to visit the Shiva temple. It was a satisfying walk in the hot dry air, the effort quickening my breath and provoking a sweat. At the peak I was startled to see a shrouded figure at the centre of the open-air temple, sitting erect and motionless with a mound of dreadlocks piled high on its head. Afraid I was trespassing, I turned and retreated downhill.

Soon I returned to the temple with the group for an evening meditation. The dreadlocked head turned out to be a Shiva lingam, the oldest idol of Hinduism, a primordial phallic tower. We chanted mantras and bathed the stone lingam in cow milk and rosewater and oiled it with ghee. Strict tradition dictates that a Shiva lingam must be tended to and worshipped every day, to quell the cosmic force of destruction.

I found my meditations at the Shiva temple the most profound. It was refreshing to acknowledge the inevitability of death and destruction, and to consider the role of this season in the cycle of creation. In contrast, New York's ceaseless worship of youth and vigour was tiring.

The summer interlude of yoga and meditation, abstaining from stimulants as mild as garlic, refined me. When I returned to New York my body responded like a voltmeter to the sheer energy of the place. Even the overlooked nature strips moved me with their beauty, and I admired the weeds and wildflowers that seeded themselves at the first moment of decay in the bitumen and concrete.

On the warm and rainy evening of 10 September I sat in the window of my favourite café. Architecture and history were reflected in dark pools on the surface of wet streets and sidewalks. A strobe of lightening mixed with the yellow flashes of an ambulance. I invested the rain with my own infatuation of the city. The water soaked up culture, mirrored the artificial lights of the night, and stained expensive and delicate shoes. The run-off followed the contours of the natural gullies and streams submerged beneath the pavement. I longed to lie down in the rain, limbs outstretched, touching the whole city at once.

MY MEMORIES OF returning to work on 11 September have ossified from repetition. Records show the first plane hit the North Tower at 8.46 am. Those of us next door noticed the sudden jerk and swaying of our building, and then a distant boom that echoed around the walls. Only junior bankers and support staff were at work that early in the morning and we ran from our cubicles to the empty senior offices, where we could look out the windows and see the lazy descent of thousands of sheets of white office paper. I was one of the last people to shake off the shock and leave the floor, after the second plane hit the South Tower.

Outside I sat by the Hudson River next to well-dressed strangers for an unaccountably long time. We could see both buildings incinerating, and paper scraps and ash rising with the heat. Finally I joined the migration north. A few blocks away I felt and heard the low rumble and turned to watch the South Tower dissolve into salt. Minutes later the North Tower imploded. I kept walking uptown and by mid-morning I stood alone on the roof of a West Side warehouse, looking downtown. The whole city seemed to be turned out of its buildings, three dimensions reduced to two. The impact inverted everything and I felt like I had witnessed the sky-scraping deity's mortality, the destruction of the grid's origin. The sound of leaves rustling in the breeze was audible for the first time on those streets.

Already, by that afternoon, enterprising individuals had tripled the price of Twin Tower postcards and collectibles. The paths I'd walked in Lower Manhattan were buried. The only footprints left were those of the towers.

At home that night I saw the neighbourhood children draw the scene in chalk on the sidewalks. The North Tower burned and a plane flew into the South Tower, with stick-people hanging out the windows, screaming for help. I was obsessed with footage of the attacks and drew my own sketches over the next few days, unable to report to work and awaiting further instruction from the firm. Still home the next week, I threw away the newspaper clippings and photos. I wanted my memories to stay fluid, registering my experience in my own limbs, not these frozen images.

THE FOLLOWING WINTER felt particularly dark and cold. For six months Lehman Brothers took over a mid-rise hotel near Times Square. The elevators weren't designed for our needs and moved with agonising slowness. We were five to a room, sharing one phone line and emergency laptops. In place of beds and nightstands we had folding tables and low-wattage floor lamps. Outside, in the synthetic twilight of Times Square, the streets were clogged with elderly patriotic Christmas shoppers bussed in from other states, sporting red, white and blue tracksuits.

Our sector, Technology Mergers and Acquisitions, was bullish and gearing up for the full force of George W Bush's 'shock and awe' campaign. Our clients included Raytheon, L3 Communications and other notable members of the military-industrial complex. Lehman stock had split and was soaring over eighty dollars per share, and my retirement investments were growing at a staggering rate.

Eventually we moved into a brand new building nearby (it had been built for Morgan Stanley, but after the attacks that firm decided to consolidate operations elsewhere) and the winter gloom lifted. However, I knew I needed to escape the holding pattern I'd been in for the past few years. Now that my job was permanent I couldn't simply arrange a three-month leave of absence to offset the months of corporate drudgery and boredom. I was closing in on thirty, had proved something to myself about living in the big city, and it was time to move on. When the time came, my boss gave me a Coach bag selected by his wife and a cheque for $1818.18, a nod to our thin bond of Jewish identity, since this figure is symbolic of giving life.

IN THE SUMMER of 2003 I moved to San Francisco for love and a more fulfilling job in the not-for-profit arts sector. In spite of my disgust with Bush's war in Iraq and my discomfort with the blood money, I was too lazy and hypocritical to reinvest my Lehman stock in something more socially responsible. Sometimes I caught myself making justifications, thinking I had worked hard for the money and convincing myself that no investment could truly wash the blood off its hands.

It wasn't until early 2008 that my partner and I, now married and living in Brisbane, made a commitment to move the money. The stock had already lost a third of its value from its peak, but we were lucky to cut our losses before it plummeted over the next few months to end up under three dollars a share by 15 September, following the Dow Jones's largest drop in a single day since 9/11.

When I read the news of Lehman's bankruptcy I wondered about my former boss, friends and colleagues, but it would have been cruel to look them up and I had nothing to offer except smug curiosity. I did look closely at the videos posted to YouTube showing various employees leaving the corporate headquarters, but I didn't recognise anyone.

There was an unusual delay before CEO Dick Fuld surfaced in the public eye, like a petulant bully complaining about not being bailed out when the Feds had already rescued JP Morgan and AIG on the grounds that they were 'too big to fail'. Fuld's hubris and sense of entitlement endeared him to no one and I found him nauseating to watch. He implied that Lehman Brothers was so intimately linked with the global economy that it was practically a crime against humanity to let it fail. Where was this guiding sense of interconnection when he and his team approved Lehman's unprecedented leveraging of mortgage assets, or when he accepted nearly half a billon dollars in compensation over the previous decade?

I realise that Fuld is an easy scapegoat for our own guilt and denial. We're wired for life, for growth and sensual gratification, and it's pleasing to believe we'll live forever and easy to justify our greedy urges. The phallic lingam itself is life-giving – but it doesn't grant us immortality.

Erica Sontheimer is deputy editor of Griffith REVIEW.

An outsider's perspective

The American flaw at the heart of global banking

Christopher Joye

I recently parachuted into the crucible of the American policymaking debate when I was invited to present alongside Robert Shiller of Yale at a private summit for Obama administration officials on the future of housing policy. There it struck me that the world I perceived was conspicuously different to the one my American colleagues could see. In analysing why, for instance, Canada's, New Zealand's and Australia's financial systems were in such radically better shape, I began to realise that there was a fundamental frailty in the foundations of America's financial architecture. This has largely been responsible for precipitating the current crisis and propagating it around an increasingly interconnected world.

The problem is ostensibly simple: the vast bulk of American home loans are not funded using the balance sheets of large transnational banks and the regionally diversified retail deposits of their customers, but through the far more complex and sometimes unstable process of 'securitisation'. This moves the loans off banks' balance sheets by selling them to third-party investors, so the lender can recycle the original capital into new loans. During periods of extreme uncertainty it can become an unreliable source of finance, supplied by a small number of sometimes fickle institutional investors that can withdraw from the market at a whim. In the rest of the developed world, securitisation, if it exists at all, has been a small yet important part of the housing-finance mix. In America it dominates home-loan funding.

This is the consequence of a credit-creation system that evolved from the parochial designs of competing states within the fragmented American federation, distorted further by government responses to the spate of banking failures during the Great Depression. Those failures were a product of the desire of individual states to regulate and control the banks operating within their borders.

The outcome of these decisions and the continued missteps of American policymakers ever since – including the 'partial' privatisation of the government-sponsored enterprises (GSEs) Fannie Mae and Freddie Mac in 1968 and 1970 – has been the effective disintermediation of deposit-taking organisations as the primary source of housing finance in America, in favour of GSE-based securitisation.

Fannie and Freddie became a synthetic surrogate for the nationally integrated banking systems that are the cornerstones of credit creation in most other OECD countries. The artificial GSE-based securitisation infrastructure relieved pressure on American governments to consolidate a geographically fractured and prone-to-fail banking system – something that should have occurred organically over the twentieth century.

What has not been identified before is that the ineluctable result of the policymakers' decision to favour securitisation was the catastrophic crisis that first emerged in mid-2007 and was quickly transmitted around the world by increasingly integrated international capital markets. Notwithstanding the relative integrity of debt securities in other countries, lenders around the world discovered that liquidity in their local credit markets was eviscerated – with dire consequences for their economies.

When a mortgage is securitised, the lender does not hold it on the balance sheet to maturity. Many economists, including me, have noted that this process makes sense if it is managed properly, enabling lenders to alleviate balance-sheet stresses and spread some of their risks to third-party investors. These investors, such as super funds, get exposure to typically low-volatility 'mortgage-backed securities' that yield higher-than-cash returns. The low risk and robust long-term performance of securitised home loans in Australia and

Canada prior to and throughout the current credit crisis is testament to the merits of this funding medium for consumers, lenders and investors.

The Canadian government's Canada Mortgage and Housing Corporation, which guarantees mortgage-backed securities in return for a commercial-risk premium, has successfully supported continued securitisation of large volumes of Canadian home loans throughout the crisis. It requires mortgage originators to contribute a 2 per cent 'first-loss' equity position to their securitised portfolios to align the interests of lenders and the ultimate investors.

Australia's and Canada's housing finance markets have been dominated by a small number of successful national banks whose balance sheets are the principal suppliers of mortgage credit. Australia now has four of only eleven AA-rated banks in the world. Canada, which was judged by the 2008 World Economic Forum as having the world's soundest banking system, also has four major banks with this coveted rating. Since mortgage-default rates in both countries remain extremely low – at less than 15 per cent of American levels – and there has been no real credit rationing, bank failures or nationalisations, Australia's and Canada's housing markets have also avoided large house price falls.

While securitisation in Australia and Canada has facilitated new competition and offered lenders valuable portfolio-diversification benefits, it has only ever accounted for around a fifth of all mortgage funding. Trouble arises when artificially strong incentives and subsidies predicate your *entire* housing-finance system on securitised forms of funding, to the detriment of the traditional deposit-taking market. In addition to stunting the growth of a nationally integrated banking sector, it exposes the financial system to potentially destabilising conflicts.

The most obvious of these is that the organisations that source new home loans, and which are responsible for assessing their credit risk, are removed from the institutions that ultimately own the assets and bear that risk. It is a classic principal–agent problem. Fannie Mae and Freddie Mac had an artificial capital-raising advantage (as investors ascribed to them the US government's AAA credit rating); they could source funds more cheaply than competitors and also enjoyed other crucial advantages such as tax exemptions and lower capital requirements. Fannie and Freddie developed exceedingly high investment-banking-like leverage ratios of 20:1 and 70:1 respectively, which rose further if all the off-balance-sheet mortgage-backed securities they guaranteed were included. Before the credit crisis they funded or guaranteed around half of all American housing finance, with total liabilities of about US$5 trillion. This compares with US$9.5 trillion of government debt at the time of their 'conservatorship' in 2008.

In the early 2000s, Fannie and Freddie were asked by the Bush administration to increase financing for low- to moderate-income regions with high minority populations. This combined with shareholder calls to improve their returns. As a result the GSEs used their AAA ratings to invest in, or guarantee, higher-risk loans. These loans had little borrower documentation, lower credit scores and/or higher loan-to-value ratios.

By 2008, the GSEs held on balance sheet or guaranteed around $1.6 trillion of these 'non-prime' mortgages (a third of their total exposures), which unsurprisingly accounted for 90 per cent of their losses. Fannie and Freddie were once again crowding out private lenders and shunting them further down the credit curve. The consequence was an increase in even riskier sub-prime lending, which doubled from a tenth to a fifth of all new American home loans between 2001 and 2005.

A RECENT OECD study on the causes of the global financial crisis argued that these effects were exacerbated by at least two other factors: the Basel II Accord on international bank regulation, which encouraged banks to accelerate their off-balance-sheet mortgage securitisation; and changes in US Securities and Exchange Commission regulations that allowed investment banks to increase their debt to net-equity ratios from 15:1 to as much as 40:1. In the OECD's opinion, the result was that banks started creating their own 'Fannie and Freddie lookalikes'– so-called 'structured-investment vehicles'.

Yet in almost all other countries where quasi-government entities do not dominate housing finance, traditional banks account for up to 90 per cent of all mortgage credit, with the vast majority of these assets permanently retained on the lenders' balance sheets. When lenders in these countries do securitise, they usually apply the same credit-assessment standards to these loans that they use with the assets retained on their balance sheets. In most western economies banks control the upfront credit-assessment process, service the underlying assets over decades, and bear the risk if borrowers default. In the US, all three critical functions – origination, servicing and funding – are separated by a 'fire and forget' approach. Without mitigating regulation this leads to inevitable conflicts of interest.

Britain's problems during the crisis can also be traced back to the vulnerabilities that materialise when securitisation starts to displace the traditional hold-to-maturity banking sector. Northern Rock, which had a 10 per cent share of the British housing-finance market, drew three-quarters of its home loan funding from off-balance-sheet sources. The sudden explosion in global risk aversion in mid-2007 as a consequence of the US sub-prime calamity propagated an indiscriminate rise in illiquidity for all debt securities, especially anything resembling a mortgage. As a result, private mortgage-securitisation markets collapsed in the latter half of 2007, with adverse ramifications for institutions that relied on them.

The emergence in Britain of a bank that predicated three-quarters of its funding on external or 'wholesale' sources of finance (as opposed to retail deposits) created a channel through which unanticipated international shocks could be transmitted. And so the initially independent American sub-prime virus precipitated the first run on a British bank since 1866; the government was forced to nationalise Northern Rock in February 2008.

HOW DID THE world's largest and purportedly most advanced economy end up with such an inherently risky credit-creation system? America's banking industry is far more fragmented that any other, with only one truly coast-to-coast institution: Bank of America. There are over 8,400 banks and savings entities, half with less than US$100 million in assets, which are highly localised in their lending and deposit-taking activities. This disposes America's banks to an astounding propensity for failure. Between 1984 and 2003, a total of 2,698 US banks and savings institutions failed according to the Federal Deposit and Insurance Corporation.

The American government's panoply of interventions in response to the problem of persistent bank failures and the collapse of its financing system during the Great Depression has, ironically, further hindered the need for consolidation of its dispersed deposit-taking system, which was the underlying cause of these failures in the first place.

The extraordinary degree of direct government involvement in America's housing and financing systems is hard for an outsider to fathom. In addition to the GSEs, the American government created the Federal Housing Administration in 1934, the largest public mortgage insurer in the world to insure the losses of private lenders to non-prime borrowers. Its market share of new mortgages in insures has risen from just 4 per cent in 2006 to nearly a fifth in 2008, with analysts predicting that it will hit a third this year.

When I described the Australian market's characteristics to the policymakers at the housing summit, their jaws hit the floor. Without any government interventions Australia has generated a higher rate of home ownership, no sub-prime lending to speak of, no bank failures, nationalisations or mortgage-credit rationing, and current and long-term mortgage-default rates that are 15 per cent of American levels.

The audience was surprised that 80 per cent of all Australian borrowers are on 'adjustable rate' home loans (viewed as devil's breath in the US), that those using fixed-rate loans only fix for one to five years, and that mortgage rates are based on the central bank's 'target cash rate'. In the US, around three-quarters of all borrowers have thirty-year fixed-rate mortgages, over which the Federal Reserve has limited control. While a thirty-year fixed-rate mortgage sounds wonderful from an affordability perspective – as it did to policymakers during the Great Depression – it has undermined the ability of the Fed to manage economic activity and the housing market in particular.

Between August 2007 and December 2008, the Federal Reserve slashed its target rate by 500 basis points. Yet the average interest rate on outstanding US home loans fell by only 15 basis points. It has been no surprise, therefore, to see default rates continue to rise. In comparison, Australia's central bank has been able to deliver a 40 per cent drop in the cost of variable-rate home loans, with 375 of 400 basis points in rate cuts passed on by lenders.

The clear point of difference between Australia and the US is government policy. While both countries are federations, America is disadvantaged by its decentralisation across fifty states. The US also has a longstanding cultural antipathy towards nationally consolidated and regulated banks. Thomas Jefferson declared: 'Banking institutions are more dangerous to our liberties than standing armies. If the American people ever allow private banks to control the issue of their currency, first by inflation, then by deflation, the banks and corporations that will grow up around [the banks] will deprive the people of all property until their children wake up homeless on the continent their fathers conquered.'

Following a bout of bank failures in 1907, Congress established the Federal Reserve in 1913 to facilitate liquidity between banks and prevent these crises recurring. Yet up until the early 1990s, laws prohibited banks from setting up branches in other states or from merging. According to the economist Charles Calomiris, 'economic logic often took a back seat to special-interest politics and, occasionally, to populist passions.'

The Federal Reserve was unable to minimise bank failures because of a bizarre patchwork of inadequate and sometimes conflicting regulators. MIT's David A Singer has observed, 'The US has one of the most institutionally fragmented…regulatory environments of any industrialised country… Banks face an alphabet soup of regulators, including the Fed, the OCC, OTS, FDIC, the National Credit Union Administration, and separate state regulators, while the SEC, the Commodity Futures Trading Commission and other regulators monitor the capital markets. Most surprisingly, the US does not have a federal insurance regulator; instead, fifty separate state regulators govern insurance firms within their jurisdictions.' In Australia there is one banking and insurance regulator: the Australian Prudential Regulation Authority.

Congress finally agreed to repeal most of the prohibitions on interstate banking in 1994 – yet by then the damage had been done. Despite some subsequent consolidation in the deposit-taking sector, the exceedingly fractured US savings system has been set in stone.

The first-order cause of the global financial crisis was not the advent of sub-prime lending, the Basel II Accord, greedy investment banks, non-recourse

lending, community reinvestment acts, or the GSEs per se (although all contributed as catalysts). The underlying driver was over a century of flawed political
decision-making that created a deeply dysfunctional and structurally fragile
system of housing finance under which bank balance sheets, and a nationally
integrated deposit-taking infrastructure, had been displaced.

The government-created yet ostensibly private GSE duopoly, which
acted as a surrogate for a national deposit-taking system, stunted the need for
the geographically dispersed and intrinsically fragile US banking industry to
consolidate and insulate itself from failure. These structural flaws were exacerbated when the highly leveraged GSEs entered the much riskier non-prime
segments of the US mortgage market. The traditional private lending sector
was pushed further down the credit curve with a consequent explosion in
sub-prime loans.

The introduction of the Basel II Accord that encouraged off-balance-sheet
securitisation activity only lent additional momentum to these dynamics. As
default rates inevitably rose and the system of securitisation instantaneously
transmitted these risks to investors around the world, the dark side of capital-
market integration and globalisation emerged. Defective mark-to-market
accounting standards, premised as they were on the belief that 'efficient
markets' always priced assets accurately (but rarely during times of crisis),
entrenched a vicious negative-feedback loop as artificial declines in collateral
values forced banks and investors all around the world to pull back on lending,
triggering further reductions in asset values, and yet another contraction in
lending, and so on.

Many of the so-called 'toxic' assets were not toxic at all: the market
failures triggered by the implosion in America's housing finance system
precipitated illiquidity for all forms of credit internationally, which then
embedded the deleveraging death-spiral that decimated asset values, parts of
the international banking system and, recently, real economic growth.

Today, the private lending market in America has all but disappeared.
The GSEs and FHA account for 95 per cent of housing finance. The remnants
of private banking are being stealthily nationalised by a questionable process
of private risk socialisation; the American government is now the largest
individual shareholder in Citigroup and Bank of America.

IT IS WORRYING that American policymakers continue to apply prescriptions that do absolutely nothing to address these dysfunctions. Stakeholders from Paul Krugman to Timothy Geithner appear to be in a state of denial – Krugman had the temerity to blame the crisis on Asia and its 'excess savings', while Geithner and the Obama administration appear desperate to bail out bankers, without any real reforms. As taxpayers are forced to internalise private risks and the role of the GSEs is repeatedly reaffirmed, the perverse moral-hazard incentives – we'll take the upside of billions of dollars worth of bonuses but only bear limited downside when we're caught short – are being re-infused into the institutional DNA.

If America is to have any hope of cauterising these problems, and preventing similar cataclysms, the administration and key thought-leaders must acknowledge the structural flaws that caused them. Applying bandages myopically in a desperate bid to avoid a cathartic recession without concomitant reforms is not the long-term answer. In fact, the administration's policies increase the likelihood of the same issues reoccurring – on another president's watch.

America's credit-creation system must be transformed to a hold-to-maturity, balance-sheet-based focus. At some point, the GSEs should be fully nationalised and, alongside other public housing-finance agencies, phased out of the day-to-day housing-finance infrastructure. Governments have a role to play supplying the public goods of liquidity and price discovery when markets fail – but only when markets fail.

In the medium to long term, the administration needs to create something that has been beyond governments since the Founding Fathers: a robust and nationally integrated private banking infrastructure, underwritten principally through retail deposits, to firmly reposition balance sheets as the main repository of credit. To achieve this, the administration must establish singular banking and insurance regulators, rather than a kaleidoscope of agencies, and remove all legal and regulatory obstacles to enable the private banking system to expand and eventually supplant the GSEs and the unnatural activities they spawned.

Christopher Joye is the managing director of Rismark International. He participated in the American Housing Policy summit at the invitation of the Rockefeller and MacArthur foundations. A version of this essay with footnotes is at www.griffithreview.com

A new globalisation

Decoupling from complexity for greater security

Jonathan West

WHEN the deepest economic crisis of the past fifty years finally ends, a changed world will be left in its wake. Capitalism will still be with us, but the new capitalism could differ substantially from the old. One key feature could be a new form of globalisation. In the current crisis it is already apparent that nations that were relatively 'decoupled' from global markets as they entered this recession have done better than the more 'globalised' ones. The lessons of their success are now under scrutiny.

Even though it's too soon to see the future clearly, the forces that will shape the new capitalism can be found in the underlying origins and peculiar character of this recession. This crisis differs from others over the past half-century, not just in its extent and intensity, but in its causes and course.

The current crisis presents two novel features. It has been precipitated by excess worldwide debt, not rising consumer prices, and the increasing complexity and integration of world markets shunted it around the globe with unprecedented speed and ferocity. How societies react to these forces will incubate the new form of capitalism. It is worth exploring further how these developments may play out, before considering how societies such as Australia might respond.

The current recession has been balance-sheet driven, not interest-rate driven. In previous postwar recessions, rising inflationary pressures typically triggered monetary tightening and a slowdown; the antidote was lower rates, which eventually promoted recovery. This time, a balance-sheet recession has stemmed from the weakened financial condition of both consumers and lenders – both have simply had too much debt.

While the crisis has surfaced in multiple forms – sub-prime housing loans, implosion of banks, collapse of automobile companies, country defaults, plunging (and skyrocketing) currencies, government fiscal crises – all are ultimately manifestations of excess leverage. Searching for causes, commentators have focused on the relatively superficial: lax financial-system oversight, overconfident mergers and corporate incompetence, and excessive executive compensation. But behind them all is the stubborn fact that global debt had simply risen to unsustainable levels.

The inevitable reaction to unsustainable debt is deleveraging – debt reduction. This will take time, perhaps several recession-and-boom cycles. But the implication is that this time, and in the future, rather than relying on ever more debt with lower interest rates to extricate ourselves from recession, global capitalism will need to learn to operate with much lower levels of leverage. It's not clear that we know any longer how to do this. Closer scrutiny reveals both how dependent our society has become on debt and how historically unprecedented are the levels to which it has risen.

While debt-to-GDP ratios have escalated furthest in the US, other developed nations including Australia and Britain face similar over-extension, and similar startling increases. To provide some sense of the disproportionate scale debt had reached prior to this crisis, at the start of the great bull market that began in August 1982, US household debt was 44 per cent of nominal GDP; by 1998–2000, it had climbed to 63 per cent; but by 2008, the ratio rocketed to 97 per cent. And that's only household debt. Add corporate and government debt, and the ratios rise to nose-bleed levels. Total US credit-market debt (households, corporations and governments) had reached almost three times GDP at the outset of the crisis, by far the highest ever recorded, and up by around five times its postwar norm.

It has been estimated that to return to its long-term average, around US$60 trillion in debt will need to be removed from the global financial system – that's US$60 trillion in buying power and assets. As total US household wealth (by far the world's largest) stood at US$51 trillion in mid-2009, this is a truly staggering sum. It dwarfs the US$3 trillion stimulus of the Obama administration, to say nothing of Australia's meagre triple-digit billions, or similar commitments in Europe.

Debt has become integral to the pre-crisis form of capitalism; a steeply rising share of all the profits of US corporations – notably including non-financial firms – now appears in financial form, largely interest on debt. Financial payments, including interest, dividends and stock buy-backs, now make up a solid majority of even US non-financial corporations' profits, and in some years virtually all net profits, up from around a third as recently as the mid-1980s. Financial assets now exceed tangible assets in aggregate. Economists have termed this shift 'financialisation'. Rather than seeking to make a return on investment by producing goods and services at a particular cost, and selling with a margin to produce profit, companies have become increasingly reliant for their profits on the movement and manipulation of money. The basis for this extraordinary shift – and it is both huge and without precedent – has been steadily rising leverage. This raises the question of what happens if debt is no longer available.

BEFORE CONSIDERING THAT, the other striking feature of this crisis is its speed and virulence. A conscientious citizen in 2007 diligently keeping up with the financial and economic news, carefully scrutinising the business pages of the daily newspapers and business magazines, digesting the reports and analyses presented there, would have had no idea what was coming.

Part of the reason is that economic commentary generally focuses on the shallow and immediate. It tends to dwell on eye-catching stories of managerial blunders or power struggles, mergers, acquisitions, business cycles, currency-exchange and interest rates, taxes or fluctuations in energy prices. But these are not the forces that shape the evolution of societies. The deeper changes underlying this surface froth and bubble generally pass without comment; staggering levels of debt had become normal.

There was another, more fundamental reason, however, that so few forecasters saw the looming problem: the world financial system, even as it teetered on a Yertle-the-Turtle tower of derivatives-upon-options-upon-debt, had also become so complex and interconnected that perhaps it was now literally impossible for anyone to understand, let alone predict, its behaviour. It had become prone to sudden, apparently inexplicable, lurches.

Complexity can make a system difficult to understand, and inherently more unstable. Because everything is connected to everything else, in sometimes unexpected ways, problems that break out in one place can rapidly impact elsewhere. More interaction can make systems further prone to surprising and sudden outcomes. Consider this: conceptually, a system consisting of only fifteen elements can interact in only fifteen ways if the interactions are linear (each element interacts only with its neighbour and in one direction); allow the system to interact non-linearly but dyadically (each element can interact with one other element not necessarily its neighbour), and the system can create any one of 120 combinations; allow the elements to interact non-linearly and non-dyadically (each element can interact with any number of other elements), and a system of only fifteen elements can theoretically assume an impossible-to-comprehend 65,535 states.

The financial system is vastly more complex than this, and a mass of interlocking contingencies. At this level of complexity, no one can predict with certainty how it will behave under stress and how change in one part will affect others. We can predict with some accuracy the odds of a single security or commodity in isolation shifting in price by a given amount, but interconnectivity and complexity make it exponentially more difficult to forecast the impact of such events on the system. Much of the time, the world appears 'normal'; assumptions about the systemic background hold, and we can analyse individual elements as standalones. Occasionally, however, complexity jars the system out of its boundaries, with unpredictable results. Under these conditions, models that predict the behaviour of individual elements are overwhelmed. Events on the other side of the world cascade through to system-wide shifts. This explains the puzzling observation that a decline in Californian sub-prime real estate prices can precipitate a chain reaction that implodes the Icelandic currency and wipes out superannuation funds in Australia.

THE UPSHOT OF this poisonous combination of debt and complexity is that nations abiding by the dominant economic prescription of the past two decades – be 'open', 'flexible', 'outward' and 'market' oriented – found themselves increasingly exposed to a global system that had become unpredictable, unstable and unsustainable. There are only two alternatives: either attempt to tame the system with regulation and 'governance', or decouple from it.

The current orthodoxy favours the former: it argues that we need better regulation, and better regulators. Interestingly, this is the response popular with enthusiasts for globalisation and many of those formerly most committed to free-market capitalism. The essential proposition is either that the benefits of globalisation outweigh the risks, if the system can be properly managed, or more simply that 'there is no feasible alternative'. Australian regulators and politicians have been prominently patting themselves on the back for avoiding the silly blunders that sank the Americans. And it would seem that indeed the Australian system has performed better than some others. But the Australian financial system is both relatively small and relatively un-complex, and it is contained within the borders of a single national government.

It's a very different matter to regulate effectively a much larger and more complex system, to say nothing of one that spans nations or is global. Reaching enforceable agreement across multiple nations and trading blocs is nigh on impossible, and if it does prove possible will surely favour the largest and strongest, whose interests may not coincide with those of smaller countries. Witness the fate of the tiny nation of Latvia: in June 2009 it was crucified by its insistence on maintaining a currency peg with the euro – its tight integration into the much larger and more complex European financial system and through that the world system. As Latvia haemorrhaged capital to support the peg, overnight interest rates hit 200 per cent, one-third of state teachers were laid off and unemployment reached 18 per cent. Latvia needed to devalue its currency and lower its interest rates, but it was locked into rates set to meet the needs of the large European economies.

And even if regulation of the global system were feasible, it would come at enormous cost. While commentators loudly call for more regulation of US capitalism, it's not as though the US is short of government-enforced rules. The *Federal Register* (which lists the rules US firms must comply with) contained 75,676 pages in 2004, a 6.2 per cent increase from 2003's 71,269 pages. The US has not been 'deregulating'. In 2004, a total of 4,101 new rules were issued by government agencies, and Congress and President Bush signed into law (a comparatively low) 299 new bills. In the same year, US agencies reported 4,083 new regulations at various stages of implementation, by more than fifty federal regulatory entities. The previous year they issued 4,266. Of these, 135 were classed as 'economically significant' – meaning that they would cost at least US$100 million in compliance – and added at least $13.5 billion a year to future compliance costs. The cost of all these rules and their enforcement is staggering: economists Thomas Hopkins and Mark Crain estimate the burden on the economy at $877 billion, equivalent to 38 per cent of all 2004 government spending. At that level, regulatory costs were more than twice the then budget deficit, or 7.6 per cent of US GDP, and exceeded all corporate pre-tax profits (at $745 billion) and both individual income tax ($765 billion) and corporate tax ($169 billion).

THE POINT IS that monitoring and controlling a system as complex as America's is already an exceedingly difficult and expensive proposition. Complexity of regulation must match the complexity of the system being regulated. But sometimes there are simply too many elements, and too many interactions. The costs impose a substantial drag on productivity. For the world system, the costs of regulating effectively would be even greater. These costs must be set against the alleged benefits of being tightly coupled to a world financial system that is becoming more complex and integrated at an exponential rate.

As well as being costly, increased regulation and oversight inevitably retard innovation. The more rules one must comply with in advance, the greater the barriers to new products or services. While a certain level of regulation is obviously necessary to avoid dangerous or otherwise undesirable products, system-wide regulation undoubtedly clogs change.

The challenges of management-through-regulation are akin to those of administering and controlling an economy through central planning – it is feasible in theory, but in practice the amount of information required and accuracy of judgements are beyond real human capacity. The system becomes slow; errors and 'system gaming' create waste on a mounting scale. The 'tame the system through regulation' school of thought advocates a watered-down version of old-fashioned central planning, with many of the same issues.

IN THE LIGHT of these dual problems of complexity and instability, we should at least explore the possibility of 'decoupling' from such a system, and in the wake of the crisis a growing number of societies are doing so.

Any such call will inevitably be met with horrified cries of 'protectionism' and 'isolationism'. But decoupling implies neither. In a world where manufacturing makes up less than 10 per cent of the economy, tariffs make little sense, and nor does 'going it alone'. What makes sense are the old-fashioned virtues of self-reliance and thrift. Being dependent on global capital to fund investment is a primary form of coupling for Australia. We spend more than we save, so we borrow from overseas to make up the gap. This makes perfect sense so long as the world is stable. But it binds us ever more closely to an unstable system.

Decoupling would begin with the recognition that becoming more self-reliant for capital and investment would be desirable. To achieve this, we would need to consume a little less and save a little more.

It would extend to the general recognition that smaller, simpler units are easier to understand and likely to be more stable than larger, more complex ones. Decoupling would not mean complete separation; that would be neither desirable nor feasible. The point, rather, is to be loosely coupled, to be able to tap the global system, trade with it, experience it, draw from it, but not have our destiny dependent on its vicissitudes.

In effect, decoupling would imply a return to the subsidiarity principle that governance be undertaken by the smallest, lowest, most local and least centralised unit possible. A now almost-forgotten foundation stone of western thought (so lost that my computer informs me 'subsidiarity' is not a word), this principle is enshrined in the US Constitution's Tenth Amendment and the

1992 Treaty of Maastricht of the European Union. It is routinely breached by both. Subsidiarity implies that social units should seek to be as independent and self-reliant as possible, within the bounds of sustained prosperity and environmental responsibility.

One immediate difficulty in moving forward with such recognition is that it has become the height of 'progressive' thinking in Australia to favour centralisation of powers and to support the expansion of regulation and control. Many a dinner party features sage nodding at the suggestion that local governments are hopeless, states should be abolished, small and simple is out of date, and powers should be passed to the national, and ultimately to the international. If the United Nations truly ruled the world, wouldn't it be wonderful!

Perhaps the current crisis will prompt some to reconsider.

Jonathan West was an associate professor at Harvard University, and is now director of the Australian Innovation Research Centre at the University of Tasmania. He lives with his wife and daughter on their family farm on the Tasmanian east coast, overlooking the Freycinet Peninsula.

A bend in the river

Hope beckons for East Londoners

Barbara Gunnell

THE opening credits of *EastEnders*, the most watched television soap in Britain, show an aerial view of the River Thames snaking west to east through London on its way to the sea. The camera pulls out to reveal the distinctive skipping-rope loop where the river dips south around a tongue of land known as the Isle of Dogs. This almost-island, with a generous spill-over a couple of miles north, west and east of the loop, is the East End, its boundaries more or less following those of London's poorest borough, Tower Hamlets. For more than two centuries, this bend in the river generated stupendous wealth in the midst of poverty of a persistence and intensity unmatched in any advanced capitalist nation. For most of London's history, ships navigated around the Isle of Dogs, bringing in everything an island could consume or transform for re-export and returning with everything a rapidly industrialising nation could produce, including convicts sentenced to transportation to Australia. The rich became fabulously rich, and so did the City of London. This teardrop of land was the crucible for creating the greatest concentration of wealth in the world.

But the wealth that drove the expansion of the British Empire did not trickle down to the hordes who scratched a living loading and unloading, stitching and scrubbing, selling services and selling sex. As commerce grew, so did the needy population of the East End, more than doubling in the nineteenth century and creating the infamous slums graphically depicted by, among others, the journalist Henry Mayhew, who recorded in meticulous detail the daily lives of London's working poor; the more florid novelist and campaigner Charles Dickens; and the social reformer Charles Booth. Like most of his class, Booth initially saw Mayhew and Dickens as peddling social-ist fiction until he investigated for himself and mapped and categorised every alley, courtyard and road in the miserable East End.

When he was writing, in the late nineteenth century, socialism was certainly in the air. The refugees who arrived at this bend in the river included thousands of religious and political dissidents. Friedrich Engels, by then living in London, believed that the East End working class would rise up as its counterparts in Europe had done. It didn't, but he lived to see the birth

---

PREVIOUS PAGE: View of the docks and warehouses on the Isle of Dogs, built to accommodate trade with the West Indies, circa 1802. *Source: unknown.*

of the union movement, born of two significant political strikes in the East End: the Bryant and May match girls of Bow in 1888, and the Great Dock Strike of 1889.

The great wealth turbine created by the Victorians shuddered to a halt when the loading and unloading of ships moved downstream to coastal container ports, during the 1970s and '80s. But the Isle of Dogs was soon at the heart of a second great explosion of wealth in which, once again, ingenuity and greed combined to make massive fortunes – for some. This time the trade generating wealth was in money itself. For some twenty-five years, spanning the final years of the twentieth century and the early years of the next, the bankers thought the free-market bonanza would never end.

AT NIGHT THE lights of the Canary Wharf towers twinkle like cartoon diamonds, reminding their low-rise neighbours in the East End that trading money is a round-the-clock business. But recently the illuminations have a gap-toothed look and blocks of black reveal missing tenants.

The landmark tower of the Wharf – at 774 feet, the tallest building in London – is the fifty-storey Canada House, designed by Cesar Pelli. Its warning beacon still flashes to warn planes flying in and out of the nearby City Airport, and its pencil-point roof still puffs out a cloud of steam, presumably the vaporised sweat of the remaining anxious bankers inside. Here, on the eighteenth floor, is the Financial Services Authority – charged, since 1997, with regulating the exponential growth in the trading of complex financial instruments, a task it undertook with such a light touch that the crisis unfolded on its doorstep before it had issued a single warning to luckless investors. Here, too, the 1,370 London employees of Bear Stearns worked until March 2008, when the investment bank was forced to acknowledge that its balance sheet included $29 billion of dodgy mortgages, most of them American. The inhabitants of the Wharf prayed that Bear Stearns was a one-off catastrophe, and the US Federal Reserve guaranteed the bad loans in order to persuade a bigger bank, JP Morgan, to take over the crippled investment bank. Ben Bernanke, the Federal Reserve chairman, acknowledged then that, without US government intervention, he feared 'a chaotic unwinding'.

Even so, the unwinding was soon apparent. In September, a second major player in the Canary Wharf ghetto of adventurous bankers, Lehman Brothers, which occupied a million square feet of office space close by, also collapsed dramatically. Too small to survive alone but too big to save, it reported $613 billion of debt, incontrovertible evidence for most bankers that the financial weather could, from then, only get bitter. Lehman's four thousand London employees provided the iconic pictures of the beginning of the crisis as they spilled onto a former quayside of the old London West India Docks with their cardboard boxes of personal possessions: an iPod, trainers, maybe a farewell card. Observers predicted that by the end of 2009 the City and Canary Wharf would lose ten thousand more jobs. But no one has estimated the size of the cull of spinoff jobs, from high-paid consultants and lawyers to the minimum-wage workers who feed, clothe, transport and clean up after the bankers. The UK's finance sector employs a million people around Britain. All will feel uncertain about their future.

The unpayable debts that stalled the world's financial system may have been American, but London's Canary Wharf, named after a small unloading quay for bananas, was the laboratory of the arcane, still scarcely understood, financial instruments that have ravaged the global economy. With a daytime population of up to ninety thousand, the Wharf is the size of an average town. But it is a town like no other. It is not London's financial area: that is still the City of London, about three kilometres to the west. It has no town hall, no schools, no charity shops. Children are found mainly in the subter-ranean shopping malls beneath the high-rise office blocks, but generally only at weekends. No old people or mothers with prams require your help through the revolving doors or off the escalators. There is not even a traffic problem, since most of the inhabitants commute in and out by public transport. There is no litter. You will never see a cat, and dogs are more likely to be sniffer dogs, alert for drugs or bombs, than pets. There are no beggars. The few poor people you meet are cleaners and service staff, usually early in the morning or late at night waiting for the buses.

Just a few hundred yards north of the Wharf is the other East End, with an oversupply of the litter and dirt and annoyances of inner-city boroughs. But if proximity to great wealth over two decades has failed to benefit East Enders, that at least now has an upside. The troubles of Canary Wharf's bankers (who, if they live in the area, inhabit the serviced riverside blocks) are likely to have less effect in these down-at-heel streets than in richer parts of London. The very informality of the East End economy has bred a certain resilience and self-reliance. You will find few of the well-known High Street names in the shopping parades, few big supermarkets, no chain restaurants or coffee bars, no chain pharmacies. There are no big employers, either. Most businesses are small or family concerns, particularly in areas of recent immigration (half the population is from ethnic-minority groups). Outside the Wharf there are few mainstream banks. In the predominantly Muslim areas of Aldgate and Whitechapel, for instance, there are Indian, Bangladeshi and sharia-compli-ant banks. Even more remote from the big banks are *hawala* schemes, cheap, efficient trust-based networks for transferring money overseas by phone. The Somali population in East London is said to send millions of pounds in this way so that money can instantly reach families back home with no bank account.

The rest of London has tended to leave the East End to its own devices. But, for the nearly a quarter of a million East Enders in Tower Hamlets, all this may be about to change.

IN 2012, THE East End will have more visitors than residents: the Olympic Games will bring around half a million workers and visitors to Tower Hamlets and neighbouring Stratford. So far, the Games have found few friends among London's middle classes and media commentators. The latest price tag of £9 billion is seen as a calamitous addition to the national debt. But the closer you get to the Olympic Park (where the main stadium structures are well under-way), the more enthusiasm you find. Thousands of jobs are being created – in construction, but also in cultural and other support services. An associated commercial centre is being built by Westfield. And by 2012 the East End will have a high-speed train link to Europe and better cross-London connections (initially to transport the athletes, spectators, and foreign great and good) than it has ever had.

Shortly after London's successful Olympic bid, I took a sceptical Will Hutton – a fellow journalist on *The Observer*, where I then worked – on a tour of the as-yet-undeveloped Olympic site, a mile from where I live. Hutton, an influential commentator, is the author of *The State We're In* (Jonathan Cape, 1995), a damning excoriation of the destructive greed encouraged by the Thatcher government. Like many Londoners, Hutton had argued that the billions it would take to develop an Olympic site could be better spent. But he also confessed to me that, like most middle-class North Londoners, he never had much reason to visit the East End.

I took him along disused canal towpaths through the metaphorical back door to the Lea Valley, an ugly ribbon of land that will soon be the Olympic Park. It had hardly seen a shilling of investment since the small factories and warehouses which once serviced the docks were bombed to blazes in World War II. Hutton saw a perspective that the many dignitaries who have visited since will not have seen and now never will. We went past dilapidated, unplanned and mostly deserted factories, under bridges where putrid water pooled, past scruffy storehouses and car repairers and paint shops. He was shocked that within sight of both the then-booming City of London and Canary Wharf an area of such neglect and ugliness could exist. In July 2006 he wrote in *The Observer*: 'The smell of sewage in the fifty yards of canal path before you arrive at Old Ford locks – junction of the River Lea and the Hackney Cut on the River Lea Navigation – is overpowering. Don't breathe in too deeply; at this intensity, it's almost certainly toxic…Ahead there is the outfall sewer that conducts most of London's sewage to the treatment plant in Beckton. This is the shittiest part of London…Where I was walking is about two miles from the City of London, one of the richest urban areas in the world, yet here everything is poor. The tracts of derelict land criss-crossed by overhead power lines, disused canals and sewage drains; the lack of infrastructure; the low incomes; the disastrous health experience; low life expectancy – everything is a tribute to neglect.'

Many are sceptical about the transformative power of the 2012 Olympics. But the Games will necessarily generate immediate local wealth, some good-quality housing and longer-term employment. London's stalled economy will certainly get a kick-start, even if the doubters are right that insufficient attention has been paid to the post-Olympic legacy. Siting the Games in this neglected part of London was without doubt the correct decision, righting a great wrong. Britain will, for once, have put its money and energies into the stubbornly derelict and impoverished East End.

WHEN WORK STARTED on the construction of the West India Docks in the final year of the eighteenth century, London had fewer than a million inhabitants. By the end of the nineteenth century, the population had increased sixfold. It was not only the largest city in the world; it was also the wealthiest. But the increase was a disaster for the East End's poor, straining already inadequate shelter beyond all limits. London's population explosion was fuelled partly by the flight of landless rural workers to the cities following the agricultural-enclosures acts, and later the failure of the agrarian economy, but also by surges of foreign immigration. Each political upheaval in Europe brought more asylum seekers. The largest group of arrivals in the nineteenth century were Russian and Polish-Russian Jews, fleeing religious persecution from Tsarist Russia. Between 1880 and 1900 their numbers grew from 46,000 to 135,000, mostly in the East End neighbourhoods of Aldgate, Spitalfields and Whitechapel. The first Baron Rothschild established the Four Per Cent Industrial Dwellings Company to construct model housing for the newcomers. The Jewish Board of Deputies was active, too, particularly in seeking other destinations for would-be immigrants – Buenos Aires, New York and Cape Town – fearing for their safety in an overcrowded East End.

There had also been what we would today call mass economic migration, including tens of thousands of Irish escaping the Great Famine. No border agency turned back those in search of a better future. As London grew, so did its appetite for cheap labour. Only towards the end of the century did the ruling class begin to fear that the large influx of subversives and radicals from Europe could foment revolution among the British working class. Most immigrants landed on quaysides in the East End and tended to stay until they had the means to move on. The stresses on this unplanned and already overcrowded patch became extreme, every now and then erupting into crisis when dwellings were torn down to build more riverfront dockyards, warehouses and roads to cater for the ever-expanding trade on the Thames.

In 1857 the Medical Officer for Limehouse reported that half of all children there died before they reached adulthood. Those who lived were likely to be stunted by disease, crippled by malnutrition and destitute. Epidemics of cholera killed thousands at a time and continued to do so until Sir Peter Bazalgette completed his program of closed brick-built sewers towards the end of the century.

Victorian England seemed blind to the misery in its midst. In 1851, marvelling at the Empire's wealth and good fortune, the 'respectable' classes flocked to the Great Exhibition. All was triumph. Britain was pre-eminent, on the way to ruling a quarter of the world. Only a handful of liberal writers, philanthropists and campaigners voiced concern at evidence of acute depri-vation at the heart of the Empire, and started to question the notion that poverty was a moral failing of the poor themselves. When Henry Mayhew told a meeting of London tailors in October 1850 that 'morality on £5,000 a year in Belgrave Square is a very different thing to morality on slop-wages in Bethnal Green,' he was challenging firmly entrenched Victorian values. The idea that poverty might be any kind of excuse for immoral behaviour was shocking indeed. Mayhew had been the joint founder of *Punch*, but proved a better journalist than businessman. Forced by bankruptcy to abandon the satirical magazine, he freelanced for the *Morning Chronicle*, with which both Charles Dickens and John Stuart Mill had connections.

MAYHEW PERSUADED THE *Chronicle*'s editor to back a detailed inves-tigation of the 1849 cholera epidemic, thought to have killed around thirteen thousand people. Mayhew believed cholera to be a disease of poverty. Likely to have been influenced by Engels' 1845 study of Manchester, *The Conditions of the Working Class in England*, his survey ultimately ran to the three-volume *London Labour and the London Poor*, published in 1851. The editor had given him three helpers, but Mayhew himself concentrated on the East End. His vivid reports revealed lives far grimmer than Dickens's graphic stories of the workhouse or the street boys of Fagin's kitchen. Unlike more lurid accounts of East End life and degradation, which concentrated on moral turpitude, Mayhew's approach is credible in its journalistic detail. He gives an account of about a dozen boys and girls, 'not one of them over twelve years of age, and many of them but six. It would be almost impossible to describe the wretched group, so motley was their appearance, so extraordinary their dress, and so stolid and inexpressive their countenances...There did not appear to be among the whole group as many filthy cotton rags to their backs as, when stitched together, would have been sufficient to form the material of one shirt.' He learns that most of the girls took to prostitution as soon as they could, and the boys to thieving.

From one boy he hears how the Ragged Schools (the endowments of well-meaning philanthropists) were places for planning stealing raids: 'I was so much struck with the boy's truthfulness of manner that I asked him, would he really lead a different life, if he saw a means of so doing?' Mayhew gave the boy two shillings (by his own calculations around ten times more than a day's pickings) and later learned that the boy and his sister had kept the family for a week by buying and reselling some sprats. A 'literary friend', perhaps Dickens, finds a job for the boy and takes on the sister as a housemaid. The mother opens a small shop, which does well. Mayhew writes that this story 'may teach many to know how often the poor boys reared in the gutter are thieves, merely because society forbids them being honest lads'.

This was dangerously progressive. Indulging the destitute was considered to encourage low morals: give an urchin a pair of shoes and you might foster a wicked dependence on handouts and a work-shy attitude. *The Economist* of 15 December 1849 argued that reports such as Mayhew's were 'unthinkingly increasing the enormous funds already profusely destined to charitable purposes, adding to the number of virtual paupers' and equated the *Chronicle* writer with a 'piteous, whining, begging-letter writer'. Then, as now, it believed that the 'higgling of the markets' had to be trusted. Trying to enrich the labourer at the expense of the master was, in the context of the 1848 uprisings in Europe, 'communism more insidious than across the water'.

The historian Tristram Hunt explains it thus: 'The Victorians considered poverty a failure of will. The idea developed that there was a character peculiar to the East End, an exotic danger. They had a prurient fascination with it. That is why the Jack the Ripper murders became a symbol of the

East End: the victims were prostitutes, the attacks savage, feeding the fantasy that it was a morally dangerous place. The poor started to be regarded as sub-human.'

The economic success of the Empire made attitudes to the 'savages' at home even worse, he argues. In *Building Jerusalem: The Rise and Fall of the Victorian City* (Weidenfeld, 2004), Hunt notes, 'Time and again [the East End] was portrayed as another world: a world of dangerous swamps and violent savages more readily suited to the jungles of Angola than the back streets of Bethnal Green. It was imagined as an alien civilisation which the age of progress had all but forgotten.' The idea of the 'alien' danger in the East End continues today, he believes, in a ready identification of the East End's large Muslim population with terrorism.

The latter half of the nineteenth century saw a spate of hysterical novels and salacious accounts of the horrors of the East End, such as James Greenwood's *The Wilds of London* (1874). Journals such as the *Pall Mall Gazette* told of 'colonies of heathens and savages in the heart of our capital'. George Gissing described 'the pest-stricken regions of East London, sweltering in sunshine which served only to reveal the intimacies of abomination', and called it 'the city of the damned'.

But amid this pornography of poverty the dissenting humanitarian voices became more forceful. In 1883 the Reverend Andrew Mearns condemned Victorian England for the consequences of desperate overcrowding. 'Here are seven people living in one underground kitchen, and a little dead child lying in the same room…Here is a mother who turns her children into the street in the early evening because she lets her room for immoral purposes until long after midnight…' Tristram Hunt describes Mearns's *The Bitter Cry of Outcast London* as 'a blunt, brilliant…indictment of the policies of church and state alike for failing to alleviate "the great dark region of poverty, misery, squalor and immorality"'.

The humanitarian crisis that became impossible to ignore in the final decades of the nineteenth century was, at root, a housing crisis resulting from the boom years of the 1850s and '60s. Trade and industry had flourished; more docks, and roads plying goods from them to the city, were needed. The building of the Commercial Road to transport goods from West India Docks to the city resulted in extensive destruction of workers' housing. Overcrowding became systemic. A docker had to live nearby in order to join the daily scramble for work and, as river traffic increased, so did the numbers of those flocking to the East End. The docks and roads around them had been funded almost entirely by private investment.

The Victorians were, in effect, conducting a social experiment in laissez-faire economics, where more work brought in more labour. Margaret Thatcher would have pronounced it a great success. But the devastation caused by the entrepreneurs who invested a few thousand pounds to make far greater fortunes was paid for in millions by the philanthropists of the later decades of that century.

By mid-century London had been transformed into a thriving commercial capital, with roads, railways and more docks. Houses were torn down and the poor pressed into the remaining inadequate housing. A few philanthropists responded to this crisis with purpose-built worker tenements, notably George Peabody, an American, and Angela Burdett-Coutts, heiress to the Coutts bank fortune and the richest woman in England at the time. By her death in 1906, she had given away three million pounds, most of it in the East End. But philanthropy was not equal to the task of housing and feeding the huge numbers still flooding into the overcrowded hamlets along the Thames. Friedrich Engels despaired at the passivity of the East Enders. Only in the final decade of the nineteenth century did they start to fight back.

TODAY, BY ALMOST every measure, the East End remains the poorest area in Britain. In 2007, the borough of Tower Hamlets had more children in income-deprived homes than anywhere else in England. Unemployment rates of around 14 per cent for both men and women were the highest across England and Wales. In the schools more than half the borough's children were receiving free school dinners, since their parents had insufficient income to pay for them. Health statistics tell a similar story: life expectancy is lower and cancer rates are higher than in any other London borough.

The government of Margaret Thatcher almost planned it thus. When the great London docks –West India, East India, Millwall, Royal, Blackwall,

Rotherhithe – were abandoned for container ports on the coast, more than 150,000 jobs in the Docklands boroughs disappeared. One in five of all jobs along the river was lost between 1966 and 1981. The Thames was left with a ghost town of empty wharves, warehouses and quays. The redevelopment of Docklands became a matter of urgent political debate in the late 1970s. But the new Conservative government passed up the opportunity for the people of the East End to share in the planned regeneration of the Isle of Dogs.

Margaret Thatcher came to power in 1979 with a zealous free-market philosophy. The former Docklands was to be redeveloped as an 'Enterprise Zone' where business could pursue wealth without obligation to its neighbours. The island enclave in which the alchemy of wealth creation was to take place need not concern itself with the sea of poverty surrounding it. Specifically, the companies who came to this free-market zone would be relieved of observing the planning laws of the borough in which they sat, and of the burden of rates and taxes that applied to the rest of London. There was, after all, 'no such thing as society', as Thatcher said in 1987.

IF WISHES WERE horses, beggars would ride and the Isle of Dogs would now be not the epicentre of the global financial recession, but a large garden suburb housing retired dockers. When the last upstream crane lifted its final load in 1981, the question of how to redevelop this unloved and unlovely part of London was the capital's primary planning issue. Docklands action groups pushed for a fair deal, finally, for the people who lived around the docks and had depended on them for their livelihood. Tower Hamlets, Newham to the east and Southwark across the river all started to plan redevelopment. The local authorities, solidly Labour, were under voter pressure to deal with persistent problems of overcrowding and some of the worst living conditions in the country. A home with a garden was the dream of every poorly housed East Ender. There was no private housing: Tower Hamlets owned virtually all of the borough's housing stock and had run out of space to build more. The council had earmarked twenty-two hectares of the former docks area for new homes. Together, the boroughs intended to double their housing stock.

But their ambitions for East Enders coincided with the advent of a leader dedicated to a free-market orthodoxy in which the poor and unemployed were perceived as victims only of their own lack of enterprise and guts. Margaret Thatcher unashamedly echoed the Victorian moralists. A thriving capitalist society, she believed, had to make capitalists of its citizens. Her lessons started in the East End. She wanted free enterprise and market values to flourish in the Labour bastion. She wanted a house-owning democracy to replace council-owned housing. She wanted a nation of free-marketeers, not of welfare dependents.

In 1981, two years into her prime ministership, she decided to take on London's left-leaning local authorities. The riverside boroughs, unable to agree among themselves on the way forward for the deserted docks, were easy opponents. A House of Lords Select Committee looking at the competing political ambitions for redeveloping the Isle of Dogs summarised the local boroughs' case thus: 'the need – if only there were the money to satisfy it – is for the provision of publicly rented small houses with gardens'. The government argued that the boroughs were looking 'too much to the past and too exclusively to the aspirations of the existing population and too little to the possibility of regenerating docklands by the introduction of new types of industry and new types of housing'. The Labour boroughs had done themselves no favours by opposing all private housing and xenophobically claiming that private ownership would bring in 'an alien community'. The government's ambitions predictably prevailed.

Geoffrey Howe, Thatcher's Chancellor of the Exchequer, was the mastermind behind the Enterprise Zones, which he saw as experimental havens where businesses could flourish free of taxes and regulation. Thatcher and her environment secretary, Michael Heseltine, saw the economic potential of isolating a twenty-square-kilometre zone of prime building land close to the City of London that could come under a Docklands Development Corporation, outside the control of socialist local politicians.

New businesses which came to the Enterprise Zone would have no responsibilities, financially or morally, for anything but wealth creation. Had political journalists not found the language of planning and zoning so dreary, it is possible that, even in 1981, Thatcher would have faced greater opposition. In fact, the audacity of putting a large chunk of the East End outside democratic rule may have given even Margaret Thatcher some sleepless nights. The House of Lords Select Committee had expressed concern that 'the transfer of development control over so wide an area from democratically elected councils to [an unelected body]…is a step which is not easily justified especially in an area such as Docklands where the attachment to local democracy was shown to be so strong.'

Nearly thirty years later, addressing a meeting in Canary Wharf in July 2008, Heseltine claimed to have had to persuade Prime Minister Thatcher. He had got her behind the idea of bypassing democracy, he boasted, only by telling her, 'The problem is, Margaret, all those councillors down there, they're communists.' Her conversion followed instantly, he joked.

What the Tory government wanted to do with the land deemed too valuable for the poor had not at this point been specified, and it would be wrong to credit Thatcher and her two ministers with a vision of the million-pound bonuses that characterised the financial city which eventually emerged. The Tories' ambitions were, in part, small-minded – to weaken the socialist boroughs of inner London – and, in part, theoretical: to establish an experimental site for their vision of a Britain ruled by an unfettered market. The homes and jobs of those who had depended on the docks for their livelihoods simply did not figure in the plans.

AS IT HAPPENED, the rewards for the ambitious and greedy were to be far greater: a new city unhampered by 'gentlemen's rules' and any obligations to the wider community. When Thatcher came to power, the City of London had just begun its transition from a gentleman's club to an international financial centre. A battle was underway between the traditional stock exchange and the modernisers who wanted London banks to join in the highly profitable world of futures trading. Deregulation of the London Stock Exchange and an end to control by the 'top hats' was a glint in the eye of the big international bankers.

The first challenge was to establish the London International Financial Futures and Options Exchange (LIFFE), which was opposed by the traditionalists. The modernisers won and trading in financial instruments began. In February 1982 the *Financial Times* lamented that few understood this market: 'Hands up who knows what a fill or kill contract is?' the anonymous Lex column asked on the eve of the LIFFE's opening. The world of swaps and derivatives and debt-trading had arrived. The 'Big Bang' was to follow, bringing international banks into the sacred Stock Exchange and ultimately allowing for electronic dealing and the rapid development of London as the world's financial centre.

But where would all these new banks be housed? Space in the Square Mile, as the City of London was known, was limited to just about that. Even when the laws were relaxed to allow trading outside the Square Mile, there remained problems of planning permission. It was nigh on impossible to get consent for a building taller than St Paul's or any that interrupted familiar vistas of Wren's great cathedral.

In February 1985, with the Big Bang fixed for the following year, Michael von Clemm, then chairman of Credit Suisse, went to lunch on a barge with the unelected Development Corporation running Docklands. Von Clemm was there not to pursue his banking interests but gastronomy. He had been a friend and adviser to the restaurateur Roux Brothers since helping them set up business in the 1960s, and was looking for a site for a packaging plant. The enterprises then springing up in the planning-free zone were small-scale commercial projects of this kind. The barge on which he lunched was moored near an old banana warehouse and von Clemm eyed it up as a suitable back office for Credit Suisse. He discussed his interest with a US real estate developer, who suggested that the warehouse should instead be developed as the front office. It was an audacious idea.

The development of Canary Wharf began in July 1987. By 1990 Pelli's landmark Canada House tower was finished. In 1991 the first tenants moved in; in 1992 the original developers went bust. But the project could not now be allowed to fail. By 1995, this monument to free enterprise and the wisdom of the market had cost the taxpayer, in development grants and tax breaks, an estimated £3 billion.

The first tenants of the showpiece Canada House were not bankers, but newspapers. In 1992, lured from their costly Fleet Street addresses by low rents and tax breaks, the *Daily Telegraph* took up residence, followed by the Mirror Group and *The Independent*. Eventually, the banks followed. John Willcock, writing in *The Independent* in November 1998, commented: 'This is what Canary Wharf offers – cheap rents and big floor plans. This is also what riles the City of London, which has seen a steady stream of its most rewarding residents – Morgan Stanley, CSFB, Citicorp, even the Financial Services Authority (FSA) – moving downriver. A lot of this was due to the massive tax breaks bequeathed by Margaret Thatcher's government to kick-start the development in the 1980s. As Stuart Fraser, chairman of Planning and Transportation at the Corporation of London, put it: "The offer of £235 million to HSBC to move two miles downstream does seem to be a generous use of taxpayers' money".'

Willcock wrote that column when *The Independent* occupied the eighteenth floor of Canada House, now home to the Financial Services Authority, which egregiously failed to protect the public against even greater losses.

TWO HUNDRED YEARS earlier, on the site that was to prove so attractive to investment bankers, another group of entrepreneurs saw the great fortunes to be made if those who wanted to make money also made the law. In the closing years of the eighteenth century, the River Thames had become impossibly congested. The tidal range of the Thames meant that loading and unloading had to be carried out mid-river, by barges and lighter ships. The cargo vessels backed up around the Isle of Dogs, waiting days, even weeks, for their turn to be unloaded. After that, unloading into smaller vessels and thence to the dockside could take days. Every delay posed opportunities for pilferage and shrinkage of the cargo. The trading companies claimed their losses amounted to hundreds of thousands of pounds a year; private watchmen and guards were inadequate to the task.

There was at that time no publicly funded police force in Britain, and considerable popular opposition to the idea. The House of Commons had been petitioned by the merchants, but shied away from something still considered alien to the British conception of freedom. Pressure mounted. In 1794, the philosopher Jeremy Bentham and his brother Samuel, a shipping engineer and architect, testified before the House of Commons for a bill aimed at 'preventing fraud and embezzlement in the dockyards'.

Parliament moved too slowly for the West India merchants, who claimed to be losing hogsheads of rum, molasses and sugar through 'sweepings' and 'samplings', at that time widely perceived by those who worked on the water as their routine and deserved rewards. The merchants wanted to deal with not just the petty thieving, but the entire riparian culture. Patrick Colquhoun, a magistrate and merchant who became obsessed with what he described as the 'matured delinquency' of the river workers, estimated that 120,000 'lumpers, watermen and coopers' were directly employed in river work, and that up to half a million men and women owed their living to the river indirectly. Many of these workers had, over more than a century, been entitled to a share of offloaded cargo; these were the 'perquisites' of the work and worth considerably more than the wages, which as a result had remained unrealistically low. The perks were the remuneration. Colquhoun was unimpressed by that line of reasoning. 'Custom and example sanction the greatest enormities which at length become fortified by immemorial and progressive usage: it is no wonder that the superior Officers find it an Herculean labour to cleanse the Augean stables,' he wrote in 1795 as he set about cleaning up the river, a task he resolved to achieve, if necessary, without parliament's help.

Colquhoun argued vehemently for the business of making money to be publicly protected. As provost of Glasgow and the founder of its chamber of commerce and manufacturing, he lobbied government for legal reforms and strategies to promote business and trade. He travelled to London in the late 1790s to confront politicians and get something done. Impatient with parliament's prevarication, he raised funds from the West India merchants trading out of London to set up a police force at Wapping.

In July 1798, fifty men with four or five boats started to patrol the river around the quaysides, to the consternation of those who for years had found ways to outwit the private watchmen paid to protect warehouses along the banks of the Thames. It was a direct challenge to all who worked on the river. The new 'river police', operating with government permission but without public funds, were hated. They enforced rules of working (daylight hours only, with meal breaks taken on board) and a dress code (goods had been smuggled in deep pockets, hats and special coats), and even supervised the payment of wages. Before the year was out, a crowd of thousands tried to set fire to the riverside 'police station' and one security guard was killed. The spark was the 'theft' of a bag of coal. The arrested man's defence was that it was the customary entitlement of those heaving coal. Sadly for the defendant, Patrick Colquhoun was the magistrate who dealt with the case.

After two years, Colquhoun believed he had made the economic case for a permanent river police: the private force had cost the West India merchants £4,200 a year but had saved £182,000 worth of cargo, he argued. Parliament now agreed to fund the River Thames Police: the first state-funded police force in Britain, predating Robert Peel's 'bobbies' by three decades.

Colquhoun's police project transformed the economy of the East End and, ultimately, the fortunes of Britain. It made possible the next giant leap, the introduction of the closed docks on the Isle of Dogs. The scope and audacity of the project – the historian and critic Peter Ackroyd describes it as 'the largest single, privately funded enterprise in the history of London' – determined the future of the capital, the nation and the world for the next century and a half.

The primary purpose of the West India Docks, on which the towers of Canary Wharf now sit, was to protect shipping from thieving locals. The Isle of Dogs provided a perfect site, an excavation at the northern end rendering it a true island for the first time. Ackroyd describes the resulting architecture of moats, high walls (guarding against thieving), warehouses and giant lakes as depicted in paintings and engravings of the time as 'an elegant prison island'.

On the eve of the nineteenth century, parliament passed the West India Dock Company Act, authorising the creation of a wet dock in the area now called Canary Wharf. The merchants had lobbied energetically for a period of trading monopoly intended to help encourage investors, much as the later tenants of the Wharf were thought to need the inducement of tax holidays. Parliament agreed but placed what proved to be generous limits on the amount of profit the company could make before reducing charges on shipping. Despite the scale of the buildings and excavations, the docks were completed with astonishing speed and were ready to be opened by Prime Minister William Pitt the Younger in 1802. Construction had taken three years and cost half a million pounds, all paid by private subscription.

The West India merchants calculated that the near-perfect security immediately saved them £400,000 a year. The Treasury, which had invested nothing, was rewarded with tax revenue of £150,000 a year. Investors received the maximum dividend parliament had allowed, 10 per cent, for the first quarter-century of the dock's operation, and the company made huge profits on top of that, soon accumulating £800,000 capital, sufficient to secure its monopoly control of trade.

Further enclosed docks soon followed: East India (now the ExCel centre, where on 1 April 2009 – Financial Fools Day, it was called – the G20 met to consider emergency measures to deal with the financial crisis), Wapping and, in 1828, St Katherine's, where the most valuable cargo was taken. These luxury goods – ivory, carpets, marble, shells, perfumes – were deemed worthy of luxury accommodation, and the magnificent Ivory House at St Katherine's dock has since become a great tourist attraction. But, as its construction required the destruction of yet more of the housing of those who worked and lived on the river, accommodation for the poor deteriorated further.

NOT ONLY WERE workers deprived of their traditional share of the wealth generated by the river trade, but the new docks created a regime of casual labour – the hated 'call-on' system, which left labourers unsure each day whether they would work – that contributed enormously to the impoverishment of the East End. By the end of the nineteenth century, in the factories, gasworks and on the docks, workers were beginning to stir. Friedrich Engels had despaired of the working classes following the example of their continental counterparts. But when they did, the revolt started in the East End and, once again, the West India Docks were at the heart of a social and political movement that would determine the course of a century.

The dockers sought a minimum shift of four hours and a wage increase; the dock owners refused, confident that the supply of cheap labour in the

East End would make it impossible for casual workers to maintain a strike. But, for once, the dockers were not without support. The year before, in 1889, the Bryant and May match girls had successfully campaigned for better wages and conditions. Their appalling safety conditions, which saw many of the women dying of 'phozzie jaw', a necrosis of the jaw bone brought on by poisoning from phosphorous, aroused the consciences of middle-class reformers. Beatrice Webb – who, with her husband Sidney Webb, founded the Fabians – wrote three decades later of 'a growing uneasiness, amounting to conviction, that the industrial organisation, which yielded rent, interest, and profits on a stupendous scale, had failed to provide a decent livelihood and tolerable conditions for a majority of the inhabitants of Great Britain'.

Not long after, gas workers at Beckton, just downstream of the West India docks, secured a reduction in working hours from twelve to eight by threatening to strike. Thus inspired, the dock labourers of the tiny Tea Operatives Union walked out. They were soon joined by the better-paid stevedores. Other docks joined in, and soon some sixty thousand dockers were on strike. The London *Evening News & Post* reported: 'Dockmen, lightermen, bargemen, cement workers, carmen, ironworkers and even factory girls are coming out. If it goes on a few days longer, all London will be on holiday. The great machine by which five millions of people are fed and clothed will come to a dead stop, and what is to be the end of it all? The proverbial small spark has kindled a great fire which threatens to envelop the whole metropolis.'

The dockers organised mass meetings by the river near Tower Bridge. Support was coming from far beyond the East End: Engels' socialist allies, including Tom Mann, Marx's daughter Eleanor and John Burns, along with William Morris and Annie Besant, all contributed. Most important, however, was their success in raising money – almost fifty thousand pounds, of which an astonishing thirty thousand came from the organised dockworkers of Australia. It proved a turning point in the strike, enabling 'relief coupons' to be given to thousands of strikers, and it demoralised the employers into agreeing to the workers' demands.

The Tea Operatives immediately became the Dock, Wharf, Riverside and General Labourers' Union, later part of the Transport & General Workers Union, for many decades Britain's largest union. Engels was delighted. He wrote: 'The dock strike has been won. It's the greatest event to have taken place in England since the last Reform Bills, and marks the beginning of a complete revolution in the East End.' And: 'Hitherto the East End had been in a state of poverty-stricken stagnation, its hallmark being the apathy of men whose spirit had been broken by hunger, and who had abandoned all hope.'

VICTORIAN ENGLAND HAD hung on to the belief that helping the poor would take from them the drive to work, the one thing that might save them from damnation. Eventually the flaws in this dogma confronted them – with lasting consequences for the organisation of British society. The dockers became a powerfully organised political force, heralding the 'New Unionism' that gave working people a voice and soon after, in Labour, a political party.

The Empire, too, came to see the sickness at its heart. In 1899, the British struggled to defeat fifty thousand Boers, and was saved from a rout in the Transvaal only by enlisting healthier Australians. The army drew parliament's attention to the problem: the poor quality of British soldiers. Poverty-related diseases of the inner cities meant the army was rejecting one in three recruits. A militant reformer, William Booth (who went on to found the Salvation Army), had in 1890 railed against the East End's 'dwarfish dehumanised inhabitants'. So wedded were the Victorians to the free market, they had failed even to safeguard the health and wellbeing of the workers and soldiers they needed to protect the Empire.

Today, it has taken a dramatic failure of the banking system to convince free-market fundamentalists that the market may not always get it right. Canary Wharf's bankers became intoxicated by the belief that their wealth-creating mechanisms were underpinned by sound scientific principles. They created fiendishly clever financial algorithms which 'proved' that parcelling up different types of debt and swapping it for other kinds of debt insulated them against the risk of loan defaults. But they did not, apparently, see the risk of widespread defaulting (of the kind you might expect, for example, when house prices crash), nor of investors and depositors getting a hunch that they should withdraw their money quickly.

The failure, when it came, was catastrophic. That is to say, the transition from apparent normality to chaos was sudden and dramatic. The financial journalist Gillian Tett was one of only a few British commentators who foresaw the problems and reported her fears as early as 2005. A former student of social anthropology, Tett did not underestimate the role of human behaviour. 'There was one dominant free-market ideology…a complete dogma that could not be challenged,' she said earlier this year in a BBC Radio 3 discussion with Britain's former chief scientific adviser, Lord Robert May. 'It is widely forgotten…that the financial industry built wonderful financial models based on Newtonian physics. But while [bankers] had taken on the idea that economics can be reduced to crude formulae, science had moved on to adopt chaos theory.' Lord May, too, was scathing. 'Some of the maths was not that sophisticated. Some of it was deeply stupid,' he said. 'Important questions were not asked [about the credit swaps]. For example, "What are the correlations in the things you bundle together?"'

But if the traders were blinded by belief in their own brilliance, why did others not see the dangers? Tett uses the anthropological term 'social silence': the convictions of elites remain unchallenged. Gordon Brown promised as chancellor that the days of boom and bust were over. But the man who staked his reputation on 'prudence' has now seen the biggest bust of his lifetime because the freedom of the market simply could not be questioned.

Inside the banks, the social silence was even more astounding. Greed overcoming caution is one explanation: bankers are paid according to the units of money they push around; the more parcelling and slicing and swapping, the better. But why, asks Tett, did the chiefs not examine the risks inherent in credit-default swaps more closely? Because, she says, in too many banks, the risk managers had lower status than the traders. 'At Merrill Lynch, for example…the chief risk officer never reported directly to the CEO. As a result, risk managers were in no position to challenge the actions of traders. Similarly, at UBS and Citi, risk managers mostly had lower status than the traders they were supposed to monitor,' she wrote in *Management Today*.

Then there are those whose business it was to advise on risk: credit-rating agencies such as Standard & Poor's, which in May 2009 upset the British government by putting a question mark on the AAA rating of its bonds, apparently saw no problem at all with the mass swapping of sub-prime loans. It is hard to understand how someone with a 120 per cent mortgage on a downtown Los Angeles house was seen as a safer bet than a major economy.

The social silence extended to individuals too. The ever-upward valuation of homes encouraged everyone in Britain to feel richer, to feel they deserved more. 'My house earned more than I did this year,' we would say of the phoney new wealth held in bricks and mortar. Personal indebtedness grew as people borrowed on their homes. While house prices remained buoyant, lenders were insouciant. And, completing the cycle, the government kept quiet, too. Voters who believed they were richer would keep Labour in power and not cavil about rising inequality and the failure of their representatives to address the entrenched poverty of areas such as the East End.

'BILLIONS OF POUNDS have been poured into alleviating poverty in the East End but the only product is strategy documents,' said Andrew Mawson when I met him at the House of Lords. Mawson is a non-party peer who chose the title of Lord Mawson of Bromley-by-Bow, one of the East End's poorest neighbourhoods, where he developed and put into practice his philosophy of social entrepreneurship. 'The issue here is not the economic crisis but the ineffectiveness of the public sector. Children are dying as a result of indecision.'

The ineffectiveness of local government, he told me, was a political failure dating back to the 'private sector bad, public sector good' mantra of the 1970s. 'It was almost a religion,' he said of that era's stymied political debate. He did not add that its replacement in the 1980s by Thatcher's 'public sector rotten, private enterprise holy' philosophy cannot be said to have fostered energetic local institutions. But he pinpoints a major problem in the East End. The public-sector ethos is strong, still overwhelming private-sector initiatives outside the former Enterprise Zone of the Docklands. Tower Hamlets still has one of the highest proportions of public housing in London, much of it in poor condition. But local authorities have been robbed of the power to improve or replace this housing. They no longer have the funds, or the skills in management. And even if they did, Britain is now under heavy international pressure to cut public debt. No future government is likely to be giving local authorities new powers to spend up big.

'The key issue is not money,' says Mawson, 'but how we use public money well. Dealing with local authority bureaucracy is like wading through treacle.' The major investment needed in the stymied economy of the wider East End cannot, he believes, start in the council offices. It has to start in the street, and the street of his example, St Paul's Way, is a few hundred yards from mine. Here, he believes, with the right private and public partnerships, a health centre and 1,300-pupil school will kick-start private commerce and housing. This is Mawson's concept of the social entrepreneur, of partnership between investors and users, as discussed by Cheryl Kernot in *Griffith REVIEW 24: Participation Society*.

The same bottom-up approach is the basis of his current project in the East End: Water City, conceived in Canary Wharf boom-time. The aim is to fully use the East End's greatest resource, its water, for leisure and commerce, housing and transport, including the underdeveloped River Lea Valley, until World War II the site of many small factories and now part of the Olympic 2012 redevelopment. The East End's canals, whose dereliction and squalor so astonished Will Hutton, are already being reclaimed for recreation. Mawson, in keeping with his philosophy of social entrepreneurship, had, when we spoke, just found a new partner. Ironically, it was the Bank of America, in which the US Federal Reserve now has a massive stake. That adds a new dimension to the idea of public–private partnership, but it also suggests one way in which banks really could begin to transform themselves and use their public subsidies for public good.

THE EAST END of the past is fertile ground for England's burgeoning passion for family history. Countless books seek to record the 'real East End'. These memoirs, written by the grandchildren or great-grandchildren of 'real' East Enders, add wonderful human dimensions to history's grim catalogue of the consequences of imperial wealth and expansion. But they also sentimentalise and glamorise. Just as the phrase 'real East Ender' has too often been used to mean 'white', so the word 'vibrant' too often precedes 'community', and means Bangladeshi or black neighbourhoods. Now, at least, internationally acclaimed writers like Monica Ali, who tells the story of a woman from Bangladesh arriving in Brick Lane, the title of her book, are demonstrating that the 'real East End' shifts, constantly reinventing itself.

When sentimentalists lament the loss of old solidarities and scorn gentrifiers and yuppies in 'their' traditional East End, they fail to acknowledge that most new waves have gentrified, if that means coming to a poor, rundown area hoping to improve it. The Huguenot silk weavers were gentrifiers in the seventeenth century, bringing the manners and skills of Protestant France to Spitalfields; so are the Bangladeshis, now a third of the population. And so were the Poles, whose work ethic during the recent boom years alarmed the more relaxed local plumbers, decorators and carpenters.

Unlike those in the soap opera, today's East Enders do not live lives of multiracial solidarity. Poverty does not encourage harmony. The British National Party is feeding a residual resentment among locals at the failure of governments to help them share in the years of plenty. My first address in the East End was off Brick Lane, then a dingy street of curry houses where the last Jewish shopkeepers were moving out and the first-generation Bangladeshis were developing what is now a chic lunch-hour destination for City workers. At that time, in the 1970s, the neo-fascist National Front sold its newspapers at one end – carrying on a tradition from Oswald Mosley's blackshirts, calling for wogs, waps and Jews to get out of the East End – and the Socialist Workers Party distributed anti-Nazi pamphlets at the other.

My second address, three decades ago, was in Mile End, where I still live. A young neighbour, then about thirty, lamented the loss of the East End of her 1950s childhood. 'They used to call this [Mile End Old Town] the Cohens and Kellys,' she told me, having correctly identified that I was neither Jewish nor Irish. She moved soon after to North London, like many 'Cohens' before her. Three connected families across the road had lived in the street since the first of hundreds of World War II flying bombs to blitz East London hit the nearby railway. When London house prices soared in the 1990s, two of them sold quickly and moved to Essex. Now my neighbours are Chinese, Polish, Sri Lankan. As teenagers, the sons of a family of second- or third-generation British Sikhs adopted the accents of North London black rappers, rather than a Cockney twang – which, despite living in the heart of the East End, I now seldom hear. Their father talks as I do: southern, slightly lazy. And there's another sound I seldom hear: the *EastEnders* signature tune ends with a cheerfully whistled phrase. Now the only whistler is the 'East End' window cleaner. Probably a 'Kelly', he drives in from Essex.

A SECOND POPULAR television program uses the signature East End image of the bend in the river. Here the credits show a helicopter clattering over the water and the high-rise landscape of Canary Wharf, towards a tower-top helipad. All is steel and glass and money. This is *The Apprentice*, a 'reality' show where ambitious young men and women compete with each other to become an 'apprentice' to the business tycoon Sir Alan Sugar. He is the son of an East End tailor (and, since June, enterprise adviser to Gordon Brown's benighted government) and talks with an improbably authentic Cockney accent, pouring scorn on their attempts to impress him with their business acumen. *The Apprentice* has proved hugely popular – partly because of Sir Alan's barked put-downs and partly because of the unashamedly raw capitalist energy of the competitors, many of them second-generation Asians. Canary Wharf is the right visual cue for this program. Over two centuries the former marshland on which the Wharf now sits has delivered hundreds of chancers their fortunes. It has done so mostly in a sea of deprivation.

That this particular bend in the river should again become the crucible for generating global wealth is an accident of geography. But the collocation of plenty and poverty is no accident. Muck and money are proverbial bedfellows. Those who need money and those who worship it find each other. The desperate arrived in London, welcomed in periods of boom and reviled when times were hard. Desperation and alienation breed lawlessness which, for rich and poor, has been a continuous thread in the East End's story.

For all the sentimental literature on the old harmonious East End, the stronger narrative is one of resilience. For a while, the life of the river and of the dockers who found their voice did provide cohesion and solidarity. But loyalties here have always been frail. Tower Hamlets has no centre; it groups together Mile End, Stepney, Poplar, Bow, Whitechapel, Millwall, Wapping, Limehouse, Bethnal Green, Shadwell, Aldgate, Spitalfields. Each hamlet has significance to its inhabitants, but no administrative coherence. The 2012 Olympics, the continuing development downstream of the Isle of Dogs and Lord Mawson's Water City will shift London's commercial centre further east. The East End could become central. The East End, with its rump of a name, could become the hub. The coming decade might be the first time – after centuries of poverty and substandard health, and of providing labour and services to enrich others – that East Enders get something back. They will not be the same East Enders, not even their descendants, quite probably not even with ancestors from the same continent. But it will be something to celebrate.

Barbara Gunnell is a London-based journalist, and an associate of the Demos think tank.

Hedging bets on the future

Sydney becomes a financial capital and pays the price

Margot Saville

IN 1985, I was a very junior lawyer in a blue-ribbon Sydney law firm. Over expensive cocktails at a function, the head of an overseas bank – the recipient of a freshly minted banking licence – flashed his gold Rolex and boasted that he had 'plenty of money' to spend and his company would revolutionise not just Australian banking but the whole country. Later, the party continued back at his harbourside penthouse, but I was tired of him and went home. He was an obnoxious, materialistic little man. Little did I know that the city would soon be full of them.

That year, Treasurer Paul Keating had granted sixteen foreign banking licences. Suddenly, Sydney was bursting with expat bankers and foreign capital. Australian businesses no longer had to go cap in hand to their local bank to get money to expand; they had a choice. The city, thanks to the reforms implemented by Premier Neville Wran, was already changing – and this new money, which arrived with the Keating-led program of financial deregulation, was the accelerant that transformed it.

While Melbourne has taken pride in being a sober, serious city, Sydney has always been in love with fast money and good times: its ethos came from convicts and the Rum Corps; even now, its government depends on the revenues from the hoteliers and registered clubs stuffed with poker machines. Gambling and gaming is in its DNA; former premier Robert Askin and chief magistrate Murray Farquhar consorted with known criminals. It's a city known for its love of bending the rules.

Like the local crims, the Australian banking system had always functioned as a cosy cartel, but by the time Neville Wran entered the New South Wales Parliament, in 1970, it had begun to open up. It's hard to imagine now, but the first credit card, the now-superseded Bankcard, was launched in the mid-'70s and for the first time people could buy things they didn't have enough cash for without applying for a personal loan. A young Paul Keating, the opposition spokesman on minerals and energy, called for the introduction of foreign banks, because the local banks were 'unrespon-sive' to the challenges and rewards of the mining industry. The *Australian Financial Review* approved his stand. In late 1977 it quoted him and called

---

PREVIOUS PAGE: Paul Keating (detail), 1998. Artist: Robert Hannaford. Courtesy of the artist. *www.roberthannaford.com.au*

for an inquiry, describing the current banking system as 'quasi-socialist in that it is effectively run by the Reserve Bank but retains the worst features of oligopolistic capitalism'.

Keating had first-hand experience of the workings of banks. In 1965 his father's company, Marlak Engineering, won a contract from the Malaysian government to build a bridge, but the local banks would not lend against the contract and the loan application was rejected. Marlak lost its chance and Paul Keating found a mission. He told me: 'That was the way they were. Deadbeat institutions run by deadbeat executives.' In *Keating: The Inside Story* (Viking, 1996) his former economics adviser John Edwards attributes Keating's fundamental understanding of markets and prices to his involvement with his father's company. Thanks to the rigid banking rules, Marlak missed the opportunity to expand and was sold to ANI eight years later.

PAUL KEATING LOVES his home town, declaring with characteristic bravado in 1993, 'If you're not in Sydney, you're camping out.' He claims credit for the city's massive demographic changes – as a result of the reforms he implemented, Sydney split into two cities: the affluent, internationally focused suburbs that cling to the harbour and the sprawling tracts of suburbia beyond.

In 2007 he said, 'When I was Treasurer, I made Sydney the financial capital. Before I opened up the financial markets in 1984, there was a $30,000 limit on borrowing, and even then you had to crawl to the bank manager. Now, any two butchers can go across the road, buy five blocks, develop them and sell off the plan. In a world awash with liquidity, anything buildable is bankable.'

Being the nation's financial capital has a downside in a global financial crisis. When Lehman Brothers collapsed the global banking system ground to a halt, and within a week its Australian branch was tipped into voluntary administration, owing up to $800 million. Immediately, local financial institutions – spooked for much of the year as companies including Allco, Rubicon, and Babcock and Brown hit the credit wall – started shedding staff; within weeks there was a panic sufficient to force the government to guarantee all bank deposits, and profoundly change the finance sector.

If you want to see what life is like when the finance sector is no longer at the top of the tree, head to Double Bay, five kilometres east of the CBD: there are dozens of empty shops; many of those still operating are free of shoppers, though plastered with sale signs; if you hang around long enough, someone will sell you their car. Postcodes 2027 and 2028 still report the highest incomes in Australia, but when the financial tsunami washed over Wall Street, the wave did not take long to hit.

For the first time in decades, Sydney house prices led the market down. In the residential heartlands of the banking and finance sectors, in the harbourside eastern suburbs and lower north shore, prices fell through the parquetry. Australian Property Monitors reported that prices in Double Bay dropped by a quarter in the year to the end of March 2009 on a low turnover. For the first time in recent memory the most expensive houses recorded the biggest falls. 'The top end of the market has always been seen as a bit of a safe haven and has generally been immune to downturn,' the RP Data senior research analyst Cameron Kusher said, but the global financial crisis 'really impacted hard on high-income earners'.

Everyone knows someone who has been affected, but trying to find one who will talk publicly about it is not easy. John McGrath has been selling top-end houses for decades: 'There has definitely been an increased number of people electing to sell below the radar. They either want to save face or don't want people to know that they are in trouble.' The saving grace is low interest rates, which have 'enabled people to rearrange their debts and avoid too much forced selling'.

Since the mid-'80s the gap between the top and the middle has widened in Sydney, skewing the local ecology. Whole suburbs are now at the mercy of one sector, and when that goes down it takes almost everyone with it. In the past year 20,000 local jobs in banking and associated industries have been cut – high-paying jobs that demanded degrees, devotion and long hours. These in turn financed an ancillary army of service providers: decorators, builders, cleaners, trainers, caterers, hairdressers and nannies.

ONE OF THE biggest problems for Sydney is that the state economy is reeling. In May 2009, Access Economics reported that unemployment would hit 9 per cent by the end of 2010. The one-time Premier State has gone backwards since the 2000 Olympics on the key indicators of growth, investment, jobs, home building and wages. It now contributes less than a third of the country's economic production. An exodus of people means its population share has also shrunk below a third, and it accounts for only 15 per cent of new home building. New South Wales receives just under a quarter of new business investment, down from a third at the beginning of the century.

Sydney split into a global city and a local one, urbane and suburban, fast and not-so-fast, in a process that started in the late '70s but received a great boost during the era of deregulation. Australia had started tentatively on that path in 1979, when Prime Minister Malcolm Fraser established the Australian Financial System Inquiry under the stewardship of Keith Campbell, the chairman of property company Hooker Corporation Ltd who examined the banking sector, tax, stock exchange and foreign exchange.

Campbell, like Paul Keating, had learned from personal experience the limits of the highly regulated Australian banking system. The ALP historian and former minister Rodney Cavalier has written extensively about Campbell in his *Southern Highlands Branch Newsletter*: 'In the 1960s a weak balance sheet denied the Hooker Corporation a loan from any Australian bank, locked in (as they were) to rigid matrixes of assets and liabilities, income and repayments. Campbell raised the funds for the survival of Hooker by selling options and warrants over Hooker shares, a true first for Australian finance.'

When the Campbell Report was released in 1981, it was 'praised as a blueprint for the future', according to the business writer Edna Carew. It 'broadly recommended that the banking and financial markets be freed of government controls so that interest rates and the exchange rates would be determined by the markets and not by authorities such as the Reserve Bank, the Treasury and government,' she wrote in *Keating: A Biography* (Allen & Unwin, 1988). 'The Australian banking system, which (with one exception) had not increased in numbers since the 1940s, should be expanded to include new and foreign banks.'

A recession sent unemployment soaring to new highs, and the Campbell Report languished until after the election. Cavalier noted, 'The impact of an inquiry depends on its political context. There is nothing so powerful as an idea whose time has arrived. When the report is substantive and the chairman persuasive, it will nonetheless go nowhere if it lacks a champion. That champion is necessarily the minister of the moment or the leader of the government. The Campbell inquiry lacked a champion in John Howard, it found one in Paul Keating. The champion was one who had changed his views on economics and regulation. Like any convert, he was a zealot as born anew.'

AFTER THE 1983 election, Hawke and Keating's victory celebrations were short-lived. The day after the poll, they were told by Treasury Secretary John Stone that the projected budget deficit for 1983/84 was $9.6 billion, $3.6 billion more than expected. Hundreds of millions of dollars had flowed out of the country just before the election. The two leaders had agreed that the old way of looking at things in Australia had run its course. Yet when Keating entered the former Treasurer John Howard's office for the first time he found one copy of the Campbell Report sitting on a filing cabinet, yellowed and faded by the sun. 'That said so much for Howard's attitude to it,' Keating recalled. 'When I came to office, there was a momentum for deregulation. Howard had let the Campbell Committee report die and I appealed to Vic Martin to do a report on that. It had to be done by someone who believed in the rationality of the markets.'

Dr Don Russell was a principal adviser to Paul Keating in the 1980s and '90s. He recalled that those unwelcome pieces of news dictated the pace of change – it had to happen quickly. On the Tuesday after the election Keating devalued the dollar, stopping an unprecedented capital outflow. Russell said they grasped that 'Australia had major economic problems. Inflation was high and we had just lived through a second wages explosion which had led to a collapse in corporate profits and an awful budget deficit...after a decade of failure there was a serious concern that the country might be incapable of fixing the problem. Australian manufacturing industry was in a shocking shape and the old philosophy of regulation, industry assistance and high tariffs no longer appeared to have the answers. Hawke and Keating came to the conclusion that they had to make Australia more competitive, which meant opening industry up to international competition.'

Finally, Campbell's time had come. He made the keynote speech from the private sector at the Economic Summit convened by the new government in April 1983. Cavalier noted that he 'won the confidence of the mainstream of Labor when he enunciated that high levels of unemployment were unacceptable as an instrument in fighting inflation. Within the week, having pushed himself beyond endurance, Campbell suffered a fatal heart attack.'

At the end of that year Hawke and Keating floated the dollar and removed exchange controls. Russell said this was a 'watershed philosophical decision', and subsequent moves to deregulate the finance sector and cut tariffs flowed from it: 'if Australia was to become internationally competitive then the controls had to be removed from the banks,' Keating said at the time. 'We, can change the financial system in a way which the so-called businessman's party never could, or never had the guts to do. I always thought it's the job of the Commonwealth Government to run the private economy well. And if you're going to do that you've got to sit down and work out where all the impediments are. Then you tick them off, clear the decks…A lot of the Labor Party is about the politics of envy. Well I don't have any of that shit in me.'

In 1984 there was another election, followed by a Tax Summit to canvass reforms, and the next year Keating was ready to announce sixteen new licences for foreign-owned trading banks. 'And they said it couldn't be done,' he boasted.

MELBOURNE HAD LONG jealously guarded its reputation as the home of the banks and the largest companies in Australia. But while the government intended that the new banks would be spread around Australia, most came to Sydney. Keating had not made a conscious decision in deregulating the financial system to make Sydney the leading financial city, according to Don Russell – but within a decade it was Australia's undisputed financial capital, the glamorous international magnet. 'Given its existing infrastructure and competitive strengths, Sydney was a natural beneficiary…It's just the way it turned out. They took the controls off the financial sector and this is what happened.'

Sydney became one of the burgeoning fields in a new global gold rush, as international bankers scrambled to set up operations. By the mid-'80s, it was becoming an exciting, cosmopolitan city. The Wran government was elected in 1976, and implemented 'reforms across the board on social measures, loosening laws on Sunday trading, hotels open on Sunday, cafés spilling onto footpaths, demands for a higher-quality bread, anti-discrimination laws, investing big in the arts and collecting institutions (new wings for the Art Gallery, the State Library), heritage laws, anti-censorship, support for the arts and arts festivals. There were tax breaks and incentives to get business here.' These were changes that enabled the city to 'express itself', Rodney Cavalier wrote.

By 1988 the city was booming. In *Sydney: Biography of a City* (Random House, 1999) the former Lord Mayor Lucy Turnbull noted that the 'federal funding to pay for public works to commemorate the two hundred years of European settlement', combined with Wran's transformation, meant that when the city took centre stage it sparkled; Sydney had 'shaken off its dull grey provincial mantle'.

The new bankers brought plenty of cash with them. As Mitchell Moss, a professor of urban policy and planning at New York University, puts it, 'Until the late 1970s, banking was a career choice more akin to being a corporate lawyer or a doctor than a high-flying hedge-fund manager. Wall Street became a high-margin business because of the deregulated environment. You basically had a casino culture operating in the financial-services industry.' And Sydney, with its love of gambling, was an ideal base for a new kind of gaming.

Some of the contracts the financial markets wanted to trade were close to the legal definition of wagers, which are unenforceable – at least by legal methods. In the early '80s, the lawyer Michael Eyers had a standing brief to review for Hill Samuel (now Macquarie Bank) the legal status of its forward financial contracts. Senior Counsel's advice was regularly sought on whether these ran the risk of being struck down as unenforceable wagers – and whether Hill Samuel could then have recourse to linked contracts and margin calls. Not until the mid-'80s did corporations legislation remove this threat from derivatives.

A CENTURY EARLIER the Victorian government had given tax breaks to companies setting up headquarters in Melbourne, and although the NSW government considered offering similar incentives to the foreign banks, they were not necessary. There were many reasons why bankers wanted to come to Sydney, and the greater number of direct international flights made the decision easier. 'People come out to Australia to set up a branch and go back to the US or the UK five times a year, and there are more flights through Sydney', the demographer Bernard Salt argues. 'Melbourne flights add hours to the journey – that's a major deal-breaker.'

The Reserve Bank director Jillian Broadbent, who was working in merchant banking at the time, concurs, adding that this gained momentum because the 'anchor' institutions such as the Australian Stock Exchange, the Sydney Futures Exchange and the Reserve Bank were all located in Sydney. The foundations of the boom which lasted until 2008 were laid down at this time. According to Michael Eyers, 'By the end of the 1980s, through deregulation and the emergence of financial markets in response, and because Australia has a world-standard banking regulatory system and a secure commercial and legal environment, and not least because technology developed to support – or permit – modern markets, the ground was laid for the twenty-year boom that followed the recession [in the early '90s] that perhaps we really had to have.'

SYDNEY MADE AN easier transition from a manufacturing to a service economy than Melbourne during this period. Over the past twenty-five years, employment in the finance sector in Sydney grew by more than 7 per cent a year. Paul Keating argues that the competition in the banking sector reinforced the growth of the high end of the service economy. 'It created a new cohort of middle-income executive people who lived within the financial-services economy. Larger salaries and emoluments and so-called success fees created a new class of individuals who expanded their wealth by using the financial assets of financial institutions.'

The international bankers brought a new pay structure as well. On top of their huge salaries, they received large bonuses. This affected Sydney's housing market, as bankers borrowed increasingly large sums of money to buy trophy homes, knowing they could pay off a big chunk of the mortgage with the next bonus.

Bernard Salts argues, 'The ability to continually trade up to a higher-priced house is part of the bonus culture... they became addicted to that and built a lifestyle around that which drove property prices in Sydney, London and New York.'

In the mid-to-late '80s, the Sydney property market rose exponentially. John McGrath recalls that at the end of the decade, 'the market went up 50 to 60 per cent – that was unprecedented in my lifetime. The rich got richer and bought into the higher-quality areas and homes. The gap between the top and the middle increased – it was the Macquarie Bank factor; people were earning money that they had never earned before, and houses became a status symbol.'

But the effects were not confined to those at the top of the income scale. Dr Glen Searle, a professor of planning, saw this first-hand. 'Sydney grew faster than Melbourne and the growth of the financial sector was a major contributor...Bankers traditionally had lived on the north shore, but you started to get the financial sector living in Paddington...I was trying to sell a house at that time [in the inner east] and in that price bracket, $130,000 to $150,000, prices were going up a thousand dollars a week.'

The economist Graham Larcombe, who is a director of Strategic Economics, also closely observed the changes. Global corporations 'nurtured the property markets and the asset bubble'. Once deregulation started, the 'role of the financial sector was much more central to the running of the economy...Sydney emerged as a global financial hub...global cities such as London, New York and Tokyo as well as Munich and Singapore became conduits for capital flows in and out of economies. Sydney was a beneficiary of that, in an economic and an employment sense.'

UNTIL THE 1980s, Wall Street accounted for only about a fifth of all corporate profits in America, but by the peak of the bubble in 2007/2008 it had grown to an astounding 41 per cent. These numbers masked the reality that it was growth based on debt. Larcombe argues: 'The type of globalisation which emphasises financial globalisation is flawed, as it is associated with growth in activities which were not sustainable in the long term.' He is concerned that household indebtedness as a percentage of Australia's national income had risen from 25 per cent in the 1980s to 160 per cent by 2007. 'That growth in economic activity and employment is driven by debt. The more the boom went on, the more speculative activities became. The extraordinary thing is that mainstream economic policymakers did not think that instability could occur. They argued that business cycles were a thing of the past.'

Now that credit has dried up and the regulation of global finance is up for grabs, the pain is being felt not only in top-end house prices in global cities. Even in well-regulated and comparatively well-insulated economies like Australia's, there is a lag in what happens to employment, consumption and production. 'The real impact on Australia is yet to come. The future is more uncertain than it has ever been. We still have not gone through the shock of the impact on the real economy, the effect of unemployment on household incomes.' This time, however, as Larcombe notes, it is 'not just the westies' who have borne the brunt of it.

John Maynard Keynes has been here before. 'A "sound" banker, alas! is not one who foresees danger and avoids it, but one who, when he is ruined, is ruined in a conventional and orthodox way along with his fellows, so that no one can really blame him.'

Margot Saville is a Sydney-based business journalist and the author of *The Battle for Bennelong* (MUP, 2008).

REPORTAGE

Greyfields

Notes on the death of a shopping centre

Mark Welker

WHEN a shopping centre is dying, its patronage slipping away, it is referred to as a greyfield. At this point annual sales have slumped below $200 a square metre. The centre slowly hollows, tenants are given notice and town planners swoop with schedules for demolition. The centre will stay open until a third of the tenants find other lodgings. The empty shops close their roller-doors and the arcades shut down in dark rows, one by one. The centre is sealed, locks are placed on the doors and the car park buckles at the edges, weeds pushing up the bitumen in anticipation.

This will happen to one in every four shopping centres. Shopping centres die in stages: like retail lepers, they lose limbs. Anchors are what keep them alive. They are the heart – a popular franchise, supermarket or department store that directs traffic past the smaller stores. Anchors such as food halls and cinema complexes are placed at the end of long stretches of glazed windows. The industry standard states that the maximum distance shoppers are prepared to walk between anchors is three hundred metres. This is called anchor drag.

Competing centres will often anchor-steal in an attempt to attract tenants and shoppers alike. When an anchor leaves, dead zones appear. Pedestrian traffic diverts like a dammed river. Blank corridors. Roller-doors. To survive, the weak gather around the strong.

Joe Raffino owns a café next to what was a large department store in Perth's Bentley Plaza, selling breakfast, lunch and snacks to the anchor's employees and passing shoppers. The day after the anchor closed its doors for good, Joe's business halved. 'We used to put on twenty-five ham and cheese croissants in the morning,' he says. 'Now I put on two.' This is the third anchor to set him adrift.

Shopping centres die every year. Rising land prices revalue a centre's worth, and property owners have no emotional attachment to an ageing complex. Closure is sometimes quick and painless: demolition can take as little as ten days. But the cost of evicting tenants often drives an ugly alternative. Property owners let maintenance fall by the wayside. Arcades become

---

PREVIOUS PAGE: Decaying Dixie Square Mall in Harvey, Illinois, USA. The mall opened in 1966 and closed in 1979. It is best known for getting trashed by Jake and Elwood Blues in the 1980 movie *The Blues Brothers*. Photographer: Lee Bey. *www.leebey.com*

sallow and bleak; leaks are left dripping, the roof blisters; shoppers leave, street urchins move in. The corridors reek of urine and mould. Roller-doors signal the end.

THE HEART OF Victoria Park was a maze of brown-tiled shopping arcades hidden behind the street. Not far from Perth's central business district, it was an area brimming with business potential covered by an ageing facade. For three years I worked in an office overlooking the centre's rear entrance.

The anchor was a dilapidated supermarket whose workers seemed to be teenagers skipping school for the day. The floors were streaked with trolley rubber; the lights – dimmed, to save energy – cast an unhealthy pallor on the sullen faces of the staff. If you stayed long enough you could hear the merry-go-round music grind to a halt, the clunk of the tape-flip over the PA system. Renovations doubled the number of registers, the cost of which halved the number of checkout staff. This was the heart of Victoria Park.

As overseas investor-owners waited for the right price to sell, the centre was left to decay. Drains overflowed after heavy rain. Electrical fittings were left bare, arcades caught in a flickering, fluorescent seizure. Two and a half years before the walls eventually came down, only eighteen of the centre's forty-two shops were occupied.

The local newspaper followed the shopping centre's demise. 'The only people that shop here are our loyal customers,' the owner of the centre's café is reported to have said. 'But it is dangerous. One lady recently fell and broke her leg.' He and his wife had been operating their shop for fourteen years. 'We stay because we have to. Nobody will buy us out.'

But even this owner is gone now. The centre was finally put out of its misery, and the space where it once stood now resembles a concealed bombsite. Only the anchor remains.

ALIVE, SHOPPING CENTRES are filled with anxiety. They fight against the retail slump, the lack that defines a failing retail venture. This can be the result of anything from an inefficient layout to what is referred to as visual pollution – which includes people, undesirables who sour the retail mix.

I made some enquiries about security at the Galleria shopping centre.

'Well,' Pam says, running a packet of frozen peas past the scanner, 'don't go near the toilets. They're purely for show: everybody knows this and everybody stays clear. The toilets are the most dangerous place in the centre; it's the only place where they can't see you.' She nods up in the direction of a camera jutting from the ceiling. 'In the toilets, nobody can hear you scream.'

I laugh, but she tilts her sunglasses down her nose so that I know she wasn't joking. 'Do you want to know why I wear these sunglasses? It's because I've been working checkout since I was twenty-two.' Pam looks like she's pushing forty. 'The lights give me migraines. It also helps distance me a bit from the customers. This way they can't see what I'm really thinking.'

I've tried talking to security about security, but my questions have been answered by slow shakes of the head, silence over the phone. Perhaps if you don't talk about crime, it doesn't exist.

'Don't use the rear car park after dark,' Pam interrupts. 'Don't park on the second floor. Don't use the stairwells. If you think someone's following you to your car, they probably are. Don't let your woman walk back to the car alone. Don't rely on security guards – they don't have the jurisdiction to do anything. Taxis will take twenty minutes to arrive, so order one early and don't wait outside. There are basic rules, and there is common sense. Don't use the rear entrance.

'The music is to deter youths from hanging around. There are studies done that say teenagers' brains are susceptible to certain kinds of classical music. It gets to them like a dog whistle. Do you know why the balconies have angular railings? It's to make it uncomfortable to lean on for any length of time. These are all policies. We only have one set of benches now.

'See those men over there?' She gestures to a group of fading Italian men gathered around a set of benches, clasping and unclasping their hands. 'They're the only people who get benches. They've been here as long as I have. Only they've always been old. They used to sit around by the shoe store until they were moved, then they were up next to the newsagent, but they kept reading the papers and then putting them back on the pile. They were out front of the manicurist for a while, until the lady found out they were looking up the skirts of the female customers. Now they're stuck between an ice-cream shop and a fishmonger. There's not much trouble they can cause there.'

She considers the length of a zucchini. 'Is this gourmet zucchini or normal zucchini?'

Gourmet.

'I've had marriage proposals from six different men in the time I've been working checkout. There's a man who comes in with his mother each week on a Tuesday and asks me to marry him. I've said no so many times that now I say yes. The other proposals are from legitimate-looking people, you could say. People like fast service, I guess.' She forces a smile.

'A lady came through the other day and threatened to call the cops on me because I asked her for her FlyBuys card.' Pam fans her fingers out in front of her face as she becomes the lady. 'FlyBuys are illegal,' the lady hisses at me. 'Why are you asking me about something illegal? You'll get in big trouble for talking about things like FlyBuys.'

Pam does a price check on a tamarillo. 'There's a certain type of person that buys a fruit like this.'

'See that man there?' She points to a man fondling a grapefruit. 'He comes in every day at 9 am dressed like he is now, in a suit and tie, and walks around till 6 pm, then leaves. Some days he buys something; most days he doesn't. One day I ask him why he doesn't just go to the park. "The park never changes," he says. And then he looks up at the lights as if he's looking at clouds in the sky.'

The man delicately places the grapefruit back on the shelf. He tucks his hands into his pockets and moves off down the aisle, trailing his fingers across the fuzz of a peach pyramid.

'A guy comes in the other day and gives me a sheet of paper that says: *Unable to talk, they are listening.* Sometimes I wonder whether it's shopping that people are after or just someone to talk to. Strewth, everyone has a different story to tell. I'm like a church confessional. It's punishment for asking people how their day's going.'

My bags are gathered like a train wreck at the end of the counter.

'Are we finished?' Pam asks.

'I guess so.'

'Good. My lunch hour's about to start.'

DEAD SHOPPING CENTRES are the tombstones of failed enterprise. In Perth the suburbs stretch a hundred and twenty kilometres from north to south, and more than fifty kilometres east. It's not uncommon to commute for more than an hour to work each day. This massive grid of barren suburbia has its own name, Greater Perth, an appalling realisation of the great Australian dream: a backyard, two cars and a Victa mower. The suburbs follow the arterial roads out, veins congested with double carports, patched lawns and swimming pools. The sprawl is made for cars, not people.

Shopping centres make this possible. On average, people will travel two to three kilometres for food and five to eight for clothing and household goods. The sprawl demands satisfaction. Yet the smell of decay is always on the wind. Retail giants squeeze the smaller shopping centres out of the market. With plans approved, sixty thousand square metres of retail space can be operational within one year. Retail gravitation takes its course, and the small centres rot as the big players draw the clientele away.

We walk under the glass-plated awning of the Harbour Town shopping centre. 'Beautiful isn't it?' My guide points to the transparent roof. 'We're bringing back the "marketplace" feel to these centres.' The tinted light casts an antiseptic gaze over the shoppers passing by. 'It's been shown that the sun has a really positive effect on a shopper's state of mind.'

Michael Tulley is a shopping-centre surgeon; he takes fading centres and reinvents them.

'This,' he says indicating a row of discount bins, 'is a new era in shopping-centre philosophy: outlet selling. Every day is a sale day.' Beside us, two large women in T-shirts and leggings sift through a pile of business ties. 'There was a massive build up of ex-season stock coming back through the distribution lines, clogging up the system to such an extent where at certain times of the year the cost of freighting goods back to the manufacturer was starting to outweigh the cost of just shredding them. It was such a waste.' Tulley talks about sale stock in the way other people talk about starving kids in Africa. 'I mean, something like this,' he says, pulling a size 14 sandal from a nearby table. 'This is perfectly good merchandise. Would you shred this?'

'I'm size 11.'

'I know! But for the right person it still holds value. Sure, maybe not as much as it did a few months ago, but still a price.' He looks the shoe up and down again, as if measuring up his own size. After a few moments he places it back on the pile. 'This style of retail is so popular that we don't even require anchors anymore.'

We slide sideways to get past a clump of shoppers crawling over a pyramid of battery-operated blenders.

'But it's not enough anymore to simply stick every type of shop you can think of into a hulking great cube. Box shops are dull, drab, austere. We spend far too much of our time in them to make them boring. The challenge is to make people want to stick around. Time spent is money spent.'

Harbour Town uses the merry-go-round retail plan. A circular arcade only has one direction. You get on at the entrance and take the ring road to the exit. It's a continuous flow of traffic that forgets no store.

Tulley talks about 'synergy' with his hands close to his chest. 'Imagine a shopping centre as a cluster of retail possibilities. Individually, these stores have to offer merchandise that is attractive or essential to the average shopper. But as a whole, customer services fit together, creating what we call the ultimate shopping experience. Shops work off each other. When a customer searches for ladies fashion they expect to find two things: range and affinity. Which shirt should I buy, and what can I buy to go with it.'

This is synergy.

'We're all looking for critical mass, you see.'

Critical mass?

'The point at which it all comes together. It's a chain reaction of expenditure: the more you buy, the more things you need to buy.' A meltdown of retail efficiency.

A growing trend in the industry is to theme centres to make them more alluring. 'This can be good,' says Tulley. Earlier he had shown me a coloured sketch of a fashion boutique arcade, all straight lines and white space. Sophistication. A themed décor or design gives context to the surrounding outlets. Food halls and supermarket sections are often combined with themes of the garden, the farm or natural elements. 'But there are mistakes. Fashions change; themes grow old and outdated. They work against you. A centre is a changing entity and you have to keep up.'

Tulley stops by a blank shopfront. Within, snakes of insulation cord lay abandoned; a small pile of dirt has been swept into the corner; a discarded chair is visible. Metres away, an escalator diverts the flow of traffic away from the store. 'Vertical circulation', they call it. Tulley points to a faded logo on the window.

'They call these "label scars",' he says softly. 'It's the mark left from the previous owner's sign.' This one is for a discount travel-goods store. Tulley rubs the spot with his fist. 'Really difficult to get rid of.'

FIVE MONTHS LATER, a yearlong renovation of the Heart of the Park Shopping Centre is finished. The brown tiles are gone; the leaks are fixed. The sagging roof has been torn off and replaced with vaulted skylights. The floors squeak like a hospital ward. Disinfectant hangs in the air. The fluorescents are steady and white in the same way you think of God's bathroom being white. The shopfronts are lathered in wet reflection.

The anchor now has express lanes, clean tiles, a health-food section and golden lights over the bakery. But the checkouts are piloted by the same sour faces. Only the girl at the cigarette counter is smiling.

Of the old faces that waited behind the glazed shopfronts, there is none that I recognise. New faces, pulled into smiles, wait eagerly by the counters. The shopkeepers seem optimistic that shoppers will return, but only the anchor is still doing regular business.

Perhaps it's the mix. Two hairdressers now compete for business; a small greengrocer battles defiantly with the anchor. At the entrance, a franchise coffee shop attracts a small crowd of middle-aged businessmen pawing their newspapers, but few venture inside. At around three, the quietest time of the day, the centre has a high-noon flavour. Shop owners are caught up in the retail silence, and stare across the empty hall at each other.

Four weeks later the bookshop has gone, its window paint so fresh I can hardly see the scar.

Mark Welker graduated from the universities of Western Australia and Curtin, and has worked in advertising for most of his career. He has recently returned to writing more 'seriously' and these days prefers to shop online.

The crumbling estate

Ten steps: the long, slow death of Australian journalism

Geoffrey Barker

NEARLY fifty years ago I walked into the Dickensian editorial offices of *The Age* in Collins Street, Melbourne, to start a cadetship in journalism. Old men in green eyeshades sat around a horseshoe-shaped subeditors' table shuffling papers and grumbling. Rowdy correspondents, full of beer and arrogance, scuffled for the few broken typewriters available in the reporters' room.

The place was worn and grubby, the air full of shouts and curses and cigarette smoke. I was assigned the daily Shipping Movements list (Due Today, Due Tomorrow, Sailing Today, Sailing Tomorrow, In Port) and the Weather, Mails and Train Times. From that first morning I was captured by the idea of unearthing, explaining and commenting on the affairs of the day.

I soon advanced to reporting inquests in the Coroner's Court, where matters of life and death, public reputation and lethal crime were presided over by the bespectacled coroner, Harry Pascoe, SM, and where sadistic coppers in the morgue behind the court delighted in showing virgin reporters their chilled clientele stretched out naked on gurneys with labels tied to their toes. It was a humbling and horrifying start for an innocent working-class lad. But we somehow learned to care about the issues of the day and about the words we wrote to report them, and we shared a naive belief in the value of free and independent journalism in a democratic society.

A COUPLE OF years ago I retired from the Canberra bureau of the *Australian Financial Review*. I had no regrets – I had run a long and enjoyable race. I had been a reporter, feature writer, leader writer, news executive, political columnist, and a correspondent in Europe and the United States. I had managed to squeeze in a degree in philosophy in my spare time (which the old sweats insisted would ruin me as a journalist). I had covered the Cold War and hot wars in Northern Ireland and southern Africa, and the rise of Margaret Thatcher and the fall of the Soviet Union. I had been with Ronald Reagan in Berlin when he called on Mikhail Gorbachev to 'tear down this wall'. And I had spent my later years in Canberra, writing on defence and foreign policy for the *Australian Financial Review*. The paper has generously allowed me to continue to write a fortnightly column and other occasional pieces.

Yet, despite all my positive experiences, I believe I am witnessing the long, slow death of Australian newspaper journalism. The craft is in decline; it is being tamed, shackled, diminished. I am conscious that old men tend to the view that things ain't what they used to be, that all around them is decay and destruction. That is not my opinion. There is much about Australian journalists and journalism that remains lively and creative, witty and informative; most Australian newspapers still do a creditable job and much of the new online journalism is effective, if handled with care.

But now-established trends are throttling the life, authority and influence out of newspapers. Circulations are falling, at best stalling; newspapers are shrinking or, in the US, going online; profits are disappearing as advertisers desert newspapers for other media. It is often said that these trends reflect changes in education and the wider sources of information now available on TV, radio and the internet, all of which are quicker and easier to consume than newspapers. But it is worth asking whether the declines in circulation and revenue result partly from decisions by companies' managers who, desperate to ensure newspapers' survival, have embraced a range of practices damaging to the craft of journalism.

THE FIRST TREND is the rise of managerialism which has displaced journalism as the dominant culture in newspaper offices. Newspapers are run by executives with little regard for serious journalism as a vocation involving a public trust. For them, journalism is a costly and troublesome undertaking; its practitioners are difficult and unhelpful, and have to be kept on a short leash. Newspaper editors now tend not to be journalists experienced in national and international political reporting, and are likely instead to be managers more comfortable behind a desk. They spend less time on editing than on staff control and corporate planning.

They want quick results: increases in circulation and revenues to boost 'shareholder value'. They want a 'fast turnaround' on stories. They are impatient with notion of careful enquiry, and uncomfortable with the exposure of public and private swinery, which can involve serious legal risks and embarrassments. Cost considerations ultimately determine how – and sometimes whether – events are covered, regardless of their national or international importance.

In this culture – a world of endless planning and ideas conferences – journalists are regarded, as one former Fairfax chief executive famously put it, as 'content providers for advertising platforms'. They are pressed to write more and to write it more quickly, to supply not only the newspaper but also its website. Journalists are valued according to the number of times their name appears over articles, meaning that the most automaton-like information processors – purveyors of what Nick Davies calls 'churnalism' – are the most valued staff. Journalists who want to take time to observe and reflect, to put events in context and put some effort into their writing, are regarded less favourably.

SECOND, NEWSPAPERS ARE engaged in a perpetual effort to cut costs and staff. While journalists were once undoubtedly profligate in their pursuit of information, they are now under strict financial constraints: travel and communications allowances have been cut so ruthlessly that journalists cannot pursue important lines of enquiry. Some staff cuts are justified: all newspapers have non-performing staff. But newspapers make little effort to replace retrenched staff with better and brighter journalists, preferring to hire young, inexperienced people because they are cheap, uncritically enthusiastic and untroubled by the demands made upon them.

Third, the way in which journalists work has changed. They are increasingly chained to the computer keyboard, the TV screen and the phone. Many lead second-hand lives, far from the action, processing information instantly as they monitor events from screens and from transcripts emailed by obliging political staffers. From a managerialist perspective this is quick, efficient and cost-effective. From a journalistic perspective it should be a last resort. Newspaper journalists in Canberra assigned to Sunday shifts have one of the most soulless jobs in journalism: they spend their day writing reports of the political talk shows, based on transcripts helpfully provided by TV networks that like the publicity. They are processing stale information for news executives for whom the Sunday talk shows are a cheap and easy source of 'news' to fill the Monday paper.

Fourth, and not surprisingly, young journalists now seem less likely to see their job as a vocation. They are more likely to regard it as a means to a more lucrative and prestigious position. A few years as a journalist are useful on the CV of a person seeking a job in political or corporate public relations. Young journalists tend to be well trained in information processing, even if they are not particularly well educated. They are taught to follow orders – which is precisely what most politicians and business executives require in a 'strategic communications adviser'. Journalism, it sometimes seems, is becoming a repository for first-rate egos and second-rate minds.

Fifth, journalists are outgunned and out-thought and out-paid by the army of political, bureaucratic and corporate communications advisers who have colonised public affairs. These advisers' role is to shield their bosses from potentially embarrassing enquiry, to spin information favourably while posing as facilitators aiding journalists in acquiring information. Getting past them is frustrating and often impossible, and weasel words crafted by flacks for politicians and executives are now among the more familiar clichés of the daily press. Recent disclosures about the intrusive role of PR flacks in a court case over the withdrawn anti-arthritis drug Vioxx offers alarming evidence of how far they are prepared to go to intimidate reporters. It is hardly surprising that young journalists are tempted to get among the big bucks rather than to struggle thanklessly to develop independent reportage, for it is easier and more congenial to be a massager of messages than a raker of muck.

SIXTH, COST-CUTTING HAS prompted Australian newspapers to buy in ever more material from notable overseas publications, including the *New York Times*, *Washington Post*, *Wall Street Journal*, *Independent* and *Guardian*. This foreign material is usually good, but it is not written for Australians; it often reflects different values and priorities. Moreover, in their search for cheap and free material, Australian newspapers have opened their op-ed and features pages to corporate and political flacks. They provide free articles for publication to advance their careers or the interests they represent. Again, there is nothing wrong with this – except the uncritical and extensive way in which the material is published these days. It further limits opportunities for newspaper journalists to develop intellectually and to do more analytical and thoughtful work.

Seventh, the practice of dumbing down – avoiding or downplaying difficult issues and highlighting sensationalist material, emphasising sex, scandal and sport – is now universal in Australian newspapers seeking to halt declines in circulation. Newspapers publish large pictures of showbiz and sporting celebrities, and make crude appeals to fear, envy and patriotism. The practice leads to serious mistakes – consider, for example, the recent publication of semi-naked photographs of a woman falsely claimed to be the former politician Pauline Hanson – and to dishonest and inaccurate reporting.

Australian newspaper ownership is notoriously limited and owners have always sought to ensure that their political attitudes are promoted. They are entitled to do so, and generally they understand that it is in their interests to allow a modicum of dissent. But these days, most notably in Rupert Murdoch's newspapers, there is a sustained right-wing agenda that permeates the presentation of news as well as the opinion pages. Much space is given over to insulting ideological opponents, questioning their motives and intelligence, and to attacking the personnel and professionalism of other newspapers, especially Fairfax publications. Newspaper readers must wonder why the press regales them with these internecine hatreds, as it cannot improve their understanding of the world or their respect for the press.

EIGHTH, AND ANOTHER product of the quest for money, is the breakdown in the separation between the editorial and advertising functions of newspapers. The long-term credibility and reputation of newspapers demands strict quarantining of editorial from advertising; both departments, as well as readers, benefit from it. But in an era of lifestyle journalism, special supplements and advertising features, newspapers compromise their independence to satisfy the demands of advertisers for some editorial quid pro quo. Perhaps no newspaper is more blatant than the *Canberra Times*. It publishes supplements in the middle of its editorial pages and acknowledges only in the tiniest visible letters that they are advertising features. Yet each advertisement on each page is accompanied by a puff piece about the product or service offered by the company that has placed the ad. Even *The Age* and the *Sydney Morning Herald* are not immune. *Media Watch* recently revealed that they published unlabelled and arguably misleading advertisements disguised as fun holiday supplements for children.

Ninth, there is now little sustained investigative journalism undertaken by Australian newspapers. Newspaper managers and editors seem reluctant to release journalists from daily reporting duties in order for them to conduct enquiries that might or might not produce publishable material. They seem appalled by the possibility that an investigative team might spend time and money on a project and then conclude that there was nothing worth reporting. There seems little sympathy for the view that the reputation and circulation of a newspaper is likely to be substantially boosted if it produces the occasional major report following sustained investigation.

Tenth, newspapers are closing expensive foreign bureaus and bringing journalists home to serve local markets. This is a result of cost-cutting, but it also reflects a desire to downplay systematic coverage of foreign and even national news in favour of local news. Major newspapers that once had international and national reputations, notably the *Sydney Morning Herald* and Melbourne's *Age*, now emphasise state and local stories involving political, administrative and criminal scandals. Their foreign news coverage, much of it purchased from overseas, tends to be limited and patchy. Vast regions of the planet are simply ignored.

AGAINST ALL THIS it might be replied, 'It was ever thus.' Newspapers have always been hotbeds of tension between the demands of journalism and the demands of commerce. There have always been managerialists whose natural inclination is to slash and burn, and there have always been journalists who defend newspapers' public trust to inform and persuade. Yet the strategic decisions made by newspapers to defend themselves against technological change and economic difficulties have only worsened their situation. Rather than seeking to raise their standards, newspapers have raced for the bottom. Rather than honouring their social role, they have chosen to cheapen it.

If there is any room for optimism, it is that few Australian newspapers are beyond redemption. Most still employ good journalists and most still publish much valuable information that is relevant to readers. But they also publish much that is dubious and, despite their vigour, newspapers are increasingly at risk from their misguided attempts to save themselves. They will remain in decline and compromised until they find a way to rebalance the imperatives of commerce and journalism. I hope they succeed in doing so. Free, independent, muck-raking journalism is more important than ever in a world dominated by political, bureaucratic and corporate authoritarians supported by armies of flim-flam communications advisers whose mission is to conceal and mislead, and who are delighted to see readers distracted with a fast-food diet of sex, sport and celebrity scandal.

Geoffrey Barker is a defence and foreign-affairs columnist for the *Australian Financial Review* and a visiting fellow at the Strategic and Defence Studies Centre at ANU. He has worked for Fairfax Media since 1960. He is the author of *The Holt Report* (Wilkie and Co, 1968) and *Sexing It Up: Australia, Iraq and Intelligence* (UNSW Press, 2003).

Slow burn

Lessons in stoicism and resignation in Japan

Colin Mills

I was initiated into the Japanese investment-banking scene in a murky Tokyo *izakaya* in early 1988. Selling Japanese stocks to international investors was a new game – foreign securities firms had been permitted by the authorities to buy seats on the Tokyo Stock Exchange only two years earlier – and everybody was learning the rules as they went along. Or making them up.

'No, no, you still don't quite get it,' my boss insisted, shunting aside his glass to create more space in which to gesticulate. Beer slopped up and over the edge of the glass, forming a little pool on the table. Around us, waitresses in bright blue and white *happi* coats weaved between the tables and emerged from clouds of cigarette smoke with trays of sashimi and tofu. *Eda-mame* shells lay scattered between the plates and on the floor.

'Look, in this business, there's this big trough of money, right? You've got to stick your snout into the money trough and keep it there! You plant your elbows like trotters in the mud, get your head down and snuffle, snuffle, snuffle! Every now and then, other little pigs will grab your hindquarters and try to drag you squealing from the trough, but you *can't let them.*'

Imposing, blunt and prone to espousing politically incorrect views with unashamed glee, James was an Englishman ten years my senior who had been transferred from his firm's London office, having found himself in stockbroking after studying particle physics at Cambridge and in Moscow. Ebullient but cynical, he didn't suffer fools and held himself and those around him to a high standard.

I spoke Japanese, but otherwise knew precious little. This saved me, as it turned out that some American with an MBA had also interviewed for the job. 'Give me the Aussie guy,' James growled at the human-resources team. 'I might be able to do something with him.' He took me under his wing, trained me and kept me sane.

From the window of our office in Akasaka, Mt Fuji could be glimpsed to the south-west when the occasional typhoon sluiced away the haze pumped out by the paper factories in Shizuoka. On the thirty-ninth floor was a bar

PREVIOUS PAGE: A businessman gazes at a share-prices board in Tokyo on 30 April 2009. Photographer: Yoshikazu Tsuno / AFP. *Source: gettyimages.com*

next to a glitzy home-fixtures showroom featuring the latest shapely multi-coloured toilet bowls with heated seats and electronic control panels, and automated bidets with hot-air dryers. After work we would sip our beers and admire the porcelain. Perched on one colleague's desk was one of those over-the-head rubber Halloween masks. This one was a Mongol, perhaps Genghis Khan: wispy facial hair, topknot. Sitting there it looked uncannily like a severed head. *Take no prisoners.*

I WAS TWENTY-ONE and had already been living in Tokyo for two years. The asset-price bubble of the late 1980s was inflating quickly, fed by low interest rates, aggressive bank lending and euphoria, but I wasn't conscious of it at the time. I was high on Japan and a youthful fervour for the exotic. Not until later did I perceive the extent to which Japan was high on itself. For me it was a can-do kind of place, where anything was possible. Disbelief is never too difficult to suspend. If stock markets teach us anything, it is that.

Across Minato-ku in central Tokyo, crude hand-painted signs hung on tiny dilapidated cottages, around which all surrounding land had been acquired and cleared for redevelopment: *Tochi wa uran*! I *won't* sell my land! The *ji-age* merchants – standover men who tried to bully landowners into selling – persevered anyway. In Yoyogi Park, hundreds of Iranian men, many of them in the country illegally to labour on construction sites, would congregate on Sundays. On weekends, I joined a group of other Australian expats in games of Australian Rules football against teams fielded by a couple of local universities. The young, fit Japanese guys ran rings around the older, fatter Aussies, who had been out drinking in Roppongi the night before. But we, the recent arrivals, were taller and by marking above their heads we held our own.

After university I had briefly been a reporter with a Japanese wire service but quickly became disillusioned with the work. It was all speed, not much creativity. At the press clubs at the Tokyo Stock Exchange and Bank of Japan, where I was assigned, I was surrounded by rumpled, perpetually exhausted Japanese reporters who hung out at their desks reading tabloids or *manga* until 8 pm, having filed their final stories for the day four hours earlier. When they then went out drinking I asked them why they didn't go home to their wives and families. They laughed, amused at my ignorance of the evening habits of *sararimen*.

Each weekday, a huge electronic stock-price board glowed like an idol gazing down over the press room. Share prices that were up that day flashed green; those that were down flashed red. The board was a sea of green nearly all the time and I was enthralled. Japanese corporations were on the brink of taking over the world, so I decided I had better find out how they were doing it. I had struggled in economics classes at university, but this was different. The stock market was the real economy in action: living, breathing, throbbing. I wanted in. That I knew absolutely nothing about stocks meant I got my wish.

WHILE WESTERN MARKETS struggled after Black Monday, the Japanese stock market took only six months to recover the losses incurred in October 1987, and then kept rising. Analysts whose stock recommendations went up considered themselves geniuses. Portfolio managers congratulated themselves when their funds posted big gains. Equity salesmen could pick spurious stock ideas from the dirtiest, raciest tabloids and puff out their chests as the phones kept ringing. When success is so easy, human beings lose sight of their limitations: hubris triumphs over humility. Most of the Japanese salespeople made no attempt to hide their contempt for the analysts, who they considered superfluous and a drain on the bonus pool. I was not only foreign but young and inexperienced as well, so I was pointedly ignored, not significant enough even to merit disrespect.

The Japanese companies whose activities we studied had little interest in shareholders' opinions and were not inclined to ingratiate themselves with anybody beyond their main commercial lender or local stockbroker. Employees, clients and suppliers ranked higher on the pecking order; investors were like pesky gnats. A quasi-socialist system in capitalist drag.

Our conversations were entirely in Japanese but we rarely spoke the same language. I would thrust with a question about a firm's plans to raise its return on equity. The company representative would block or parry, asking if I could use chopsticks or liked Japanese girls. We were tolerated but not welcome, like distant relatives who invite themselves over and stay too long.

Some of the younger investor-relations men opened up, though, especially if I plied them with liquor. One myth soon exploded was the idea that Japanese companies were somehow collaborating under the banner of 'Japan Inc.' to gain an advantage over western competitors. I discovered that Japanese companies' greatest rivals were each other, and much of the time there was no love lost.

'I despise Nintendo,' growled a representative of a major electronic component manufacturer as we sipped our fourth bottle of sake in a dim Kyoto bar one evening. His necktie was askew and his pink cheeks glowed. 'At least the stuff we make is used in things that improve the quality of people's lives: TVs, phones, cars. All they do is turn kids into lazy zombies, and they make billions doing it. Parasites.'

The clouds began darkening as the stock market approached its peak, in December 1989. Valuations were already stretched to ludicrous levels. Foreign fund managers had either given up on Japan in disgust or were playing the spurious game because the benchmarks of their international funds meant they had no choice but to try and keep up. The market became less interested in earnings per share or even underlying asset value, and more intrigued by thematic stories that could supposedly lead to profitable opportunities for certain stocks or industry sectors. Investors bought first and asked questions later – mostly in pump-and-dump style. Superconductivity, room tempera-ture fusion, waterfront, geofront: these were the precursors of the internet bubble of a decade later. And then it all went down.

IN HINDSIGHT, THE easiest part of adjusting to life after the bubble was the three-year period through to 1992 when the stock market halved, a process which quickly burned off unrealistic hope, incinerated much of the ego in the atmosphere, then extinguished itself. Fine, I thought. The correction we had to have. The cycle will kick in. And so I waited.

By 1998, Japan was approaching the end of its first 'lost decade' after the bubble, but the fire under the stock market had yet to reignite. A correction followed each rally, a bit of greed but then more fear, and eventually it became clear that all we had left was a hot ember. After collapsing from nearly 7 per cent in 1988 to virtually nil in 1993, real GDP growth had only once flickered briefly above 2 per cent, in 1996. By early 1998, the stock market was back at its level of six years earlier and later that year would sink to yet another new low. Prime Minister Hashimoto had hiked the consumption tax the previous year, throttling a nascent recovery and knocking the country back into recession. The banking system was basically insolvent.

As the years passed, I barely noticed my expectations being lowered. It was an insidious process, being ground down, conditioned to hope for less as the business cycle was smoothed out. Japan was rotting under the surface.

I loved the work but disliked the job. The research was absorbing. I learned how a semiconductor chip works and how a hard disk is made, why the shelves at 7-Eleven were always stocked no matter the hour, which textile companies were diversifying successfully into plastics and which just made denim fabric and fire hoses, why Japan's biggest warehouse operators are really property-leasing companies and how a Japanese trading house makes money (you think it merely trades?). If the stock market wasn't often up, there was still plenty of fodder for my curiosity. I was like a little boy on the floor surrounded by his toys, oblivious to his mother calling him.

The job, though, required much more. An equity analyst needed to be something between an evangelist and a stand-up comic: knowledgeable, sincere and, above all, *entertaining*. To be paid, analysts had to sell, had to earn. All the knowledge in the world was useless if you weren't well ranked in the annual analyst survey, in which fund managers voted for those analysts they regarded as most helpful or influential. Institutional investors looked at the poll when allocating their commissions to brokers, and corporations looking to sell shares or bonds sought the bank with the highest-ranked analysts. Unfortunately, presenting to clients bored me. So did phoning them, lunching with them and drinking with them. Selling the information wasn't half as rewarding as acquiring it. Aware that I was not likely to succeed as a top-ranked analyst, I made a fateful decision in 1996: I went into management.

TWO YEARS LATER, I was rapidly approaching burnout. I had now moved firms twice since 1988, a mercenary with an Excel spreadsheet, and was head of a department of about forty analysts and support staff at yet another European investment bank. I was a resource allocator, dispute mediator, recruiting agent, kindergarten cop, bum-wiper and whip-cracker. I hated it, weary of the politics, appalled at how much certain individuals thought of themselves and how much the bank felt it needed to pay to retain them.

'And so,' I said as the door of my little office clicked softly shut, 'this year the bank has decided to award you a bonus of two hundred and fifty thousand US dollars.' Kohno sat motionless but I could tell his mind was working. His dark eyes were unmoved behind thick-rimmed glasses. He was doing the maths. Was it more or less than he was expecting, more or less than he could get from a rival bank, more or less than he was *entitled* to? Should he appear aloof and unimpressed in the hope that he would get more? Perhaps the bank would cough up a bit extra if it thought he might defect to a competitor, but was it worth alienating the firm? How much was he prepared to piss *me* off?

After a moment, he mumbled, 'Uh, okay,' and permitted me a small smile before leaving. I realised he had not thanked me, and felt unutterably depressed. Money emboldens, strokes your sense of self-worth, especially if you have little of either to begin with.

I felt my sense of reality dissolving when I was required to mediate a dispute between a Japanese analyst and her assistant. Seated beside each other, the women despised each other so much they communicated only by email. Neither party wanted peace, only victory.

'Stop whining,' James would tell me over beers after he left the finance industry to run his own internet and media company, in 1996. 'Get your nose back in the trough.'

LIFE IN TOKYO in the late 1990s hadn't changed all that much, but the smaller regional cities that I would occasionally visit for company interviews were withering on the vine. Bridges had been built to nowhere, international airports erected in tiny regional towns linked by four-lane highways, but now the expenditure was petering out. With property prices in freefall, land-owners no longer needed to hang signs on their houses to ward off greedy *yakuza*. Golf clubs across the country were going bust. The Iranians had vanished almost overnight from Yoyogi Park, deported en masse after demand for their labour evaporated.

My partners and I quit our investment-bank jobs and established our own money-management firm in 1998. We were tired of bank bureaucracy and, despite the risk, preferred the eat-what-you-kill simplicity of working for ourselves. I loved the solitude, and company interviews were more fun now that I wasn't writing reports for publication.

The internet boom came and went; another head fake, another rally, another decline to a new low in 2003 before Prime Minister Koizumi pumped two trillion yen into Resona, putting a floor under the banking system.

In my little office in Kamiyacho, I was forced to hang up the phone when the ultranationalists charged south along Sakurada-dori, headed for the Russian Embassy, unintelligible propaganda blaring from the loudspeakers atop their huge black trucks. The middle-aged barber in the basement made me uncomfortable with tales of his sex-tourist jaunts to coastal Chinese cities, his sense of entitlement unsettling me. Each month, the fawning representative of the landlord would stop by, ostensibly to hand-deliver the rent invoice but really to keep an eye on me, his enquiries about the likely length of my stay masking a desire to replace me with a tenant in a more familiar or respectable line of work.

By the time Koizumi sang 'Love Me Tender', in 2006, Japan looked as if it had finally shaken off its post-bubble blues. Many Japanese companies had at last begun to realise they were better off engaging their shareholders. I began to feel empowered.

Over the four years to early 2007, corporate earnings rose to a high, and the stock market more than doubled from its 2003 low as exports boomed on demand from China and the US. Corporate governance improved; dividend payouts and share buy-backs achieved record levels. Company balance sheets piled up with cash after years of restructuring, and foreign ownership of Japanese shares hit a historical peak of 28 per cent.

By then I had my hopes up again. It was the last time.

IN OCTOBER 2008, the benchmark TOPIX stock-price index skidded to a twenty-six-year low, down three-quarters from its peak of nineteen years earlier. Then, I had believed stock markets in developed economies experience peaks and troughs but generally trend upwards over time. Japan turned out to be an exception, with the nadirs of 1992, 1998, 2003 and 2008 all lower than the one before, the market smouldering endlessly but unable to ignite. And no economist or stockbroker can quantify the spiritual rot that set in somewhere along the way.

Our little company – small but perfectly formed, my business partner and I used to joke – had seven employees at its peak but by last year was reduced to the two of us. In October, the decision to liquidate our sole fund was made for us: after ten years' slog, we had to salvage what we could. We resolved to distribute what was left of the money to unit holders, and let the screen go blank.

In March 2009, the Tokyo stock market ebbed to yet another low for the quarter-century – below even the level recorded last October – before rebounding a little. GDP growth for the first quarter of 2009 was minus 15 per cent, the worst result since World War II. The OECD is expecting Japan's gross public debt to increase to double its GDP in 2010.

The Nobel economics laureate Paul Krugman wrote recently, 'Japan's lost decade – yes, growth was slow, but there wasn't mass unemployment or mass suffering – is actually starting to look pretty good.' True, depression was averted; but mass unemployment and mass suffering still lie ahead if Japan can't address its low return on capital, ossified political institutions and anaemic domestic-consumption growth. An American friend – a long-time Tokyo resident now married to a local – told me Japan has become a 'can't-do culture'. He's relocating to San Francisco to ensure his infant son has more opportunities than Japanese boys.

Six months have passed since I ended my association with Japan. I'm puzzled by an absence of emotion: some of the stoicism and resignation of the Japanese has rubbed off on me. I am desensitised to crisis. Whatever regret I might have felt is offset by relief that I'm back home and not broke. I'm out.

Colin Mills is a former investment banker and portfolio manager who lived in Tokyo for more than seventeen years before returning to his native Brisbane.

A short prehistory of the future

Table manners of the global middle class

Tom Morton

> Ah, the old questions, the old answers, there's nothing like them!
> — Samuel Beckett, *Endgame*

> Above all, the bourgeoisie produces its own gravediggers.
> — Karl Marx, *Communist Manifesto*

FOR me, the history of the crisis begins with a sound. It's a chilly spring afternoon in Berlin in March 1990, the day before the first and last free elections in what was then still East Germany, the German Democratic Republic. I'm taking a walk along the Berlin Wall, on the western side, when my attention is caught by a chinking, clinking sound echoing in the frosty air. I turn on my tape recorder, put on the headphones and move closer. Up ahead, a small group of Turkish guest-workers are busy chipping pieces off the wall with hammers and chisels. The chips will be sealed up in plastic bags and sold to tourists as souvenirs.

I still have that recording. At the time, the clinking of the hammers seemed to me a perfect metaphor for the historical process that was unfolding in Germany: entrepreneurial capitalism chipping away at the Eastern Bloc's most potent symbol, sounding a tiny but insistent death knell for fifty years of communist domination in Eastern Europe.

The following day, the citizens of the German Democratic Republic voted decisively for the Christian Democratic Party, the deutschmark and reunification. '*Jetzt waechst zusammen, was zusammengehoert,*' declared the former Social Democrat Chancellor Willy Brandt: what belongs together now grows together.

Shortly after the fall of the wall, one of the GDR's most venerable writers, Stefan Heym, published a short newspaper article decrying his fellow citizens'

PREVIOUS PAGE: Street art on the Berlin Wall. *Source: unknown.*

appetite for all things western, as they stormed the supermarkets of West Berlin and returned to their homes in the east with shopping bags bulging with consumer items. For decades Heym himself had walked the tightrope of dissidence, a 'critical-loyal' writer who was tolerated by the East German authorities. Now, wrote Heym, fifty years of socialist tradition was being tossed on the rubbish heap, and what for? Bananas.

Heym's tirade drew a swift retort from another former East German writer, Monika Maron. She had left the GDR in the mid-1980s, after publishing a novel which exposed the appalling environmental degradation caused by the East German chemical industry in the city of Bitterfeld. Never one to pull her punches, Maron accused Heym of speaking from a position of extraordinary privilege: under the old regime, he had been allowed to travel to the West and buy western consumer goods, a privilege normally reserved for senior party officials. Heym's sanctimonious rebuking of his fellow East Germans over their appetite for bananas, she declared, amounted to nothing more than 'the arrogance of the well-fed who are disgusted by the table manners of the starving'.

That pithy exchange between two German intellectuals seems to me to resonate, along with the clinking of the hammers, just as insistently twenty years later. The central question posed by the global financial crisis is a simple one: should we apply the old remedies, jump-start the sputtering global economy with a fresh injection of high-octane growth, a new orgy of consumer spending? Or is growth itself the problem, rather than the solution?

It's all too easy for well-meaning, well-heeled and well-educated intellectuals in the West to declare that it's time to put an end to the tyranny of consumerism, to toss out our flat-screen tellies, downsize our kitchens and opt for a simpler, slower, less cluttered existence. And there's an undeniable environmental logic in this position. But are we really prepared to tell two billion people in the developing world, a generation who see the promise of a western lifestyle finally becoming a reality, that they should forego exactly the same consumer goods which we have taken for granted for the past fifty years – not even flat-screen TVs or SMEG kitchens, but items as ordinary as a family car? Isn't that tantamount to the well-fed tut-tutting at the table manners of the hungry?

It's perhaps no accident that a professor from the Chinese Academy of the Social Sciences, Jiahua Pan, was reported recently to have told an audience at the Australian National University that the planet 'could not afford countries like Australia and the US having wasteful and luxurious lifestyles'.

A COUPLE OF weeks after the 1990 elections, I interviewed the East German writer and dramatist Heiner Mueller. At the time, Mueller's production of *Hamlet* was running in East Berlin. The performance lasted nine hours. Characters made their way across the stage at the glacial pace of actors in a Japanese Noh drama, taking a good ten minutes to make the journey from the wings to centre stage. Each time the ghost of Hamlet's father appeared he was accompanied by an eerie, crackling voice: a recording of Stalin from the 1930s.

Sipping Glenfiddich and smoking a Cuban cigar, Mueller explained some of the ideas behind his staging of the play. He'd deliberately slowed down the production to mimic the pace of life in the GDR. The working day in the former land of 'real existing socialism' was nine hours long, but a good part of it was spent killing time. 'You worked for two hours but were paid for nine,' Mueller wrote in *On the State of the Nation*, a collection of essays and interviews published around the the same time. 'Naturally that was terribly inefficient.'

A few days after the elections, on the factory floor of a foundry in Leipzig which employed eighteen thousand people, I asked some of the workers why they'd voted for the Christian Democrats. 'We want to do a proper day's work and be paid properly for it,' they told me. 'We need investment and the Christian Democrats have the connections to West German capital, they'll bring it here.'

Looking around the factory hall, it wasn't hard to see why they felt that way. It looked like something out of Dickens: filthy and stuffy, badly ventilated and badly lit. The workers told me that some of the lathes they worked on dated back to the 1920s. Aren't you afraid that you'll lose your jobs if the foundry has to compete with West German firms? I asked. 'We're not worried – the economy will take off and we'll find jobs elsewhere.'

When I went back to Leipzig in 1993, the foundry had closed down. No one I asked seemed to have much idea what had happened to the eighteen thousand workers who'd lost their jobs; no doubt some of them had found new work, but despite the hundreds of billions of deutschmarks poured into the east after reunification unemployment rose rapidly, and has consistently remained more than twice as high as in the west. At the same time, entrepreneurial capitalism in the east has generated some astonishing success stories: Bitterfeld, the 'dirtiest city in Europe' in Monika Maron's novel, has now become the headquarters of Q-Cells, the world's largest manufacturer of solar cells.

According to Mueller, the basic contradiction between the two systems lay in the way the flow of time and the pace of everyday life was regulated. 'In the west, the governing principle of society is all about speeding time up, total acceleration. In the east, it was all about deceleration, slowing life down.'

After sitting through nine hours of *Hamlet*, the Western members of the audience undoubtedly had some idea of what this principle of deceleration felt like in practice. The atmosphere of claustrophobia and paranoia in the state of Denmark mirrored the paralysis and ossification of the GDR. But what was the connection between Stalin and the ghost of Hamlet's father? I asked. Mueller chuckled mirthlessly. 'Hamlet's dilemma is the dilemma of the GDR,' he replied, 'caught between Stalin and the Deutsche Bank.'

Mueller was sceptical about the possibility of any middle way between the two, and the reunification of Germany proved him right. But, Mueller argued, there was a kind of utopian, oppositional potential in the slowing down of capitalism: 'I'm interested in how one can create a positive quality out of deceleration.'

To paraphrase Mueller, we could say that 'real existing socialism' in Eastern Europe acted as a brake on the process of modernisation. For the two decades since the fall of the wall, acceleration has been the order of the day. In the late '90s, it seemed that capitalism had overcome the laws of economic gravity and reached escape velocity; pundits sang the praises of the 'weightless economy', a kind of neo-liberal utopia in which growth was freed from the traditional economic constraints and propelled by the dramatic expansion of 'weightless' goods – principally computer software.

What put the weightless economy into orbit was, of course, the internet. In the first decade of the twenty-first century it is the mobile internet that has caused the acceleration of the knowledge economy – and the speeding-up of everyday life. There's good reason to think that the speed of global communications and the sheer volume of information ricocheting around the world were contributing factors in the financial crisis: turning points, such as the collapse of Lehman Brothers, sent the electronic herd into a stampede of selling that would have been hard to imagine before the advent of the BlackBerry and the wireless internet.

It's too early to say yet how much the crisis will slow the acceleration of globalisation itself. In the short term, it's clear that there is already a degree of 'deglobalisation' occurring – a term coined by Walden Bello, one of the leading theorists of the counter-globalisation movement. Seventeen of the G20 countries have introduced protectionist measures in the wake of the crisis, world trade is falling rapidly and international capital flows have declined. This is what some sections of the counter-globalisation movement have been advocating for over a decade. Others in the movement have argued that what's necessary is greater democratic control over the key institutions of globalisation, the International Monetary Fund, the World Bank and the World Trade Organization. It's probably fair to say, however, that all share scepticism about the pace of global modernisation over the last two decades, and sympathy with Mueller's notion of 'deceleration' as a kind of counter-dynamic.

What is really at stake, in the longer term however, is not just the speed and direction of globalisation, but its legitimacy as a process supported by the billions of human beings it affects. For this reason, it's worth drawing breath and attempting to look at the crisis and its causes and consequences with a longer perspective.

IT IS EASY to forget now how much the history of the last two decades owes to those clinking hammers chipping away at the Berlin Wall, and how much energy and confidence global capitalism derived from the humiliating defeat of its antagonist. As Heiner Mueller said presciently in 1990, Soviet communism had acted as a brake on capitalist modernisation; now the brake was off. Not only did the collapse of communism and the disintegration of the Soviet Union open up new markets, and end the competition between East and West for influence in the developing world; they also seemed to spell the end of any serious ideological challenge to the legitimacy of liberal capitalism.

Since World War II, that legitimacy had rested in no small measure on the democratisation of consumption. The forms of liberal capitalism varied considerably across the West, from Australia to Britain, Scandinavia, Germany and the US; but what united all of them was a consensus that the state would insure its citizens against the kinds of economic risks which had resulted in the Great Depression – and paved the way for the rise of fascism. Just as importantly, all across the West states underwrote a redistribution of wealth and an expansion of spending power, which enabled whole sections of their populations to buy things and do things previously reserved for a privileged minority. In Beveridge's famous formulation, they created a ladder and a net, and up that ladder several generations climbed into the middle class.

That achievement, perhaps more than any other, was the postwar West's most durable insurance against a challenge from the militant left or the appeal of Soviet or Chinese communism. In the 1970s, however, the consensus which had underpinned it began to break down, and in the Anglo-Saxon world Keynesian, social-democratic capitalism was driven from the mainstream and replaced by a neo-liberalism inspired by Hayek and Friedman. The triumph of neo-liberalism is a familiar story, but there are one or two subplots to that narrative which helped to pave the way for neo-liberalism's spectacular fall in 2008.

The first has to do with what the financial-services industry refers to as the 'democratisation of risk'. This attractive-sounding euphemism is shorthand for the process whereby governments and employers shed the responsibility for providing retirement incomes and transferred that responsibility to us, the citizens and workers. The massive expansion of pension and superannuation funds since the 1980s occurred because we took on the risk previously managed by governments and financial institutions.

The effects were profound. A vast reservoir of capital flooded into the global economy, looking for investment opportunities and driving innovation.

According to Mike Clowes, author of *The Money Flood: How Pension Funds Revolutionized Investing* (Wiley, 2000), the retirement savings of American workers provided the seed capital which enabled firms like Hewlett-Packard and Intel to launch themselves into the marketplace and grow. 'If you look at when the American high-tech industry began to take off,' Clowes writes, 'it coincides almost perfectly with the flow of pension dollars into the venture capital industry.' By the early years of the twenty-first century, around half the shares in American companies were held by pension funds.

The downside of this is only now becoming fully apparent. So far, the financial crisis has wiped US$5 trillion off the value of pension funds in the United States, Japan, the United Kingdom and the Netherlands. According to the World Bank's Robert Holzmann, the impact of the crisis will fall disproportionately on people aged over fifty, and governments will need to strengthen the role of state-funded pensions 'to prevent individuals from falling easily into poverty in tumultuous times'.

Coinciding with the democratisation of risk was the 'democratisation of credit' in the 1990s. As Zanny Minton Beddoes, economics editor of *The Economist*, wrote recently, the current crisis has its roots in the biggest housing and credit bubble in history – driven, at least initially, by the appetite of British and American householders for debt-financed spending, and the easy availability of consumer credit. For many consumers, easier access to credit was a good thing, allowing them to own homes which would previously have been beyond their reach. But in the 2000s, 'asset and credit bubbles formed in many countries simultaneously'.

These bubbles in the developed economies were funded and inflated by capital from emerging economies. In other words, the good times that consumers in countries like Australia have enjoyed until recently have been financed by the savings of workers in the east and south of the globe – in particular, China.

IF, AS THE Chinese academic Jiahua Pan says, the world can no longer afford Western consumers having 'wasteful and luxurious lifestyles', what does this mean for the democratisation of consumption in the emerging economies?

In *The Expanding Middle: The Exploding World Middle Class and Falling Global Inequality*, a research paper published in July 2008, the Goldman Sachs economists Dominic Wilson and Raluca Dragusanu predicted that the global middle class will expand by up to two billion people by 2030. Driving this will be a shift in spending power away from the richest countries, towards middle-income economies – including some of the world's most populous countries: India and Brazil, and members of the 'Next Eleven' (N11), such as Egypt, the Philippines, Indonesia, Iran, Mexico and Vietnam. To qualify for membership of this exploding middle class, new entrants must have annual incomes from US$6,000 to $30,000. Wilson and Dragusanu draw on earlier work showing that once people earn above $6,000 their demand for energy increases, and above $9,000 a year they can begin to afford consumer durables such as cars.

Just how the global financial crisis might affect these predictions is unclear. But there's evidence that some of the most successful companies in India, China and Brazil are banking on a burgeoning global bourgeoisie. Tata is an Indian conglomerate with operations in eighty-five countries that has recently bought up assets ranging from the Tetley tea company to the car firms Jaguar and Rover. In July this year Tata launched the Nano, a two-cylinder 'people's car' with a price tag of US$2,000, in India. As Matthew Bishop said in *The Economist*, the Nano is aimed first and foremost at the lower income bracket of the Indian middle class. But its price puts it within reach of newly arrived members of the middle class in other developing countries.

What Tata is doing for drivers in the developing world, the Chinese computer company Lenovo is doing for a new generation itching to get online. Lenovo was founded in 1984 and built its growth on the domestic market in China. It bought IBM's personal-computer business in 2005, for about US$1.75 billion. Lenovo has been hard hit by the global crisis, losing more than $200 million in the first quarter of 2009, mainly as a result of falling sales in the US, its largest market outside China. But the company is betting on an unlikely new market to put it back in the black: Chinese peasants.

According to Lenovo Group's chairman, Liu Chuanzhi, also a deputy to the National People's Congress, Lenovo aims to sell five million computers in rural areas over the next three years. These cut-price, stripped-down 'netbooks' will sell for 3,000 yuan (US$439) and, as part of the Chinese government's massive stimulus package, villagers will get a subsidy to buy them and other electronic equipment. A century ago Lenin famously declared, 'Communism equals Soviets plus electrification'; in twenty-first century China, communism equals local assemblies plus laptops.

Can the world afford a vastly expanded global middle class equipped with low-cost cars, laptops and other consumer goods? Even if the manufacturer's claims are true and the Nano is a low-emissions, eco-friendly vehicle, it's mindboggling to try to imagine what an extra two billion Nano drivers would add to global greenhouse-gas emissions. But if consumers in the West are prepared to finance their lifestyles with easy credit from the East, why should governments in China, India, Indonesia and the Philippines attempt to rein in their citizens' expectations that they too should be able to enjoy a western lifestyle? If globalisation is to be environmentally and politically sustainable, politicians must begin to utter the unspeakable truth: that living standards in the West will have to fall as they rise elsewhere.

As Zanny Minton Beddoes writes in *The Economist*, it's clear that the whole direction of globalisation will change. In the short term, at least, the financial markets will be reregulated, governments will reassert their control over crucial areas of the economy such as food security and commodity prices, and the economic clout and intellectual authority of America will decline. But these changes alone do not amount to a more democratic global economy. Development economist Robert Wade has pointed out that neo-liberal globalisation 'has a mixed record on its central ostensible aim of emancipation and prosperity. It has a much clearer record of success on its much more concealed aim as a class project: to redistribute income upwards to the very top percentiles of the population and consolidate political power in the hands of the wealthiest sliver of society.'

THE CONTINUING LEGITIMACY of liberal capitalism cannot rest on the 'democratisation of consumption' alone. The crisis offers the potential for a much more far-reaching democratisation of global institutions, the global public sphere and global capital itself. There are a number of concrete and feasible directions this might take.

Just as the 'democratisation of risk' exposed the retirement savings of a generation of workers in the Anglo-Saxon economies to the vagaries of the market, it also created what the late Paul Hirst described as the largest pool of socially owned capital in history, in the shape of pension funds. At present, the owners of this pool of capital exercise little control over the way it is invested and the consequences of its use. It might surprise many members of Australian superannuation funds, for example, to know that fourteen of the largest industry funds hold investments which directly generate nearly six million tonnes of carbon dioxide emissions a year.

My financial interests as a stakeholder in a super fund may not coincide with my interests as a citizen who is worried about global warming and the kind of world my children will live in. Neo-liberal capitalism created a dismembered citizen whose interests as shareholder, consumer, parent, partner, child and individual subject of the democratic process could somehow be compartmentalised, partitioned off from each other. A more democratic liberal capitalism would attempt to put the dismembered citizen back together, and recognise the common interests of the individual owners of capital in broader forms of social solidarity.

But this is not enough to restore legitimacy to globalisation as an economic and political project. If this is our goal, we will need to end the domination by the developed economies of institutions such as the World Bank, the International Monetary Fund and World Trade Organization, or replace these institutions with new ones which can better reflect the interests of people in the developing world – and, in particular, the poor.

Just as western governments after World War II set about redistributing wealth within their economies, a democratic global order can and should seek to redistribute wealth from richer to poorer citizens of the global economy. This may sound like a utopian project, but in fact one simple mechanism for doing so, the Tobin tax, was first suggested more than thirty years ago. The tax, now known as a currency-transaction tax, would impose a small levy on international currency transactions and use the proceeds to fund development projects. It is, as the former French President Jacques Chirac said, a tax on the benefits of globalisation, albeit a minuscule one, amounting to a 'development levy' of 0.005 per cent. Such a levy would yield an estimated US$33 billion, which could be invested in the Millennium Development Goals adopted by the United Nations in September 2000. The practical means of collecting and distributing the revenue has been explored in research by the North-South Institute in Canada, and the UN Secretary-General, Ban Ki-moon, has supported its proposals.

As Marx wrote in the *Communist Manifesto* in 1848, the bourgeoisie has played a revolutionary role in history. The bourgeoisie of the developed world has reaped huge benefits from the first phase of neo-liberal globalisation, and it can continue to play an important role in a new phase of democratic globalisation; but only if it can find a new language in which to speak to the citizens of the developing world, stripped of the moralising tones of the well-fed.

The ascendancy of a new bourgeoisie in the South and East will not, of itself, guarantee the emergence of a more democratic and liberal global order. This will only happen if the global poor – the slum-dwellers, landless peasants and migrant workers of Africa, Asia and Latin America – receive a greater share of the benefits of globalisation.

The essential questions Marx asked – questions about human dignity and social justice in the conditions of modernity – are no less urgent now than they were more than a hundred and fifty years ago. Marx's answers to those questions were wrong, and the history of the twentieth century is littered with the corpses of tens of millions of people who, if they could be raised from the grave, would bear witness to how wrong they were. The global financial crisis marks a turning point no less significant than the collapse of communism in 1989: in Heiner Mueller's terms, we have moved beyond the point where the only choices open to us are between Stalin's ghost and the Deutsche Bank. But unless we can find some new answers to those same old questions, we will produce nothing but a new, global generation of grave-diggers in the twenty-first century.

Tom Morton is a broadcaster and writer. His essays have been published in *Griffith REVIEW: Webs of Power, The Lure of Fundamentalism, Re-imagining Australia* and *Family Politics*. He is the author of *Altered Mates: The Man Question* (Allen & Unwin) and his most recent radio series for Radio National and Triple J is *Wide Open Road*.

No soft landing

Europe after the crisis

Ryan Heath

'Tis against some men's principle to pay interest, and seems against others' interest to pay the principal.

— Benjamin Franklin

FOR a continent following the trajectory of the Great Depression, Europe exudes a surprising calm. In politics, no new phoenix is rising from the ashes of past policies. And in the media, the crisis plays to a weary audience. Lacking the heroes, villains and global relevance of the American debate, and the naked assertions of power that the crisis has encouraged in China, Europe is snoozing.

Complacency is a mistake. The countries most affected may be small and the losses largely on paper, but Europe is missing its last chance to change its economic culture and individuals' behaviour before a much bigger crisis hits: a pension crisis. With more than A$6 trillion in loans, guarantees and direct aid given to banks in the past year, European governments are stretched like bungee cords. Yet *The Economist* predicts that the coming pension deficit will involve figures up to *ten times* that size.

While the current crisis renders the future of some private pension funds uncertain, and new debts diminish the capacity of states to meet their pension commitments, the systemic problems long predate it. Neither public policy nor private savings have adjusted to greater life spans. When Bismarck created the aged pension, in 1889, you had to be seventy to qualify – well above the average life expectancy. In 2009 Europeans live far longer but qualify for the pension earlier. The average retirement age for men is below sixty in Belgium, France, Hungary and Italy, and millions more aspire to early retirement.

This seeming social progress sits uneasily with the shrinking ratio of workers to retirees, and rising unemployment rates. Today's generosity may be tomorrow's fiscal nightmare in a region where public pensions can be up to three times as generous as Australia's. Even before the postwar baby boom is added to the bill, pensions are already costing more than 14 per cent of GDP in some Western European countries. With A$5 trillion of private pensions funds 'up in flames' – as the OECD delicately puts it – in the past year, pensioners are likely to demand even more of politicians in the future.

Twenty years of patchy and incremental pension reforms have not prepared European pension systems to meet these demands. If anything, close observation reveals a repeat of the patterns that generated the sub-prime crisis: a failure of government to keep up with a changed economic landscape, allowing systemic risk to develop; a culture of trying to squeeze too much from a financial system, generating economic shocks; and the misuse of other people's money. The difference is that when the pension crisis unfolds, governments will have little fiscal ammunition left to fire at the problem.

Even if governments can agree to continue an aggressive monetary and fiscal policy for a number of years and then correctly time their transition to more conventional policies, European leaders will struggle to win political acceptance for the tough debt-repayment plans that may give them a chance to tackle the pension problem. However, other potential disasters – like the collapse of a car-industry pension fund alongside a parent company – may conspire to send pensions policy in the other direction.

To guard against this, European governments must start the unenviable task of pursuing cultural change and more radical pension-policy reform, while also managing the recession. The cultural issues will be the hardest to address, because legislation alone cannot solve them. Europe has become a continent of modern-day Marie Antoinettes, funding lifestyles with credit cards, asset bubbles and loans denominated in foreign currencies instead of hard work. Europe's public sector unions reinforce this culture in their united belief that no one should have to sacrifice their 'rights' to relatively early retirement and generous pensions. Even the well-off – and market-oriented – staff of the European Central Bank are striking over proposed reforms.

The best thing would be for government leaders to convince Europeans that they need to lower their expectations, that they must accept pain in the next economic upswing to reduce long-term difficulties. But with confidence already low and attention distracted by the current crisis, it is easy for politicians to delay this discussion. Predictably, citizens are not clamouring for such tough-love approaches. Indeed, because many stand to gain at the expense of their children, they have strong incentives to stay silent or punish those who act tough. Younger generations, meanwhile, are focused on more immediate and fundamental matters, like getting out of insecure temporary jobs, and do not see beyond the immediate future, let alone save for it.

> *I might not even have a job in two months. Why do I care what I might get when I am sixty-five? That's why I pay tax – so the government will think about these issues for me.*
>
> — Adele Vanthournhout, 31, Belgium

IN THEORY, THE European Union exists to think about seemingly intractable big-picture issues like pensions on behalf of Adele Vanthournhout and her peers. Yet the EU is absent from this debate, providing only a toothless secretariat, the Committee of European Insurance and Occupational Pensions Supervisors, to monitor market developments. This policy vacuum is a product of the tension between the EU being the world's biggest democratic experiment and it being made up of national governments who hold the purse strings.

Without centralised executive powers – the *gouvernement économique* of President Sarkozy's dreams – the diversity of Europe also works against top-down change. Today's economic outlook ranges from Latvia's forecast 18 per cent 'negative growth' for 2009 to Poland's actual growth. The financial cultures stretch from Britain's credit-bingeing property-flippers to Germany's discount-supermarket-addicted savers. What hope do Spaniards and Italians have of coping with a common pension policy when they cannot afford a universal unemployment benefit?

When the workforces of Western Europe begin to shrink from 2011, as they are forecast to do, will that fragile safety net break altogether? It is hard to know, because no one can predict a country's total liabilities – though the OECD thinks the average is 200–400 per cent of GDP. The maths is simpler than unravelling toxic assets – the living are a good audit trail – but we can't know how long people will live or when their private savings will run out. With each year of increased longevity adding 3–4 per cent to liabilities, even a small adjustment to calculations can make a great difference. Such uncertainty is compounded by state secrecy: nearly all European governments keep future liabilities off public pensions on their balance sheets.

> The size of Europe's monumental public debt is only surpassed by the hidden liabilities accumulated in Europe's short-sighted public pension schemes.
> — Dr Martin De Vlieghere, University of Ghent

EVEN POLITICALLY DIFFICULT policies to lower debt and raise the pension age to sixty-eight are the equivalent of treading water when it comes to pensions. European pension liabilities outweigh declared public debt, and for many countries they outweigh GDP. Indeed, the gap between liabilities and dedicated assets is so great that today's thirty-year-old Italians would have to contribute 127 per cent of their salaries to the state pension scheme to guarantee receipt of the current pension.

Some nations are making progress, almost all of them smaller nations. This year Latvia, under threat of national bankruptcy, cut pensions by a tenth, while Hungary cut them by nearly that much. Denmark is moving to a system where the official retirement age moves up with life expectancy, and the Finnish Prime Minister, Matti Vanhanen, warned in June that he will be forced to deliver years of 'painful cuts' to meet the costs of ageing.

Germany is alone among the largest European countries in undertaking significant change. German-owned companies, under government pressure, now contribute an average of £3.27 for every pound of new pension benefits credited to employees (after years of covering less than two-thirds of their pension liabilities with dedicated assets). For its part, the German government is seeking constitutional limits on budget deficits and has allowed schemes that ensure almost a third of labour costs are devoted to building up pensions.

The heart of the problem is that most European pensions are pay-as-you-go schemes. Like Germany's formerly wayward private schemes, most public and private schemes are not funded by accumulated assets, as in Australia's employer-funded superannuation system or Norway's oil-driven Sovereign Wealth Fund. Nor do retirement savings follow workers through a career. Instead, current workers fund previous generations of workers, and each generation passes its bill to the next.

This will suffice if the workforce and economy grow strongly, but when they shrink, a nation's low birth rates or loose fiscal policy can no longer be masked. Now that retirements last twice as long as they did forty years ago, some of these systems face collapse. For European workers, who rarely have private savings to fall back on and own homes at lower rates than do Australians, this scenario could be devastating.

An example of particularly bad pension management is the UK's Civil Service scheme, of which I am a member. This is one of the defined-benefit schemes to which seven out of ten British workers belong (compared with just one in ten in the more affordable defined-contribution schemes). While high entitlements combined with a forced retirement at sixty are personally agreeable, this is certainly not sustainable when the UK spends four pounds for every three it now collects in tax. Yet it continues to rack up pension liabilities equal to paying 19 per cent super contributions to each civil servant.

While it has been running up this bill, Britain has chosen to use its North Sea oil revenue on anything but pensions, in sharp contrast to Norway, its oil-field neighbour. The Norwegians now have a fund so strong that they saw the 2008 share wipe-out as an opportunity to cherry-pick underpriced assets from scared investors. Spain – without oil, and desperate to catch up to Europe's front-running nations – also took the easy road. There, more than two-thirds of people believe the state should be 'primarily responsible' for pensions, yet these same people encouraged a property bubble as their back-up plan, rather than save for retirement. Spain's state depended on that property bubble for income, and now that the bubble has burst it faces rapidly increasing deficits and unemployment already spiralling beyond 18 per cent.

Everyone knows the money has run out...we will not see such riches again until my generation has paid off every last unfunded public-sector pension liability, every last bit of debt kept Enron-style off the books, and all the other components of the structural hole in the public finances. That hole is 'recovery-proof'- it will still be there even when the economy recovers.
— Camilla Cavendish, 40, columnist for *The Times*

ONLY IMMEDIATE RADICAL reform will address these issues. Some favour even the abolition of formal retirement. While that is politically impossible, lower or delayed access to entitlements, higher taxes, higher employment rates and more working-age immigrants are essential. Leaving reform too late will mean massive social tension or a suffocation of economic growth as governments desperately struggle to maintain entitlements.

How then might attitudes shift? Assumptions about retirement entitlements need to be remoulded. Europeans may offer in-principle support for private retirement savings, but they also equate state pensions and low retirement ages with social progress. They must accept that comfortable retirement now requires private savings and working until the age of seventy.

The most pragmatic approach is to ensure the pension bill is paid by all, not only the workforce. With some European states sucking up half of GDP in taxes already, it will be easier and less economically harmful to redistribute the tax burden rather than increase it sharply. The OECD concludes that property and indirect (consumption) taxes are the least harmful to long-term growth, which dovetails neatly with the need to maximise the number of people footing the bill. Europe will also have to figure out its attitude to migrants: can it shoulder the social pain in return for the economic gain? Anti-immigration parties fared well in the 2009 European elections, and countries from Spain to the Czech Republic are already paying immigrants to return home.

Whatever route Europeans take to rebalance their pension books, Norway's disciplined use of public funds and, on the other side of the world, Australia's mobilisation of private funds – through compulsory employer contributions – will feature in policy discussions. Norway's strong incentives to work until seventy make sense when you realise that their choice is born out of a culture of responsibility, a tangible belief in the benefits of 'generational accounting'.

If Europeans take one lesson from this crisis, it is not that capitalism is broken, or that governments should attempt to solve every economic problem. It is that in dealing with money – whoever is doing the dealing – planning, saving and discipline can save a great deal of trouble. The economist Dambisa Moyo offers a proverb for dealing with failed policies: 'The best time to plant a tree is twenty years ago. The second-best time is now.' For Europeans, their eventual return to economic growth is also their final chance at effective pension reform. The economic clash between Europe's ageing population and a young, rising Asia already resembles the *Titanic* hitting the iceberg. Europe would do well to make sure the lifeboats are in order.

Ryan Heath is based in Brussels as a speechwriter for the European Commissioner for Competition. He is the author of *Please Just F*** Off: It's our turn now* (Pluto Press, 2006), and his essays have been published in *Griffith REVIEW: The Next Big Thing* and *Essentially Creative*. www.ryanheath.com.au

MEMOIR

Tobias passing

A meditation on facing the axe

Brett Caldwell

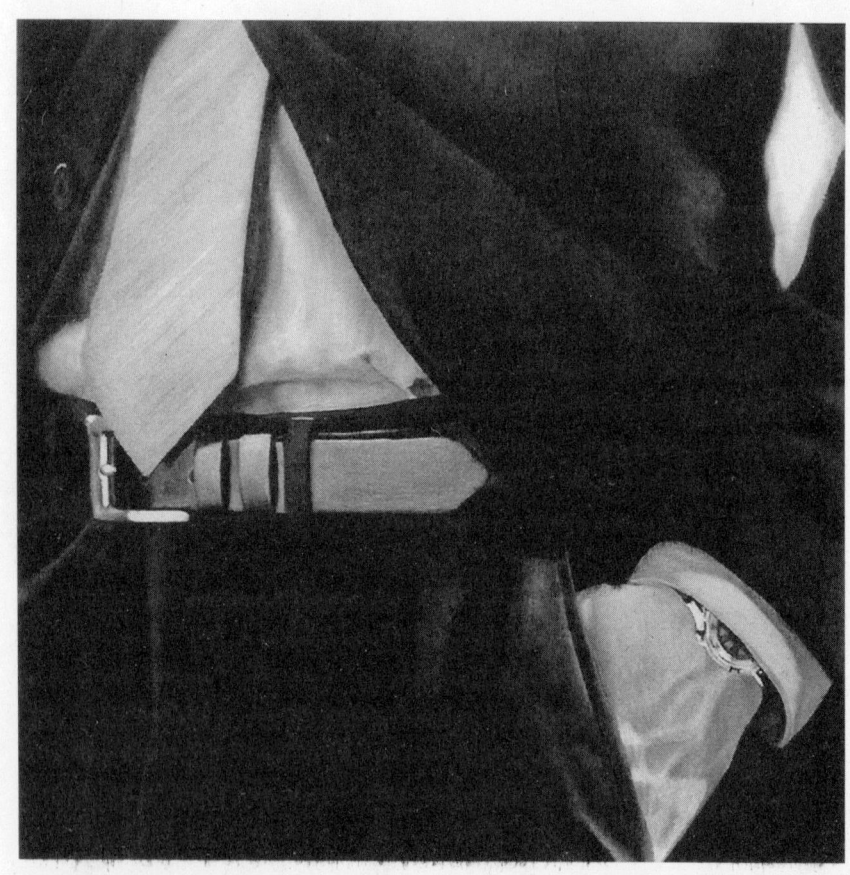

TOBIAS Fox, vice president of sales, arrived at our Canberra sales office by taxi. This was the last stop on his nationwide recession-chasing tour. For some weeks prior to his arrival, motivated by primal emotion, our team pored over spreadsheets, deals and opportunities, trying to construct a future. Our creatively optimistic forecasts failed to obscure the fragility of our predicament. The numbers looked terrible, and for Tobias the numbers meant everything.

Growth is a fundamental imperative of capitalism, and for some it is an end unto itself. For more than a decade the world forgot that endless growth is unsustainable. That's why we have great recessions – to remind us. Since the late 1990s my wife and I had reclined on a bed of puffed-up middle-class comfort. Like so many we were oblivious to the growing troubles and ignored the debt hole beneath our mattress: a mortgage, school and university fees, HECS debts, tax debts and big-boy's-toy debts.

Before the recession, Australia's economy roared. In Canberra, industry flourished with ripe government contracts. Companies grew fat; sales managers made fortunes and some entrepreneurial ex-public servants even made *BRW*'s rich list. Most ignored the faint voices warning of trouble ahead. And for a while Canberra was sheltered by its isolation and the public service; but eventually the financial plague came to its bushland suburbs.

MY COMPANY EMPLOYS several hundred thousand people globally and reaps tens of billions in revenue every year. Tobias rules the Australian roost; our clients are mostly government departments and agencies. In October 2008 business started to recede. The recession sucked the marrow from some of our most loyal clients. They delayed, reduced or abandoned acquisitions. Profit and loss ratios and budget cuts dominated boardroom discussions – survival plans replaced expansion strategies. The Rudd Government set forth on a crusade early in its tenure: bands of bureaucrats and high-powered consultants roamed Canberra's byways, lanes and alleys, seeking out inefficiency, duplication and waste – and there was much to find.

PREVIOUS PAGE: Mauve, 2000 / 12.6 x 12.6cm, Oil on board. Artist: Michael Zavros

When the crisis hit, our company's corporate surgeons panicked and cut deeply into muscle and bone. The first to go were the middle managers, followed by the backroom sales support, administrative people and the inventory they managed. The sales force thinned as revenues declined. Senior managers celebrated the profit savings that buttressed their own positions, but they mortgaged common sense and forced untenable sales numbers onto the few ragged troops that remained. Some of the slack was taken up by low-paid Malaysian and Philippine workers, who took to the phones armed with naive enthusiasm, phone lists and scripted introductions.

Anything that smelled like a perk came to an end: office managers stopped buying newspapers, stationery and the Tuesday fruit basket. We could buy coffee for clients but not fat-boy lunches. In order to save power and costs we were encouraged to work from home. Tobias cancelled our hallowed sales symposium and stopped inviting ex-Olympian motivational speakers to motivate us. One final indignity remained: the CEO asked each employee to 'volunteer' for a pay cut of 'only' one-tenth. 'Your small sacrifice will assist us avoiding "hard" decisions,' we were told. 'Hard decisions' translated as mass sackings, but there was no guarantee that a pay cut would save any job. I hedged my bets and voted yes.

OUR CEO ALSO took a pay cut, but he earns more in a few days than I do in a year. He earns more over a long business lunch than some of our Malaysian teleworkers earn in three months. An e-net magazine reported that the company's board awarded him $32 million in cash last year, a $1.8 million salary and $30 million in bonuses. The figures were posted on the day of President Obama's inauguration, when he declared: 'Our economy is badly weakened, a consequence of greed...a nation cannot prosper long when it favours only the prosperous.'

Our company favours only the prosperous. Tobias could sack me on a whim. He can cut my commission, or change my accounts, my role and conditions without consent. I wondered how many people Tobias would sack once he had examined our business. How would he do it? I read that a Singapore company activated the building's fire-alarm bells. When the employees assembled in the car park, a security officer appeared and read a message: 'Dear employees – with sincere regret I have been asked to announce that for many of you it will be your last evacuation drill. Due to the recession, the company is laying off almost half of its employees. So when this announcement finishes, I ask all of you to move back into the building and if your building pass does not work then it means you have been laid off, in which case you will not be allowed inside. Hope you have had a rewarding career with us and all the best ahead. Please move back in and try your luck.'

Later I read the story was a hoax, or that the event occurred in Houston in 1994, when an oil company downsized. Regardless of veracity, it made me nervous.

Tobias commenced the one-on-one interviews early on Friday morning. When I'm nervous I eat doughnuts and listen to music, large headphones jammed on my ears and a sign attached to the back of my chair: 'Please Do Not Disturb.' I cannot hear the talk of sackings or alarm bells as I savour my sugary deep-fried dough.

A workmate taps my shoulder, startling me.

'You're next in with Tobias, but not until Monday morning. Make sure you take your account plans.'

'You still got a job?' I ask, smiling.

'Maybe. Make sure you enjoy the weekend.'

I DON'T WANT to think about Monday morning. I'm taking my family away from Canberra, away from the recession and fear of failure. We drive to Dubbo for the weekend. On the northern side of Yass the land turns from Canberra brown to fertile green. We pass fields of canola spread across the countryside like lemon butter, and scattered mobs of sheep and alpacas grazing, unmindful of human things.

There are only a few cars on the road. We overtake a truck stuffed with cattle and a tractor towing bails of hay; we pass tired-looking old men towing caravans and a Greyhound bus crammed with Chinese tourists who wave and photograph us.

The country town of Burrowa is overflowing with people, ewes and wethers. The annual 'running of the sheep' is finishing and we stop to gawk at the remnants of the spectacle. I wander along the swarming street and for just a few dollars I buy a huge jar of homemade marmalade from the Country Women's Association.

We eat a late lunch at the Japanese memorial gardens in Cowra, where we explore the traditionally styled Japanese house with its sunken bath and impossibly small bed. None of us contemplates too deeply the reason the gardens exist, but take pleasure in their meditative beauty and enjoy feeding the koi.

My daughter buys a postcard to send to her Japanese penfriend. I glance at a newspaper. The recession has faded from the front page, replaced by news that North Korea has fired a missile across Japan's bows and America has deployed a squadron of F-22 fighters to Okinawa – just in case. Curiously, the jobs-vacant section remains thick.

Late in the afternoon we arrive at the Dubbo Western Plains Zoo and set up camp. We meet our polite uniformed guides and drink tea as a furious storm erupts. We walk through the zoo that night in torrential rain, our squelching pathway lit by lightning and the guides' spotlights. I smell the rancid stink of the Galápagos tortoise before I see her massive, rain-sodden bulk. She is a hundred years old and may yet outlive me, although her kind may not see another century. She has already lived through two world wars, the Great Depression, the Spanish flu pandemic, and the rise and fall of thousands of tides.

I RETURN TO work on Monday morning. Tobias and a HR acolyte bivouac in the conference room. I avoid them with busy work and phone calls. At the photocopier I speak quietly to Sam, a veteran of the last great cull. He provides sage advice. 'Say as little as possible. Be confident. Don't ask questions. Just give them the numbers. Oh, and under-commit – it sounds more realistic.'

Sam and I walk to Psychedeli, a nearby coffee shop. I am a voyeur; my usual seat is next to a window where I can watch the streetscape. My table is also close enough to the caffeine crowd for me to hear snippets of gossip and smidgens of conversation, but today nobody seems to be talking much.

We chat quietly. Sam and I have worked together for several years; he is one of the best sales guys in Canberra, an ex-submariner though he seems too tall to have poked about in small spaces aboard some of the most powerful and dangerous machines invented. He has four years left until retirement. Sam's a lucky bugger: his patch covers Centrelink, a major account. He's confident the selling season will pick up; Centrelink needs to expand to meet the expected influx of customers from hard times.

The café is my refuge. Great and failed expectations cast me upon its shore. In 2004 a good friend started a domestic grey-water treatment company. The drought and harsh water restrictions shrivelled gardens and house values, so the market seemed primed for the product. Avarice and thrill called me to join them on the venture – how could I resist? The technology was brilliant and the business vision clear. We won accolades and prizes, grants and contracts. The *New Inventors* hailed our grand design and the *New York Times* wrote about us. We installed our grey-water systems in homes, a prison, a youth-detention centre, a residential college at the ANU, and in office and apartment blocks. Investors and carpetbaggers, at times indistinguishable, courted us with their promises. We schemed and plotted: we dispatched a team to California; we made inroads in the Middle East to treat the water used in mosques; we pitched to Chinese mega-companies – but the tide of wealth never rolled in. As the manufacturing costs climbed, the technology coughed and spluttered. Our sea of credit soon dried up, leaving us in a land void of hope. Fear and failure morphed into blame and retribution. We turned upon each other, like dogs fighting over a poor man's food scraps. I jumped ship and scuttled back to the superficial familiarity of IT. Six months later the company went into voluntary administration. Now it's gone.

SAM AND I finish our brew and return to the office. The dreaded meeting arrives too soon. Tobias Fox sits on the far side of the wide conference table. He doesn't offer his hand in greeting, or smile when I joke about the weather. He explains he wants 'Just the facts.'

Tobias has tight skin and Arctic-blue eyes. He grills me for an hour about my accounts, clients and opportunities: quarter by quarter, month by month and deal by deal. I search the spreadsheets but they remain void of the magic numbers I need. I stop struggling and sink to the muddy bottom as Tobias takes notes. I'm sure he knows I'm a fraud and should have been sacked months ago.

After the interrogation I drive to a meeting but my enthusiasm has waned. I pass the sprawling campus of the ANU and the iconic buildings around Lake Burley Griffin's shores: the National Library, the High Court and the National Gallery. A wrong turn brings me to Old Parliament House and the Aboriginal Tent Embassy, with its flags flying proud amid a collection of ragged tents and demountable buildings.

Finally, I arrive in the foyer of the client's department. A security guard protects the reception desk and takes my details, handing me a pass. I call my client's mobile and she answers quickly but is busy, locked in a conference and unable to meet today. Apologising, she promises to send an email to rebook the meeting. I tell her not to bother, and hang up. Then my mobile beeps: it's an SMS from the office. Tobias wants to see me. Now.

ON THE WAY back to the office I call my wife and tell her I'm about to be sacked. I'm still on the phone when I almost drive into the back of a stationary taxi, drawing the attention of a small tribe gathered in front of the Salvation Army coffee shop. I see them there most days when I walk past on my way to lunch or a business call in my pinstriped, sunglassed superiority. I recognise the windscreen washer, with his scruffy beard and broken, stained teeth. I recognise the ice-faced young woman, an occasional busker whose violin resonates with artful beauty. I wonder what she thinks about before she falls asleep.

I glimpse my car's reflection in the coffee shop's window and see a tired old fool in the driver's seat. He should be driving a Winnebago, heading for baby-boomer nirvana, not running around Canberra selling stuff to public servants. I hope I get a redundancy payout.

The mood in the office is sombre. Tobias calls me into an empty office and asks me to sit down, then comes to the front of the desk and sits near me.

There's nothing between us except cold air. He explains calmly that times are tough, the toughest he has experienced in his thirty years in the industry.

Sweat dribbles down my side, soaking my white shirt.

Tobias believes that even tougher times lie ahead and that the recession is yet to sink its teeth into Australia's hide: 'When it does, the damage will be brutal.' However, he also believes that Canberra will survive the mauling better than most cities. Nonetheless, he explains that he has made five people redundant.

Sam is one of them. I am not. The news shocks me. I'm a fraud and he doesn't know it. I shake his hand, promising not to let him down. He says, 'Just make your numbers,' and leaves.

Tobias Fox and the recession pass out of the building.

I spy Sam heading for the basement car park, struggling to carry a large cardboard box. I take his briefcase and walk beside him; he looks pale and seems shorter. He says, 'Mate, who would have thought this would happen?' I point out that he'll have no problem getting a new job and suggest he should celebrate a little – after all, he got a very generous package. We travel in silence down to the basement.

As we get out, I ask him to meet me at Psychedeli some time. I want his advice about how to handle the Centrelink account. He calls me a lucky bastard and walks away.

After a few paces, he turns back and throws me his security pass. 'Mate, hand this in for me. There's no hurry, though – it doesn't work anymore.'

Brett Caldwell is a Canberra-based author who changed the names and identifying details of his friends and colleagues in this piece. His stories have appeared in *Griffith REVIEW: The Next Big Thing*, *Up North* and *Cities on the Edge*.

FICTION

THE OTHER SIDE OF SILENCE

CHRIS WOMERSLEY

IT'S true I wanted him dead and would gladly have done it myself. I wonder about the days before fingerprinting, before CCTV, forensic analysis and Google Earth: how easy it would have been to do away with someone. It's hard to believe to look at me, but it goes against nature when a child predeceases her parents and one might assume I was acting in an unnaturally emotive manner at the time. Revenge, I have since discovered, is merely the wish that no one else experience the life denied the person you have lost.

In the modern, *friendly* courtroom, where the sentence was handed down (a mere two years! on a prison *farm!*), it felt as if the entire world were a poorly constructed billycart that had lost a wheel, only to continue careening down the asphalt, chunking up sparks as it went. After sentencing, the judge, a chap called Roger Hilliard, a fellow I actually knew of through friends of friends, plumped his papers and swept from the courtroom, steadfastly refusing to meet my eye. Well might he have been ashamed at his part in a system that had so obviously failed to punish adequately the man who killed my daughter. The entire thing was a disgrace.

Meanwhile, the dolt in question exhaled noisily like the pig he was, turned to his dumpy wife and smiled a tight smile of *Oh well, honey, it could have been worse,* while she dabbed at her lurid mascara. They referred to the crime as an accident, which was true *technically,* but let's face it, nobody forced the man to drink twenty glasses of beer, jump in his ute and speed through the first red light he encountered. Nobody had a gun to his head.

MARIE AND I struggled to have a child at all, and as a result Carol had been much hoped for, much loved and occasionally much spoilt. It is true that parenthood erases utterly the life you lived before, but even after the child has departed it is impossible to return to the things that might otherwise have occupied your time. The massive space that develops in one's heart to accommodate a child does not, womblike, shrink after the child is gone. For a long time afterwards, both Marie and I woke early in the morning and wondered what to do with ourselves. What we did before Carol came along had been, in the early days of parenthood, the question we asked ourselves. Now the question was: what could we do now she had gone?

I felt Carol's loss deeply but it was Marie who mourned for her most elaborately. She visited her grave regularly, often alone, and hoarded her personal items for longer than was necessary. They were the closest mother and daughter I had ever had the pleasure of knowing, distinguishable from a distance by their characteristic manner of walking arm in arm in a clumsy but touching pas de deux. Marie moved a framed photo, in which Carol was at her most beautiful and at her most assured, to different locations throughout the apartment – now on the bedside table, now on the bookcase, now to the kitchen bench – as if she might give our beloved daughter the animation she now otherwise lacked. More than once she dialled Carol's number for a chat, only for her to realise, with a horror that never really dims over time, that she was calling a number now registered to a complete stranger.

I'd have done anything to ease her pain and it is no exaggeration to say that I would gladly have swapped places with Carol – stepped off that kerb into the path of that speeding truck – if it meant that she and Marie could have enjoyed more years together. Grief is not one of life's human *journeys*, as those saccharine New Age mystics might tell you, nor is it a destination; rather, grief is an entire continent, apparently endless, with its very own topography and foreign tongue, a nation in which one loses one's passport and papers and must spend the foreseeable future.

After the hullabaloo diminished, Marie and I resolved to take a few weeks away from our interfering families and the inevitable follow-ups from the dogged press. On a whim we decided to revisit the coastal town of Mallacoota, where we had spent two weeks thirty years earlier, before Carol was even born, a place we remembered with great affec- tion, a place where our sorrows might even be unknown to the general public and thus more easily forgotten. It was a simple and isolated place. There was a time when, having been elevated to such lofty heights in our personal history, we would use Mallacoota as a sort of touchstone when assessing the worth of other destinations. We would shake our heads and say – laughingly, but also with complete sincerity – things like, 'The Dalmatian coast was nice, but it was no Mallacoota.'

In this way, the humble Victorian seaside town assumed almost mythical proportions and I suppose that was part of the appeal of revisiting: the hope that, after all the tragedy of the past few years, the solitude and peace might offer us solace, rejuvenation, a chance to set the world to rights. And so it did, but in the most peculiar of ways.

We arrived at night, as we did three decades ago, located the house we had reserved several days before and received our instructions from our landlady, a gnome of a woman with energetic eyebrows that tumbled and leapt across her forehead like a pair of lithe gymnasts. She activated the utilities, explained the neighbourhood, such as it was, and showed us how to work the automatic garage door. Before she departed, she issued us with a photocopied sheet with a map and a list of names and phone numbers for various services we might require in the township: boat hire, takeaway food, massages and so forth. She assured us we would be undisturbed and urged us to call her should we require anything at all.

The house itself was large and comfortable, almost as tastefully appointed as our own apartment. We unpacked our supplies and it wasn't long before we were nestled on the couch with a fire blazing in the hearth and glasses of red wine cradled in our hands. The silence was deep and tranquil, interrupted only by the occasional crackle and pop from a burning log or the call of an owl in the night.

That night we lay in the unfamiliar bed, deep and warm, under heavy blankets, and stared into the darkness, into the past and into the future, such as it was. I wondered what the man who killed our daughter was doing and hoped that, at that precise moment, 3.15 am, he was being abused in a dreadful fashion by some lunatic prison inmate.

OVER THE WEEK we began to recover some of our former selves. We both knew it would be a long haul, but at least there were the beginnings of some sort of adjustment. We would rise early to eat toast spread with local marmalade on the sunny lawn overlooking one of the series of lakes fed by the nearby ocean. Contemplatively, we watched boats tacking back and forth in the late afternoon breeze. Arm in arm we walked the pier to inspect the catch of the men and boys fishing there. Marie, with her binoculars always to hand, sought out birds, checking them against a book bought especially for the purpose of identification. At night we watched DVDs or read quietly, rising now and then to prod the fire or refill our wine glasses. A view of the horizon and the nippy sea air, carrying on it the scent of distant places, combined to make us feel more positive, more hopeful. Even Marie seemed to display flashes of her former self.

There was, it was true, an occasional melancholy that settled upon us when we were reminded of Carol's absence – often by the most obscure object, a TV show, say, that we knew she would have enjoyed or a jumper in a local shop she might have liked – but these episodes became more manageable, almost *companionable*, like adjusting warily to the presence of a stranger.

The peace and quiet came to a halt, however, one night when a group of about fifty descended on a neighbouring house and proceeded to have the loudest party I have ever heard. I had observed them with some foreboding as they arrived by the carload throughout the afternoon. Marie chastised me for being a fuddy-duddy when I expressed my fear they would disturb our precarious solitude, but it turned out my fears were well founded. From 8 pm, the night was full to the brim with a brew of the most appalling thudding music, the screech of drunken women and the hoarse arguments of young men.

At first we tried to ignore it and passed the evening as we had passed the previous seven. I told myself that it was all fair enough, that I had most likely kept a few people awake during my more reckless years, but as the hours wore on I became increasingly agitated. As a man, one feels the burden of having to do something on such occasions, so when 1 am rolled around and the noise gave no indication of abating, I got out of bed and dressed.

'What will you do?' Marie asked.

I shrugged in the darkness. 'Just ask them to stop. Have some consideration for us.' It sounded pathetic, and I knew it.

Marie sat up. 'Well. Be careful. Don't say anything foolish, Clive. Please.'

I pulled on my sandals and reassured her, but she insisted on getting out of bed and said she would observe proceedings through her binoculars. I knew the set of her voice and declined to talk her out of it, even as I thought it a pointless idea.

The two properties were separated by nothing more than a large stand of pine trees, and as I padded beneath them and out into the party's penumbra of light and noise I felt as if I were entering an obscure circle of hell: people thronged about in various states of undress and evident intoxication; girls huddled here and there on the lawn. The music was obviously, unbelievably, even louder. I was aware of people observing my progress with slightly bemused contempt, as they might a dog walking on its hind legs, and yet I pressed on.

The house was larger than the one in which we were staying and was lit up like a film set. People danced. A tide of young people ran past me, yelling and calling to each other. They all shone from a day at the beach and were smartly dressed, evidently enjoying the hospitality at the beach house of one of their parents. I crossed the lawn, ducked beneath a tangle of coloured lights strung across the terrace and stood on the threshold to a living room. In the short walk across the lawn I had run through a variety of scenarios, all of which involved me emerging victorious from whatever altercation I was about to engage in, but now I was here, in the thick of it, my resolve ran from me like water. I gazed around at them, at the way they sprawled on couches and bounded up the stairs. It was horrifying in a way that only dimly came to me as I stood there being jostled by passers-by; what galled me most, I realised after several minutes, was that they all had life, were fairly bursting with it, while my daughter, dear Carol, lay crumbling in a box in the earth, cold and alone, miles from us. A couple smiled at me as they squeezed past. I wondered if Marie were observing me through her binoculars and felt my masculine pride under scrutiny, but retreated nonetheless; back to our temporary home, back to bed.

'What happened?' Marie asked when I was under the covers, ten minutes later.

'Nothing, really.'

'You didn't talk to anyone?'

'No.'

'How old were they?'

'Were you not watching?'

'Yes,' she admitted.

'Well. They were in their mid-twenties, I suppose.'

Marie drew breath. 'Carol's age.'

'Yes. Carol's age, more or less.'

WITH SEEMINGLY ENDLESS goodbyes and the slamming of car doors, the party finally dissolved sometime shortly before dawn. Marie and I got up early nonetheless and set out for a walk just after sunrise. The day was misty but, if the past week were any guide, would clear up by mid-morning. We didn't mention the party in detail, or only to say how tired we were. I felt positively ancient, beyond living. We walked along the road for a short distance before cutting down a sandy track to a headland that looked over the curving beach. We stood and the wind whipped about our legs and sang through the stubby tea-trees. Marie peered through her binoculars out to sea in an effort to spot some bird or other she hadn't yet managed to tick off her list. I huddled in my coat and watched the progress of a person surfing far below. A man, I eventually discerned, who determinedly paddled out on his board through the roiling surf and waited for the right wave to ride back into shore. He didn't seem particularly good at it and was dumped repeatedly, often before he even had a chance to ride the board for more than a few seconds.

I found myself willing the surfer on, urging him to stay upright longer, and felt unaccountable disappointment at his failures. After fifteen minutes of this, he appeared to get into difficulty. The board that had been lashed to his ankle came free in a particularly smashing wave and he found himself past the breaking waves in evidently deep water, flailing somewhat, his black, wet-suited arms waving about amid the foam like a beetle drowning in milk. A quick scan revealed there was no one else on the beach, indeed no sign of humans at all as far as I could make out, even though I knew the township was just beyond the scrubby dunes. Immediately I tapped Marie's shoulder and told her there appeared to be a man drowning down in the surf.

She swung her binoculared gaze to where I had indicated. 'Clive. Have you got your mobile phone?'

I fumbled through my pockets and located the damn thing, as small as a Matchbox car.

'Call someone. Call Triple 0. Quickly. They can probably get the rescue people out there. A boat. Save him.'

I was wrestling with the mobile phone, struggling with the tiny keypad when Marie, still with her eyes glued to the binoculars, placed a hand firmly on my forearm. 'Wait,' she said. A pair of gulls wheeled down out of the sky, landed on the grass nearby and shrugged their wings. 'It's one of them.'

I managed to unlock the phone and was dialling. 'What? Who?'

Marie's voice was astringent. 'One of those…*arseholes* from last night.'

It was extremely rare for Marie to swear. Even throughout the trial, she had managed to withhold her anger, even if I could detect its presence by the tight-lipped set of her mouth. I waited with phone in hand. The wind buffeted us where we stood, out there on the headland, exposed to the elements. We didn't speak a word. I was aware of Marie, my beloved wife, steadying herself against the gusting wind. I was aware of her short brown hair flicking this way and that, of her unzipped jacket flapping about as if the fingers of the wind were searching for something hidden about her person – some grief, most likely – that might be taken away and discarded. Marie kept her hand on my arm. Her grip tightened slightly, almost imperceptibly. I understood at once what she was communicating.

It was then I saw us as if from a distance – as one of the wheeling seagulls might have – two old things in their all-weather jackets on a windswept headland, made tiny by nature. I dropped the phone back into a pocket and we watched, Marie and I, somewhat *greedily*, I am ashamed to say, as the surfer struggled against the tide, his head disappearing and reappearing within the creaming waves, his dark mouth, visible even at this distance as it opened hungrily for air, until he reappeared no more.

BY THE TIME we made our way down to the sand, half an hour later, a small crowd was hovering around the fellow's body like birds. As if she had read my mind, Marie coughed into her fist and began to speak above the sound of the wind. 'Do you know,' she said with some satisfaction, 'that the collective noun for herons is a siege? A siege of herons.' Our progress was unwieldy; the sand was heavy and thick, our old bodies tired. We huddled and bent into the whipping wind until we approached the group, who were by now standing around with their arms across their chests, obviously waiting for the ambulance or police. We did not stop. One or two of their number looked up but if they recognised me from the party the night before they showed no sign of it, and we offered no greeting of our own. We kept on and by the time we left the beach, stamped our shoes free of sand and went into the house – now quiet, now peaceful – I expect the ambulance would have arrived and pronounced the fellow dead.

Chris Womersley is the author of *The Low Road* (Scribe, 2007), which won the 2008 Ned Kelly Award for First Fiction. His short story 'The Possibility of Water' won the 2007 Josephine Ulrick Prize for Literature and was published in *Griffith REVIEW 20: Cities on the Edge*.

Material or post-material?

Renewing the search for meaning

Paul D Williams

THE American political scientist Ronald Inglehart argues that 'the basic value priorities of western publics' shift in affluent times 'from giving top priority to physical sustenance and safety, toward heavier emphasis on belonging, self-expression and the quality of life'. Inglehart calls this shift in values 'post-materialism'. It's an idea that can be traced at least to the mid-1960s, and perhaps even to the pre-Depression 'flaming youth' of the 1920s, though it was the late 1960s – the period I call Aquarian liberalism – that saw the most significant shift away from the old politics of base materialism and toward the new progressivism of human rights, environment and community.

Public sentiment about the individual's relationship with the state has fluctuated like fashions since the nineteenth century. Following the depression of the 1890s, Australians – so often cast as rugged individualists, models of pioneer self-reliance – came to embrace a vigorous union movement, progressive political organisations such as the Protectionists and the Australian Labor Party, and a federalist political structure that would protect them from womb to tomb. Conservative policymakers from Prime Minister Stanley Bruce down later warned against excessive welfare, for fear of transforming Australia into a 'nation of mendicants'. But the 1950s saw a return to a bipartisan commitment to what Paul Kelly has labelled the Australian Settlement and, in particular, the welfare state. State paternalism was mandated by both citizen and government.

That changed by the mid-1970s, when oil shocks and stagflation ended the western dream of uninterrupted economic growth. Despite governments' best efforts, state patronage of the working and middle classes no longer propped up prosperity and employment. Taking its lead from Margaret Thatcher's determination to end what she considered the stifling of individual incentive, western capitalism abandoned Keynesianism and borrowed from, if not completely embraced, the 'supply side' economics of Milton Friedman's monetarism. By the mid-1980s, Australians had witnessed the greatest political paradox of their age: a Labor government, led by former Australian Council of Trade Unions president Bob Hawke, deregulating the Australian economy. The impetus of globalisation, freer trade and small government thereafter changed Australian values. 'Big government' – notwithstanding the expansion of middle-class welfare in the 1990s – again became unfashionable.

The current financial crisis is likely to change all that yet again, at least for a while. As more government assistance is offered to individuals, and to such industries as tourism and car manufacturing, deeper and longer-term attitudinal changes are likely to follow. It's likely that Australia's middle classes will reassess their relationship with the state when they face real need. Moreover, Australians' experiences may produce electoral shocks. Just as the English middle classes' exposure to evacuees' extreme poverty contributed to the unexpected 1945 defeat of wartime hero Winston Churchill, in favour of the unassuming welfare champion Clement Attlee, by 2010 Australians may well be even more accommodating of big government. Indeed, despite the non-Labor parties remonstrating about Labor's 'squandering' of the Coalition's budget surplus, Australians don't at all appear dismayed at the prospect of a $300 billion debt. In one Newspoll, nearly four out of five surveyed Australians declared they would like to see government stimulus packages spent on social infrastructure, such as roads.

ATTITUDINAL SHIFTS, NO matter how enduring, constitute but one legacy. A second level of change – and one buttressing the first – can be expected socioeconomically. Many in upper income brackets, such as those in medicine and law, will be quarantined from the crisis by virtue of their profession. Many more, despite previously strong earning capacities in such sectors as tourism, finance or mining, will be less fortunate. Yet more, on middle and lower incomes, will be financially ruined through unemployment, underemployment, declining wages and conditions, or eroded superannuation. While cavernous income gaps will continue, economic recession may flatten out middle and lower-middle income streams, with those on the lowest rungs – pensioners, the unskilled and the unemployed – the most severely affected. As such, many Australians will once again become disposed to government paternalism. Whether this will be a permanent conversion is impossible to say: for some it will; for others it will be short-lived, soon thrown off in a laissez-faire rebirth at the first hint of economic revival.

A third change rests on how we spend our increasingly precarious incomes. It surprises no one that the consumption of luxury goods nosedives in times of economic trouble. But cultural shifts are rarely simple and – if economic forecasters are to be believed – the length and severity of this current crisis suggest domestic cultural changes may be more enduring.

Newspapers and magazines have already had fun in speculating on the types of commodities families are, or will soon be, removing from weekly budgets. Restaurant dining, cinema tickets and new vehicles are the first places discretionary spending is cut, and it appears synthetic diamonds are now the vogue as a measure of a new-found personal responsibility for brides-to-be. But *Time* also reports sharp slumps in sales of more practical items, such as batteries, light bulbs and kitchen gadgets. Conversely, there are those consumer goods that soar in sales as families seek cheap ways to feed, clothe and entertain themselves. But again, less expected items – such as birth-control products – have also grown in popularity. In short, we might say western consumption following the financial crisis is reducing to the Three Cs: cans, condoms and conservatism. In purchasing canned foods, families hunker down for what they are told will be a long and bleak economic winter; in purchasing condoms, couples are wary of bringing into the world yet another mouth to feed; and in their overall conservatism, people eschew the risks of the outside world, looking instead to the warmth and protection of hearth and home.

It's this last trait – a propensity to look inward domestically – that represents the greatest cultural shift, morphing us from a globe of engaged, intertwined networkers to households of cultural homebodies. Either by necessity or by choice, Australians are likely to rediscover extended families over home-cooked meals. By contrast, work colleagues, club members and casual acquaintances – for so long the focus of the busy business networker – will be eschewed. And where networks are kept up, their principal instruments of communication may well be online, on Facebook and Twitter.

Yet there's a fourth level of change that may at once be the most contentious, the most profound and the most difficult to measure. Morally and spiritually, Australians could emerge from this crisis transformed. Indeed, we may change twice in a short space of time.

Clive Hamilton and Richard Denniss labelled the West's material obsession a spiritual illness – affluenza – in which ethical and moral values are corrupted in an endless self-seeking cycle of material gratification. But this malaise extends much further than money: it has created a generation of Australians obsessed with making public their individuality. And while individuality can be a good thing when it means demonstrating difference from our neighbours, it quickly becomes a pernicious quality when it means wanting to be *better* than them. Very quickly, the West appears to have been transformed from a 'community first' to a 'me first' mindset. I call this phenomenon the spoiler society – a reference to not only individuals' spoiled nature, but also specifically to the type of cars we drive. Who hasn't noticed the number of spoilers now on even the most prosaic sedans? Once an expensive accessory, these appendages are today attached as fashion statements in a vain claim to superiority over fellow road-users.

Just as the Great Depression helped bond pre-war communities, though, this economic downturn may also remind people of the need to look out for our neighbours. This may translate into, for example, increased church attendances. We're also likely to see a rise in volunteer rates as recently retrenched workers, with time forced upon them, look outward to maintain skills and keep connected.

THESE PREDICTIONS ABOUT individuals are only speculative; but predictions about how governments will emerge from the crisis are more certain. Despite any new-found love of state paternalism among taxpayers, governments are unlikely to return to Keynesianism at the expense of the economic rationalism adopted a quarter of a century ago. They simply cannot afford to, financially or politically. When the global economy recovers, any democratic administration unilaterally continuing a big-government approach risks attack from an opportunistic opposition. Charges of high debt and financial irresponsibility are easy populist points to score with a cynical electorate.

And this remains a risk, even amid heightened rhetoric against the free market. Kevin Rudd wrote earlier this year in his *Monthly* essay that 'the great neo-liberal experiment of the past thirty years has failed', and that, to recast the role of the state, 'social democrats would need to draw, in part, on a long-standing Keynesian tradition'. There's little doubt Rudd and other western leaders are committed to smoothing the rough edges of neo-liberalism. But to suggest that governments will totally abandon the macroeconomic framework of the past three decades is absurd. Perhaps the best evidence of a world not really wanting to return to the 1970s is the near-unanimous call to maintain free trade, and to resist the temptation for nervous states to retreat into their protectionist shells.

So how material or post-material can we expect the post-crisis village, state and globe to be? The choice is ours, but the constants will far outweigh the differences. Keynesianism will not be resurrected; market economics will merely continue, with governments playing a slightly more active role, if only temporarily. This not a value judgement of monetarism: it's simply an acknowledgement of the deeply entrenched economic and political realities. Yet, if voters and policymakers retain even a shred of the post-materialism garnered from the crisis, the effects of the next economic collapse might be tempered just a little.

Paul D Williams lectures in politics and journalism at Griffith University. He is a columnist with the *Courier-Mail*, and a commentator on politics. He is co-editor, with John Wanna, of *Yes, Premier: Labor leadership in Australia's states and territories* (UNSW Press, 2005).

The leaving of Pudding Island

English expats marooned in Europe

Tony Barrell

I spent much of 2008 in France, Spain and Greece, living among British expats, some of them relatives or friends and some complete strangers, all of whom had decided over the previous two decades that they no longer wanted to live in the country of their birth. What started out as a pleasant journey of exploration and reminiscence ended in a jolting confrontation not only with the collapse of capitalism as we know it, but with a more urgent imperative to survive.

The decisions made by the people I knew were mostly based on romantic dreams they had harboured in their twenties but could only realise in middle age. The accelerant was the decade-long power of the British pound, whose strength against the euro gave owners of modest homes from all over the United Kingdom the opportunity to sell up, buy a little bit of continental Europe and live there on quite low incomes or pensions. Sterling peaked in 2000, when a euro could be bought for 58 pence, but in January 2009 the two were at parity, with the pound falling. It was a disaster the English had never imagined.

Whether Provence, the Ardèche, Tuscany, Umbria, Amalfi, the Adriatic, the Algarve or all the costas of Mediterranean Spain, 'the Sud' has been more or less overrun by refugees from what Lawrence Durrell once vilified as Pudding Island. In the mid-1930s, Durrell removed himself forever from a life infused with the overpowering fragrance of brown Windsor soup and the dreary preoccupations of men in Fair Isle cardigans who smoked pipes by the fire and only ever left the house to go to the shed.

Durrell's discontent resonated with many who grew up in the 1960s with a frustrated feeling of entitlement to a life in the Midi, the Riviera, the Aegean or anywhere 'away'. Many came to Australia, still the favourite destination of the evacuating Briton, but in the 1950s, aside from Durrell, the only foreigners who lived in the Sud were other writers – Somerset Maugham at Cap Ferrat, Robert Graves on Majorca – or a film-star-turned-princess like Grace Kelly in Monaco. Durrell's books – *Prospero's Cell* and *Reflections on a Marine Venus* – started the undertow of desire for the Mediterranean idyll. Without him there would be no Club Med, *A Year in Provence* or *Mama Mia*. Now three million Britons live in Europe, a third of them in Spain.

PREVIOUS PAGE: The Gran Hotel Bali, Benidorm dominates the skyline. The image shows the relentless development of the coastal region. *Source: unknown.*

WHO WOULD HAVE guessed that in some of France's village schools, settlers from Pudding Island would one day make the native tongue the second language taught and the French a minority in their own land?

Nonetheless, I was shocked three years ago when my younger cousin David Chenery told me he was leaving his ancestral home of Combs, Stowmarket, Suffolk to live in a remote village in Burgundy – 'for good', he said. David was not a career person; he'd done jobs in factories, retail and social work. I had never suspected he might decamp to France.

I'd told him I'd got lost looking for his house in Stowmarket, and he said that's just how he and his wife, Pauline, felt: lost in their own space. They had been walled in by glass and besser-brick warehouses and mysterious factories, and their 'village' had morphed into that dreary light-industrial estate shown in the opening credits of *The Office*.

Watching from Australia, I often wondered if the 'English village' David missed still existed outside the constructed rustic eccentricity of television series like *The Vicar of Dibley*, a place safely removed from city murk and yobs with seven-inch blades, where the church bell tolls the hour and cows wait patiently to be milked. Even morbid television serial-killer stories are set in quaint country locations far from Britain's urban and suburban worlds, where ambulance sirens scream constantly. Listening to David, I realised his idea of contemporary England converged with the social mayhem portrayed in *The Bill*.

My cousin was not brought up on fifty-year-old literature pining for the Sud but, shrewdly, he'd discovered that France in general – and Burgundy in particular – was full of half-empty villages. Pauline put it plainly: 'I realised that to get a decent pension in Britain I would have to keep working until I was seventy-one!'

By the time it dawned on them that a house in Suffolk was worth two or three times one they could buy in rural France, the rush was peaking. They sealed a deal just in time. Two years before the credit crunch loomed they found an old stone semi in Faverolles-lès-Lucey: a medieval farm hamlet deep in rural Burgundy, with a thirteenth-century church (*sans* priest), wheat and barley fields, pastures full of pink and white Charolais cattle, threaded by a small but full flowing tributary of the Seine; with all the wild bird species that have disappeared from Suffolk, and spacious woods with free firewood, mushrooms and nuts, wild boar and fallow deer.

There are no shops (bread arrives daily by van) but eight kilometres away there's a butcher-charcuterie, a baker, a grocer, a doctor and pharmacy and, at the nearest real town, Chatillon-sur-Seine, growers and providores markets with sausage, cheese, meat and fish, fruits from the farms and a help-yourself bar-cum-restaurant with as much as you can eat from the cold meats and pie table (followed by a main course from the kitchen) for twelve euros a head – a mere eight quid in 2007 money. Another half-hour on the road and they can browse the wineries of Nuits St George and Beaune.

They never guessed how soon this would change, how they'd be 'at the mercy of the exchange rate'. Even governments seemed oblivious to what was coming. The credit crunch was like global warming: plausible, even probable, but it might never happen. As recently as 2007, before 'sub-prime' found its way into everyday speech, Gordon Brown made the astounding claim that his policies as Britain's Chancellor of the Exchequer had ironed out the normal boom–bust business cycle.

Despite the tumultuous descent of the sterling last year, David and Pauline insist they will never return to England. Yes, they are living on pensions and investments from the sale of their home that are worth less than when they moved, but it's not just a matter of economics: 'There's no respect back home,' says David. 'It's all yob culture.'

His closest crony is a retired gendarme who is trying to interest him in the crevices of French culture. When I left, Daniel was feeding David a daily diet of Jacques Tati DVDs in return for generous slugs of good malt whisky. Body language was the key, he explained, and showed David how to bow, suck a pipe, doff his hat and jerk up and down on his heels, all in one movement in the manner of the ever-jaunty M. Hulot of the 1950s – a different time, in a different France. A few months later I rang to ask how things were going and David explained that their really good friends in Brittany had decided to sell up and go back to Pudding Island. But they couldn't find a buyer for their French house.

My next call was to have been to a friend in the Dordogne, a 'professional' expat who had been chasing work for decades all over the world, until he was lucky enough to buy an old stone house in a 'perfect little French village'. He was always close to the edge financially and, when he developed cancer, wrote to say there was no way he would 'go home' now because the French medical system was, in his view, superior. He met the cost of winter heating by decamping to Spain for three months. Sadly, the French medical system failed to save him before I could see him again and hear his views on the economic catastrophe.

THE FURTHER I moved away from the lush green meadows of Faverolles, towards the crispier Mediterranean Sud, the more obvious and, in many cases more shaky, I found the British expat presence. On Spain's Costa Blanca I found friends not seen since 1991: Rip and Sally Rippingale, who live in the mountains forty kilometres inland from Alicante. They met in the late 1950s at the University of St Andrews, where they first played golf – a pastime without which they admit life would be empty in Spain. In the '70s they bought a cheap holiday home in the French Ardèche and dreamed they would one day move there for good.

Rip gave up his day job to buy and sell rustic pine furniture, and drove around France in a van picking up farmhouse chairs, tables and corner cupboards which he would strip, wax and paint with floral designs to sell in their shop in World's End, that little extension of Chelsea into Fulham. At the time of the last big economic crash, in the early 1990s – just as they were thinking of quitting and heading for the Sud – they had to sell everything, including Ardèche and their Bayswater flat, to pay off the bank. It took years to get rid of their business, so they lived on a boat on the Thames at Limehouse. Eventually they 'sailed' through the canals of France and on to Corsica, and then transferred to the vast marina at Alicante. After a few years cheek-by-jowl with hundreds of other yachties (many of whom never went to sea) they decided it was time to move back to dry land. They never considered returning to Pudding Island. Their best option in Spain was an eyrie a thousand metres up a mountain behind the almond town of Xixona, famous for *turon,* nougat and all kinds of marzipan.

Their mountain 'community' isn't old and has no name. The 'villagers' are foreign and Spanish retirees and holiday-homers in stucco ranches scraped into raw, steep land so far from the coast that the distant sea is often invisible. In 2007, a summer wildfire swept up the hill and singed the edge of their beautiful garden; in winter, fierce winds and torrential rain keep everyone indoors. Now that the value of their investments has shrunk, they are more or less stuck in the last house below the ridge, wondering what might happen should their health fail.

They take me down to Benidorm, to see coastal overdevelopment. Twenty years ago it was a tiny village; now its Gran Hotel Bali is the tallest in Europe. There are apartments and townhouses, concrete esplanades and car parks but, early in 2008, property prices collapsed, credit disappeared and dead cranes took over the skyline. By midyear there were 650,000 unfinished or unoccupied apartments, and by year's end thousands of real-estate agents had gone out of business, industrial production had slumped, unemployment was soaring (now around 20 per cent) and the economy was heading into recession.

At the Sunday market, English couples sell off their possessions or the bric-a-brac, furniture and clothing they've bought at local auctions. One woman of about fifty, deeply tanned and overweight, wearing the minimum for decency, tells me she too is hoping her health holds out. She and her husband are living in a caravan. She would rather be in Queensland 'but it's too far'. Would she go back to England? 'What, and live in Grimsby? No way.' Others tell the same story. A trailer park in Benidorm still beats Birmingham. Their faith in bricks and mortar as the basis of wealth, however, has taken a fearful battering. Selling out and scuttling back to Pudding Island means taking a heavy loss.

Few understand why. Most suspect they got here by luck, and it's hard to know who to blame now it's run out. No one wants to hear about the property bubble, about how the Blair–Brown team thought shifting costs off the national budget by privatising debt – cutting taxes, reducing state services, making the user pay and plunging into private-finance initiatives – was respectable economic management. Until last year what cash people had simply bought more in France and Spain.

Rip and Sal get by – but, they say, 'any wine that costs more than three euros is out of our range'. Doubtless there are gourmet opportunities at Xixona's weekly street market but they are content with simple local ingredients twisted into mildly eccentric recipes eaten in the living room, on the terrace or next to their modest plunge pool.

Golf has expanded with the influx of the British – there are nearly a hundred and fifty courses in Andalucía alone – and KPMG reported in 2008 that Spain was still the most favoured location for golf 'resorts': greens, fairways and clubhouses integrated into apartment complexes, although the trend in the past year was to forget the greens and just build the apartments. The day Rip and I go around the Bonalba golf course, between Benidorm and Alicante, he points out a new development of flats lining the back nine. 'The year they were finished they all got flooded,' he says as we zip down the fairway in his electric buggy. 'Now they can't sell them.'

At a group lunch at the clubhouse, the conversation moves from handicaps on the green to obstacles to easy living. A retired Scottish RAF sergeant says the services and daily expenses that used to cost less than half what he paid in the UK are now much more expensive. It's well known that members shower at the club to save on their home hot-water bills. Others who speak no Spanish or have little interest in Spanish culture (aside from sun and wine) have been slowly realising that unless you've immersed yourself in the new, alien environment, the paradise you dreamed of can evaporate as soon as things go bad.

Sal Rippingale admits that she used to be more 'involved' in public and local issues, and was active in the British Labour Party and Amnesty; now, she says, she confines her political actions to 'getting up the noses of the British club members who want to chop off the hands of thieves'. Her other activities are swimming, crosswords and rolling her own cigarettes. Neither she nor Rip is fluent in Spanish, but with the help of an English-speaking local Rip looks after community-association business (a job he says the local Spanish won't do), writing reports, checking the water supply, and processing requests and complaints from his neighbours.

MOLIVOS IS A picturesque Greek village on the north-west corner of Lesbos, close to Turkey. I've known a few British expats there, but the eastern edge of the Aegean has never appealed to mass resettlement. Lawrence Durrell went only once. There are a few empty houses – some quite grand, others collapsing hovels, a few 'dowry houses' waiting for a granddaughter to get married – but they are all overpriced. Homes can be picked up cheaply in less fashionable villages, but these villages are often remote and most likely entirely Greek. There are a few Pudding Islanders, like Jeff and Belinda Paffet, who have bought a cottage in Vafios, high up in the lee of Mt Lepetymnos, but they don't mix with the other English couple in the village and are learning Greek.

Ten years ago they came for a holiday with their sixteen-year-old daughter, Naomi. When they were due to return, she announced she wanted to work on as a waitress. They agreed, but at the end of the summer she told them she wanted to stay – and live with her Greek lover, Vangelis, a restaurant manager seven years her senior. Jeff and Belinda were shocked but trusted her (and him) enough to go along with it. Belinda insists their decision to buy in Vafios was not to 'follow Naomi' but to leave England, a desire intensified by disenchantment with the Labour government.

Naomi speaks Greek fluently, and with Vangelis (who is equally proficient in English) started a travel business they hoped would survive the slump in tourism. Their relationship did not. Naomi's waiting table again, but the Paffets are not going back to Pudding Island. 'This,' insists Belinda 'is home.'

Lesbos is the eastern edge of Europe. The shoreline that runs east of Molivos is backed by scrubby valleys, rocky headlands; the beaches are longer, wider and stonier, less populated, treeless. This is the coast closest to Turkey, which is about eight nautical miles away. There are a few low-rise hotels, studio apartments and single-storey summerhouses. I stayed for a fortnight with my wife, Jane, between the resort and a small market garden farm worked by an Albanian family who can't make enough money and are going home. Back among the trees there's an English couple in a bungalow. They claim to have stayed here every year for three decades, but have no plans to move in permanently. The farm and the hotel are both bordered by a road which runs along the water's edge and a stretch of narrow unshaded shingle with a beachcomber's shack. Adonis has been living there for years, oblivious to sunbakers plodding by.

On the night of 11 August 2008, just before midnight, a storm breaks, thunderheads crackle around the mountains for hours and the gentle hiss of a steady downpour ends just before dawn. By the late afternoon, as we sit drinking tea, gazing at the farm, the beach, the sea and Turkey, there is no sign of the turbulence. The storm has cleared the air, so minarets, villages and small resorts are quite distinct. At around half past five we hear voices calling, a plaintiff *aaayyaaayy* sound repeated slowly by two or three people, together and separately. It reminds us of a sports chant, but it seems to be coming from Turkey, and there, about a kilometre out, something different is in the water: a group of people standing in an orange inflatable dinghy. About fifteen or twenty of them, crying out in relays for attention. The onshore breeze is bringing them slowly towards us, but without engine power or paddles they are afraid the dinghy might founder and so, I guess, they are calling out to the people on the beach to start up one of the idle runabouts on the shingle and come and rescue them.

We run down to the water's edge but our enterprise is thwarted as the high-powered Molivos coastguard powerboat races around the headland. In about ten minutes it has brought the dinghy alongside, taken the men and women aboard and swiftly set off west around the coast to the main port of Mytilene with the group huddled on the foredeck. Mytilene has a notorious overcrowded detention centre, as do several Greek islands along the coast of Turkey.

Afghanis, Iraqis and even Somalis frequently land here at night – Adonis found a body in his nets a couple of years ago – but rarely do they arrive in broad daylight. I can only guess that this group was held up on the Turkish side by the storm. Nobody will tell you how they make their journeys – across Iran perhaps, or from the Horn of Africa to Yemen and Saudi Arabia – but despite the hardships of the journey they keep on coming. I think of Michael Winterbottom's *In This World*, about a pair of brothers on the hair-raising journey by truck from Pakistan to London.

IN 2008, 150,000 'illegals' landed in Greece; around twelve million now live in Europe. Most who arrive on Lesbos have no qualms about Pudding Island. They want to get 'to England' and on the Turkish side of the strait there's a busy cottage industry selling dinghies – for as much as a few thousand euros – to people looking for landfall a few nautical miles away in the nearest part of the continent.

Needless to say, refugees from the Middle East and Africa who make it are not looking for a Greek island paradise. Their desire to move into Europe is a bit different from my adolescent yearnings for a sybaritic life in the Sud. They want the 'West', and if that means a job in far north Scotland, so be it. While the International Labour Organization says tens of millions of jobs will disappear worldwide by the end of the year, talk of hard times in 'the global economy' means nothing in Afghanistan and Somalia.

The ironies are stark. While economic refugees have been clamouring to be let in, three million Britons moved offshore to enjoy the benefits of a strong pound – or to get away from immigrants – in European villages partially deserted by people fleeing poverty. Whatever else the tough times bring, the movement of people will not be deterred by collapsing home prices in Slough.

References available online at www.griffithreview.com

Tony Barrell is a writer and broadcaster. ABC Radio National broadcast *Stranded in Paradise*, his documentary version of this piece, on 29 August. It can be downloaded from www.abc.net.au/rn/360/stories/2009. His essays have been published in *Griffith REVIEW: Up North, Cities on the Edge* and *MoneySexPower*.

Glimpses of heaven and hell

Dubai confronts the limits to growth, consumption and greed

Hilary McPhee

THE Eighth Wonder of the World had already been proclaimed well before the grand opening in Dubai of Atlantis, The Palm, in November 2008. The thirteen acres of artificial palm-shaped archipelago jutting out into the shallow waters of the Arabian Gulf featured a forty-two-acre water park of sixty-five thousand fish and the soon-to-be controversial Dolphin Education Centre, the whole thing anchored by the vast pink luxury hotel, its 1,539 rooms full for the occasion with the world's celebrities and tycoons. This was to be an Event like nothing on earth, and the $20 million fireworks display would be clearly seen from outer space.

But the timing and scale of the opening of Atlantis, The Palm could not have been worse. International derision was guaranteed. 'Dubai's Last Hurrah,' trumpeted the cover of *Newsweek*. *The Guardian* cited Ozymandias: 'The dunes will reclaim the soaring folly of Dubai.' And *The Independent* kept putting the boot in: 'The Shangri-la of the Middle East bites the dust…a city built on credit and ecocide, suppression and slavery.'

The news that Dubai, like everywhere else in the over-developed world, was feeling the force of the global recession was endlessly repeated. The real-estate bonanza had indeed slowed; some of Dubai's more spectacular projects were on hold, their indentured labour redeployed or returned to Pakistan and Bangladesh. But the tall tales about the end of the world rapidly assumed the shape of a manga: three thousand luxury cars abandoned at the airport, keys in the ignition, their owners fleeing to avoid jail; once-rich wives deserted, selling their bling and sleeping in the dunes in their SUVs; empty apartment buildings as far as the eyes could see; every second business retrenching staff and dishonouring contracts; not a crane moving on the horizon. And, through the cracks in the edifice, the desert sands had started to creep across the highways.

Emiratis and the professional expatriate community fought back as best they could on blogs and in interviews to Arab media, which was more inclined to listen. Dubai will not be allowed to fail, said the World Bank's Tariq Yusef on Al Jazeera. Dubai, he said, has become a model of accelerated growth for

---

PREVIOUS PAGE: Camels stroll along a tourist beach in Dubai against a backdrop of commercial and residential towers. *Source: gettyimages.com*

others in the region; its belief in itself as a grand hub of trade routes and ideas is an ancient one which the Arab world celebrates and intends to realise again. A failure of Dubai would be a failure of the whole United Arab Emirates.

Eventually the British government weighed in, distancing itself from the mockers. The British have longstanding links with the region. The seven sheikhdoms which form the United Arab Emirates were a British protectorate from 1820 to 1971. The UAE is one of Britain's top ten export markets, and 1,783 British companies operate in Dubai. The Brits, including the egregious Beckhams, have been the most enthusiastic purchasers – after the Russian mafia, so the stories go – of expensive and hyped real estate off the plans. Investors reaped huge returns in the good times, buying and selling when rents were leaping by up to 40 per cent a year, but the credit crunch caught the over-extended, major developments slowed, vacancies rose and rents began to fall. The place is now a renter's paradise, says Dubai's *National*, the impressively staffed and resourced *Guardian*-lookalike English-language newspaper – the world's newest print journal and surely its last.

THE DISCOVERY OF oil in the mid-'60s transformed the small Bedouin fishing and pearling ports along the strip of land on the southern shore of what is now called the Arabian Gulf. Today the Emirates are essentially seven cities of varying sizes and strategic roles, with unimaginable amounts of money to invest in fast-tracking modernity.

Abu Dhabi, the conservative capital within commuting distance of Dubai that possesses most of the UAE's land and oil wealth, dominates the federation. It aims to be the cultural centre, investing heavily to develop institutions and cultural projects such as the prestigious and extraordinary Saadiyat Island, where Frank Gehry will deliver his biggest Guggenheim yet and for which the Louvre has accepted a billion dollars to share its exhibitions and its name. But it is Dubai, with limited oil and natural gas reserves accounting for less than 6 per cent of its revenues, which has embodied the narrative of globalisation – ahistorical, diverse, unsentimental, its economic goals transcending all others. Here the constraints of culture and nationalisms have melted into air and a 'world-class' megalopolis has emerged in which Spider-Man would be at home.

By mirroring and exploiting the West's own excesses of consumption and greed, catering to every whim and fantasy of the newly rich, Dubai made itself a perfect target, rapidly becoming one of the world's greatest carbon footprinters. The green golf courses and lush parks and private gardens reaching down to the sea require more water per capita than anywhere else on the planet. But much of the criticism is rather like accusing the Arabs for doing at top speed, with maximum hubris and minimum regulatory impediments, what developers have been doing in the West for decades: knocking down, building up, producing skylines that look the same everywhere, creating cities that further deplete the world's finite resources, which isolate people whose chief value seems to lie in their capacity to consume.

Dubai is crass but it is not alone. Britain's developments on the Costa del Sol are neither pretty nor environmentally sensitive; nor is the Australian Gold Coast, nor the proliferation of gated communities on Egypt's Red Sea Riviera, nor Florida. The new Westfield Mall in London's Shepherd's Bush, 'the largest urban shopping centre in Europe', which opened this year on the site of the 1908 Franco-British Exhibition halls, is a glass-roofed, climate-controlled cathedral to consumption and luxury, glittering with chandeliers, full of food flown in from around the globe, and featuring the same upmarket labels as the malls of the United Arab Emirates. Without the flack.

FOR THOSE WHO hadn't been watching, the first sign of the UAE's regional and global strategy was the launching of the Emirates airline in 1985. Two years later, Emirates was running daily nonstop flights to London and the European capitals, enticing shoppers and tourists with cheap fares to make stopovers in Dubai. Twenty years on, the Dubai International Airport is a hub for world aviation. Terminal 3, which opened a month before Atlantis, The Palm, is not only the largest building in the world in floor space (1.5 million square metres) but is located twenty metres below the taxiway area. Terminal 4 is on schedule to open in 2013 and, forty kilometres away in the desert, the Al Maktoum International Airport – the world's largest, planned to cater for up to 150 million passengers annually and twelve million tonnes of cargo – is already underway.

The night we arrive at the glittering Terminal 3 there are no queues and the duty-free shops selling alcohol are empty, but the arrival hall is so enormous the crowds may well have been somewhere else. A smooth immigration official in a *dishdasha* and *keffiyeh* admires my Italian spectacles and waves us through. The English-language newspapers on the plane have carried an extensive interview with the Vice President and Prime Minister of the UAE and Ruler of Dubai, His Highness Sheikh Mohammed bin Rashid Al Maktoum, reassuring the world in the bland language used by prime ministers everywhere that all is well, that the Emirate is on track, that the downturn is global and Dubai is exceedingly well placed to emerge stronger than ever.

The news of the injection a few months earlier of ten billion dollars in bonds from the UAE's Central Bank was interpreted by most western pundits as oil-rich Abu Dhabi propping up hapless Dubai by buying into its economy. This was firmly denied by the President of the UAE, His Highness Sheikh Khalifa bin Zayed Al Nahyan of Abu Dhabi, who cited the conditions of Islamic banking, which preclude one party profiting to the exclusion of the other, and the region's grand plan. Obviously Dubai had been playing by other rules, profiting from the lifestyles of expatriates and tourists from all over the world, and thriving on speculation and the same kind of debt-trading instruments that brought the western banking system to its knees. By the end of 2008, Dubai's foreign debt stood at 148 per cent of GDP, while monthly retail interest on a Platinum Visa Card issued by the National Bank of Dubai was 2.99 per cent – both well into the realm of *haram* for Sharia-compliant Muslim institutions. Now, it seems likely that the combined financial strategy with Abu Dhabi may be emerging with a different mix including a range of state-funded Sharia-compliant development projects.

'Rest assured that between Abu Dhabi and Dubai there is no buying and selling,' said Sheikh Khalifa. 'Everything in Dubai belongs to Abu Dhabi and the rest of the UAE, and all that is in Abu Dhabi belongs to Dubai and Abu Dhabi and the rest of the UAE.'

ARCHITECTS AND URBAN planners from around the world started pouring into the region over a decade ago. There were the stars – Norman Foster,

Rem Koolhaas and Fernando Donis of OMA, Atkins, Zaha Hadid, to name a few – their teams usually young and drawn from all over the world. They were encouraged to develop concepts on a scale and complexity that only China building for the Olympics could match – and were attracted, in all likelihood, by the prospect of seeing projects fast-tracked, unencumbered by the bureaucracy most have to deal with back home. The Ruler of Dubai is often described as a one-man band. Certainly his executive team is small and hands-on. This is a kind of e-government: accelerated decision-making with minimal regulation, which provides at least the impression of easy access to power.

Debate about the future shape of Dubai and the problems caused by its accelerated growth is far from discouraged, according to the planners and architects I spoke to, and there's been a good deal of it in recent years. But in a speculative climate of rapid returns, hard-hitting advice from consultants and advisers may have been compromised by the power structures. Sustainability is one of the UAE's greatest concerns but it sometimes sounds more like a buzzword than an imperative.

The Dubai Urban Development Framework, commissioned in 2007, has still not been released. This is expected to resolve a number of issues, including the structure of the development entities, and to systematically confront the massive environmental concerns facing cities built on sand at sea level, although the Dutch are already helping with dyke technology. The largest and most fantastical of the recent developments have been put on hold, the manmade Islands of the World and the Universe, and the second and third great Palms, constructions that would add another 150 artificial kilometres to the coastline. But professionals described slowdowns rather than outright cancellations – projects on the backburner while the current downturn lasts.

Several layers of infrastructure are still missing, they say, because Dubai has grown so fast without a coherent urban vision. A secondary road system barely exists and superhighways swirl through the city, segregating the older, poorer areas of small businesses and cheap restaurants, and limiting the life they could give to the city. Walking is almost impossible. A consortium of Japanese and Turkish contractors is building a metro with air-conditioned pods for stations which will include prayer rooms, shops and cafés, but car journeys will still be required to access most of it. Expat mothers will still have to ferry their children to school in huge SUVs and the poor will still be piled onto grim buses and trucked to building sites.

But in the New Zealand-owned Lime Tree Café near the beach in Jumeirah, where young expatriates from all over the world hang out at the weekends, where the espresso is great and the food like home, the talk is about the Idea of Dubai, and the opportunity it now has to slow its breakneck pace and fill in the gaps – in institution building, in regulation, in content development. And at night on the Dubai Creek, where the sparkling urban skyline frames the life on the water – *dhows*, wooden trading boats, carrying small cargo from Iran, India, Yemen and North Africa as they've been doing since the 1830s, when the Maktoum tribe established a free port, and the *abras*, cheap water taxis, ferrying people back home, and the smell of the *shawarmas* cooking on stalls on the banks – you have a sense of what talented people here get excited about, the unique opportunity they have to mix with all races, cultures and religions in an increasingly tolerant cosmopolitan Arab city that is inventing itself.

IN JULY 2002, the rich Arab world's complacency was shattered when the United Nations released its first *Arab Human Development Report*. Written in Arabic by the Egyptian statistician Nader Ferany, it described two decades of failed planning and developmental decline and drew humiliating comparisons with the developing world. The report's main thrust was that poverty and deprivation were about empowerment and literacy at least as much as income, and that the region was way behind global standards of economic, scientific, social and political development. Three hundred and fifty foreign books are translated into Arabic each year throughout the Arab world, with its population of more than three hundred million – a fifth of the number of titles translated in Greece, population eleven million. A clear measure, surely, of a lack of openness to the rest of the world. Israel was the only country in the region to be on a par with other developed nations. China was doing better on most counts.

The report also showed how threadbare was the much-trumpeted tradition of Arab generosity, the oil-rich nations having utterly failed to bring on the hinterland and the peoples of their own region. Millions of Arabs are among the world's poorest, still dependent on foreign aid, in countries where literacy levels and schools are often atrocious and libraries rare.

Since then there have been changes, hopeful signs of a new pattern slowly emerging, serious state-of the-art planning and investment in educational infrastructure at all levels. Philanthropy and volunteerism are being encouraged at last, especially among over-privileged and under-occupied rich young people, with Dubai, Abu Dhabi and Qatar leading the way. Sharia-compliant micro-financing and the mandatory charitable giving through *zakat* are unlikely to solve the structural defects that keep the rural poor trapped in their fate, so any substantial alignment of Islam with social justice is surely a long way off – but money is starting to be invested in people as well as real estate.

The Maktoum Foundation's mission statement is, 'Our region's success depends on creating an environment conducive to knowledge and providing tomorrow's leaders with the motivation to build a better future.' A year ago Sheikh Mohammed, through the foundation, announced the establishment of a $10 billion fund for education throughout the Middle East – by all reports, the world's largest humanitarian investment from a single source. Literacy is the target.

'Reading is an essential tool towards building knowledgeable and innovative societies,' said Sheikh Mohammed, announcing a program to encourage reading and to donate books to underprivileged Arab countries. These would include, he said, 'international literary classics presented in a simplified and attractive manner...to widen the horizon of children and educate them in virtues such as co-operation, tolerance, honesty, integrity, among other typical values of our Arab culture.' Writing books for children would also be stimulated by a program of grants for authors across the Arab world, encouraging them 'to contribute to the noble goals and explore this important literary genre'. This is a start, and a huge one.

Shopping, too, is worth another look. The giant malls are refuges from the heat, which can rise over fifty degrees, places where people work out early in the morning, where community groups meet and people come for all kinds of entertainment. Each February the Dubai Shopping Festival draws people from all over the Arab and European worlds. The slopes of Ski Dubai in the Mall of the Emirates and the ice rink in the recently opened Dubai Mall are thronged day and night. So are the gigantic bookshops and themed malls created as sites for education and culture, where Emirati school parties can be seen taking notes. Here are meticulous and elaborate recreations of the journeys of the great thirteenth-century traveller Ibn Battuta, and displays proclaiming the achievements of the Arab countries he passed through – which cannot be dismissed simply because they lack the authority of western museum culture.

Dubai employs the rhetoric of innovation and creativity constantly, but there is not a lot of beauty yet, or not until you get out into the desert – or so it seemed to me. The light on the rubble from demolitions and roadworks is harsh, the vast swathes of green anachronistic despite their branding as oases. The city feels like a collection of individual, often spectacular, statements. There are some graceful buildings, others gimmicky and pretentious, and more so dull their designers must blush for the missed opportunity. Dubai's narrow economic goals have so far defined it.

But the gaps are starting to be filled in – making those connections to the wider world of art and ideas that are essential for a sustainable, modern Arab city. There is an annual film festival, and earlier this year the first internationally marketed contemporary-art fair drew artists from around the region and dealers from the West, despite the downturn – contemporary Middle Eastern art having been declared the next big thing. Its curator chose to focus on small venues in Dubai's tiny historic quarter of old stone houses, and in an industrial area near the airport some political and hard-hitting new work, especially from Iraq and Palestine, was on display. Not only was Australia playing Pakistan in Twenty20 cricket in the enormous new Dubai stadium while I was there but WOMAD was in Abu Dhabi for three days of non-stop free concerts, with performers such as Senegal's Youssou N'Dour, the Algerian *rai* star Khaled, the British rock band Coldplay, Niger's Etran Finatawa and Tunisia's Dhafer Youssef. Both events attracted huge crowds.

UMM SUQEIM ON the Beach Road, where we are staying with friends, reminds me of Melbourne's affluent low-lying bayside suburbs in high summer: the light and the silence, the occasional palm tree, the sand and the sea at the end of the street, the city skyline in the distance.

Just before sunset I walk to the public beach through the empty streets. Except for two men polishing a black limo, there is no sign of life behind the huge gates and high walls of the compounds. But at this time of the evening the beach is crowded: family groups with picnics, workers from the neighbourhood, a few maids from the Philippines sitting together, men playing cards or chess or strolling past tourists in all stages of undress, Australians in T-shirts identifying themselves. At last count there were about fifteen thousand of us living and working in Dubai and dealing with jokes about the lack of surf.

There seem to be few expatriate mothers and school-age children on the beach. Later I am told that early evening is peak hour for mothers, who must arrange their day around school programs that start at 7.30 am and often do not finish until after five. Driving on Dubai's roads to schools in outer areas can take several hours a day. There is little part-time work and the expat mothers' website, www.expatwoman.com/dubai, carries pleas for car pools and playgroups in Fun City. There are fitness programs on women-only days in the parks, and heartfelt advice on how to survive.

On the fine white sand brought in from somewhere else, I sit and watch the young families, grandmothers setting out food, grandfathers smoking *nagilas*, the women in black *abayas*, the men in jeans and T-shirts. A very young baby is being tossed up and down and dangled in the sea by its proud father. The mother, her abaya tucked up, paddles beside him taking photographs.

In the distance there are yachts silhouetted against the beautiful billowing shape of the Burj Al Arab hotel, and a lone swimmer out beyond the net meant to prevent people being carried away by the currents. The water is warm and waveless and everyone watches as the huge red sun falls into the Arabian Sea.

When I walk back through the dark streets, the local *majlis* is glowing with neon. The majlis, the place of assembly where men congregate to exchange views, is still a feature of male life in parts of the UAE. Traditionally, anyone from the street, however down at heel, could come and sit in the majlis and take part in the debates of the day. Through the open door I can see men in white *dishdashas* lying on divans, smoking their *nagilas* and holding forth.

Our friends' house is one of eight around a pool with a common garden in a compound rented to foreign nationals, most with young children. It is spacious and cool, with marble floors and rugs, and is filled with books and family treasures from Egypt and Europe. I can hear the music before I open the door.

The boys, just home from school and still in their English-style uniforms, are practising their performance for their father's birthday party this evening. Adam, in a green and yellow Australian cricket cap, is playing blues on his saxophone with great feeling. Jo, his young brother, in a Rugby League cap, accompanies him on the piano and makes jokes. They both move effortlessly, sometimes in mid-sentence, between Arabic, German and English, as do their parents. Nadia, the youngest, in her swimming costume, headphones on, is at the kitchen bench making an elaborate birthday card.

The gathering this night includes friends from journalism, finance, education and the law. Some are neighbours from the compound, which is shared by families from Mexico, the US, France, Russia, Germany, Malaysia and Iran. At least four languages are spoken at the table and I struggle, as always. Most have been in Dubai or other parts of the region for some time and clearly regard themselves as part of the place.

The talk at first is about the downturn. Everyone knows someone who has left or might have to, and there is concern, but the consensus here too is that Dubai will emerge stronger, with better institutions and some long-overdue clarification of legal systems. At present there are federal laws, local laws and Sharia – and much confusion. (The current *Guidebook for New Residents* gives lengthy practical advice on 'what to do if you are nicked'.) And someone points out that one of the new universities is offering a degree in Luxury – whatever that might mean.

THE KORAN WAS playing in the cab and the driver didn't look at me or answer when I first gave him directions. Not realising he was praying, I repeated the name of the mall I'd been told to visit. How long had he been in

Dubai, I asked. Six years. He is permitted to go home to see his wife and three children in Islamabad every year. He manages to do so every second year. He lives in a room with a cousin and two Pakistani friends, so that he can send his family most of his meagre pay. Life is very hard, he says cheerfully, but heaven is waiting, God is good, I am a good man and my children are very clever, my wife is a good woman. My life is very very hard but God is good. I am happy that I am a good man and that I will go to heaven.

Without the consolations of religion, life must be hell. Two-thirds of Dubai's foreign-born residents are from India and Pakistan. Three hundred thousand of them live in labour camps between the great arcs of the freeways, hidden from sight. Only if you take a wrong turning as we did, and manage to get through a couple of checkpoints, can you see the camps. Our friend tells the armed guards she is lost. They go through the motions of leaning into the car but we are not turned back.

We drive through endless rows of metal huts with washing strung up between them. Some have old air-conditioning units; most have satellite dishes and benches out the front. Here live most of the indentured labourers who build and maintain Dubai, men who leave home on the promise of better wages and on payment of an upfront fee to an agent who takes their passports and sends them to labour in the UAE while their health and strength last. Once they have paid back their fares, they send home what they can to their impoverished families. Their life expectancy is less than forty-five years.

After the damaging report last year by Human Rights Watch, widespread bad publicity in the western media and some protests by immigrant workers themselves, the men were allowed to form a union. But nothing much has changed. Living conditions have improved a little, overflowing sewerage is 'being rectified', and working during the hottest part of the day in summer is no longer enforceable. But too much still hinges on workers' compliance. Sending money back home is essential.

A large proportion of the GDPs of many of the poorer countries in the region, including Egypt, depends on these remittances from the Gulf; and governments, more often than not, are complicit in maintaining the status quo while trying to secure larger quotas for their workers. This is a world that works because there is no other way for the poor. It works because it is taken for granted by those who benefit most by it. It works because the hierarchies and inequities are ruthlessly maintained.

All imported labour in the UAE is regulated by laws that favour the employer. People can leave their jobs or cancel contracts only if their employer agrees. Domestic servants are utterly dependent on the kindness of their employer. Some treat their maids abominably. Others help them, pay hospital bills, teach their children to share the pool with the maid's kid. Most maids have left their families behind and send them money and gifts, but some husbands and children manage to arrive, living for a time in servants' tiny rooms, perhaps regarding themselves, as did the early immigrants to Australia and North America – also fleeing poverty and persecution – as having the opportunity of a new life for their children. Some may even be allowed to paddle in the sea.

DUBAI, BUILT ON the twin pillars of high living and consumption, is a bellwether for much more than the global recession. The Muslim world is drawing on its own legacies and traditions and substantial moral underpin-nings in its race for modernity – playing by its own rules as well as the rules of the globalised West – and therein lies its fascination. It is worth looking at, it seems to me, and worth remembering that many things get lost in translation.

A young Emirati blogger wrote recently, 'Our export isn't oil, it's hope. Poor Egyptians or Libyans or Iranians or Pakistanis grow up saying, "I want to go to Dubai…" We are showing how to be a modern Muslim state, not an Islamist one.'

The region is on to something.

Hilary McPhee is a Senior Fellow at the University of Melbourne. A writer and editor, she has been living and working in Italy and the Middle East. Her essay 'Seeds of hope' was published in *Griffith REVIEW 24: Participation Society*.

The Ministry of Going In

Christine Paice

This is what happens
I go in
sweep the floor
clear the dishes
interview the Secretary of State over a flat white
and lamington
and ask about Afghanistan and postmodern democracy
in a political vacuum
I forget to ask if she wants sugar with that

This is what happens
I go in
sweep the floor
stack plates
dry cutlery
make sure the knives
are really really shiny
and ask the Minister for Dreaming
if I need a new paradigm to contain my thoughts

There was a knife once that was not
as shiny as the others
it was held up as an example
of what can happen
if you're careless
an unclean knife
half a second and your whole life changes

I go in
sweep the floor
foam the milk
and wonder
if there is too much importance
placed on the size of a takeaway cup
milk jugs are full
of constant fluctuations
and I ask the Minister for Intermittently Good Behaviour
how he is adjusting to the global downturn in fortune cookies
he says there is always another biscuit to be had

This is what happens
sometimes I don't go in
I run in the wind
a gory phantom with a large
coconut shell necklace
I say gory on account of the beetroot I have peeled
and I ask the Minister for Outsized Accessories
if I have gone too far
in my quest and she says
she would wear that far mountain and two intertwined planets
if she could get them round her bloody neck

This is what happens
I go in
there are people
waiting at the counter
I take one not-so-shiny-as-it-should-have-been knife
and excise my bad intentions
and I ask the Minister for Procrastination
is it always as bad as they say
he says not if you catch it in time and do something about it

This is what happened
you went in
made muffins
and cappuccinos
ordered milk and bread
and did something about it
but didn't catch it in time
you asked a doctor what the results were
and he said you'd better come in

You went in
swinging your wooden spoon
like a pendulum
backwards and forwards
into the dark
big black crow cleared his throat
and crow ordered fast
before you had time
to catch your breath
crow caught it for you

You and crow
riding a spoon
into the cold mysterious night
crow's fierce black wings
beating the sky
and I asked the Minister for Last Things if it was true
that after you die you turn into a star
and he said he was looking into it

This is what happens
I go in
water has flooded
from the fridge
I swim round tables
like a dolphin
and I ask the Minister for New Beginnings
what she does when waves threaten to engulf her
and everyday feels strange
she says take a larger boat and throw your guilt over the side

This is what happens
I go in
my hair the shape
of a dolphin's fin
someone hums the music from *Jaws*
and I ask the Minister for Psychic Disinformation
how many times he has blamed poltergeists for his own bad temper
and he says I am in the wrong film

This is what happens
I go in
sweep the floor
rearrange shelving
stare at your photo
and stack my own
small bones
in with the coffee cups
I get everything right
it is one of those rare sparkling days
and I ask the Minister for Myself when I was last elected.

Christine Paice has published two poetry collections, *Mad Oaks* and *Staring at the Aral Sea* (Ginninderra Press, 2003 and 2008). Her work has been featured on Radio National and Jazz Alive.

MEMOIR

The fire this time

Notes on the vernacular of Australian catastrophe

Robert Hillman

THE bushfire debris descends from the night sky with a strangely graceful motion, as if swimming. Leaves and twigs settle softly on the grass, on the flowering plants, on the divided planks of the veranda. A strip of bark a metre long describes a slow spiral around the extended limbs of a weeping spruce before drifting down to the lawn. More charred debris arrives, appearing out of a haze the colour of Coke. I stand enchanted in the suffocating heat of the evening.

There's fire in the mountains and it's coming this way. If the fire reaches our town Anni and I may die. We have gambled on a predicted wind change, absurdly determined to remain loyal to the trees that surround our house. We're not sentimental about trees – we don't believe that they're home to dryads or earth spirits, or that they benefit from being embraced – but it seems wrong to run away while the trees remain staked by their roots. The oldest tree, the weeping spruce, is in its nineties and will burn like a torch if an ember touches it. What do we hope to achieve? If the wind stops the fire on the mountain slopes, the trees will survive without us. If the fire keeps coming, nothing we can do will save the trees, and nothing will save us.

The waiting, though, is pure poetry – the swimming debris, the motionless air, the silence, a patch of sky as bright as mango away to the north where the fire rages – but only because of all that we don't know. The town of Marysville, just over the mountains, has been incinerated – we don't know that. Many people up there had the life scorched from them in seconds as they ran from the towering tongues of flame, but we don't know that. The blast-furnace intensity of the heat at the fire front, capable of igniting a timber structure without the agency of raw flame – that's not the sort of thing we would believe, even if we'd been warned. 'Listen,' says Anni, quietening the hiss of the hose in her hand so that I can hear what she can hear. It's the sound of nothing. The melded play of noises normal at this time of night, when birds sprint for home and dogs try out a few final recreational whines and cars on the Warburton Highway send a muted burr over the river and up the hillsides – gone. We grin at each other as people do

PREVIOUS PAGE: The road between Marysville and Healesville after the 1939 fires. *Source: Department of Primary Industries, Victoria, Australia.*

when they recognise a moment that other, more easily alarmed folk would consider spooky. Because of all that we don't know, we think of ourselves as not easily alarmed.

A HELICOPTER BEATS its way east, and then another. All that we can see are the travelling haloes of their lights. When the pulse of the helicopters dies away we revisit our response to that unnatural hush. Perhaps this *is* genuinely scary? When was the night ever this quiet? And for that matter, where are all our neighbours? Uneasy in a way we weren't five minutes earlier, Anni and I glance at the car in the driveway. If the fire comes we'll have to rely on a harum-scarum dash down the paved road to – to somewhere. To the river? Do people survive in rivers if the bush is burning above them, sitting on the pebble bed with only their heads above the water? Or do they expire like matches, blackened skulls lolling on unburnt bodies?

The cat agitates for a feed. We shrug off the anxiety. Within the house the radio is broadcasting a report from Whittlesea, not so far from Kinglake, where people have died and the charred remains of homes lie smouldering on roadsides. A young woman is interviewing a mother who escaped the inferno with her three children. The mother can barely control her distress, but everything she says is as gripping in its brevity as the verses of an ancient ballad. The fire came. She had two minutes in which to act. Flaming debris fell around her as she ran with her children. She saw horses sprinting in a paddock. A stranger stopped his car and bundled her and the children inside, then made the dash that saved them all. Thank God for that good man. When do we hear voices like this on the radio? When a correspondent is reporting from some hellhole across the seas and a mother is speaking of the massacre in her village. The fire in Kinglake and Marysville is what Kalashnikovs and mortar shells and implacable young men in combat camouflage are to lands more in the news than our own.

Reports come through of probable deaths at Marysville. Although what transpired there in the space of sixty minutes a few hours earlier is still being spoken of cautiously, it's clear enough that the final count of victims will be high. Anni and I return to the garden, damping down vegetation in a way that we are now aware will make not the slightest difference if the fire reaches out for Warburton. But the tranquillity of the night and its lulling influence persists, and I find myself gazing in reverie at the dark humps of the mountains across the river. I can distinguish a faint violet glow beyond the topmost trees. If I were to start walking due north and press on until within that light, I would be in Marysville. I project images of the Marysville I remember, the day-tripper destination where you would stop to admire the tall trees and wander about thinking in a Willy Wordsworth way of nature as the nurse of the soul, and call into a Bide-a-Wee bakery for a pink lamington and a takeaway latte. And then I think of the fire rearing from the kindling of the forest floor, throwing arms of flame into the oil-laden foliage, striding into the town like a living thing, a monster of appetite, limbs ablaze and red mouth roaring.

LIKE THE PEOPLE in Marysville in the years before the fire came, like people everywhere, I have meditated on curtain falls: car crash; cancer; too far out from the strip of sand where my beach towel lies folded; dancing about the dinner table with a lump of gristle wedged in my windpipe; whatever. But not fire. And this is what came into the lives of people in that pretty mountain town: the death you dare not contemplate. Why should it not be my death, and Anni's? Why should I not become the written about rather than the writer – the guy among the big trees in Warburton (and this is tragic) who stood with a hand-held hose while the monster was leaping valleys toward the fodder of his combustible garden?

The cat cries out from a secure distance, uneasy about the bright shaft of water I'm directing one way then another. I soothe him affectionately, but what I'm thinking is: does fearing so dreadfully one particular type of death prevent it coming for you? It didn't work in Kinglake; it didn't work in Marysville. I call out to Anni, 'Should we go to Carlton?' Anni has a house there, on the fringe of Melbourne's CBD; no bushfire will ever trouble Carlton. Anni replies, 'Should we?'

I gaze up at the weeping spruce, the lacework of its highest boughs silhouetted against the sky like a mantilla. Anni won't go unless I go. It would seem to her too trite for words if I were to order her into the car, kiss her goodbye, then face the flames alone. Her generation of women is easily irritated by men acting out fantasies of valour. So what I ought to do is jump in the car with her and the cat, because she wants to go, I can tell that; she thinks we're now more stupid than stubborn, and every wrenching voice we hear on the radio endorses her new conviction. All that we don't know notwithstanding, all that we *do* know should persuade us to run. On this day that's taking so long to pass, Victoria is among the hottest places on earth, forty-seven degrees and higher, with embers fattening with the nourishment of a north wind. And this smallish state sprinkled with place names from a pair of pretty islands that have never known a bushfire has been turned to tinder by a decade of drought. Listen to the people on the radio – listen to them. 'It came from nowhere, I had ten seconds, I just grabbed the kids and ran, I don't know about the others, I think they're dead.' I can't set a match to the kindling in a fireplace without thinking of *autos-da-fe* and the horror of administered agony. Do I intend to scream out the last of my life while the house and the trees hiss around me like a sentence pronounced?

'SO, DO WE go?' Anni calls from the blurry darkness somewhere near the birch.

'Let's wait a bit. Do you think?'

'If you like. Seems rather futile.'

So we stay. We wander dazedly about the place with our plastic hoses. The leaves of liquid amber rattle briefly as a vagrant breeze runs up the trunk. I have no idea of what I'm doing, of my real motivation. Maybe it's snobbery? So many people have run away. I saw a man down in the main street much earlier in the evening. 'The fire's jumped the lines!' he shouted. 'It's jumped the lines!' Then he sat down to wait for the 6.20 bus to Lilydale. That man was in a panic of a certain sort, and he was wearing a *Big Brother* T-shirt. I would never shout anything in the streets. I would never wear a *Big Brother* T-shirt. The shouting man has come to represent in my imagination the type of person who runs away. My disdain for a *Big Brother* T-shirt is strong enough to overcome my dread of death by fire. And even if I knew everything that I don't know, I would still refuse to associate myself with the sort of person who shouts in the street and wears a *Big Brother* T-shirt. This is a curious thing, because when I was researching heretics for a book I'm still writing I was distressed by the refusal of all sorts of people – Spanish Jews of the fifteenth century, English Protestants persecuted by Thomas More, Chinese intellectuals critical of Mao – to throw their beliefs overboard and escape the stake, the noose, the garrotte.

Meanwhile, more of what we don't know is about to enter the state's annals of disaster. The Bunyip State Forest to the south of Warburton is ablaze, and veins of flame are running up Brittania Ridge to the west. The fire storm that destroyed Marysville has raced down the gullies of the O'Shannassy catchment to the north-east, wiping out approximately fifty times the area of forest that Anni and I (in the prissy manner of green folk everywhere) were trying to save from loggers. Another fire, due east, has broken into the Upper Yarra Dam catchment; to the north-west, beyond Mount Riddell, the Kinglake fire has leapt into small towns to the west of Healesville. The body count on the radio is stalled at four, but the actual number of dead is almost fifty times that, and almost all who are to die in this summer's fires are already dead. The complex of blazes known for the time being as the Murrindindi Mill fire is also being carried north through forest and pasture, towards Yea and Alexandra on the Goulburn River. All of these things that we don't know would reveal, if we knew them, that the towns of the Upper Yarra – Warburton, East Warburton, McMahons Creek and Reefton – sit in the hollow of a huge horseshoe of fire. Only freakish good fortune and the wherewithal of some thousands of firefighters will save the whole of the Upper Yarra from destruction.

AT THREE IN the morning, Anni and I take what we know and what we don't know and go to bed. We'll sleep in shifts. Anni opens *Revolutionary Road* at chapter one and when I next open my eyes, she's at page fifty. The normal morning show on the radio has given way to a service dedicated to the fires. The presenter accepts calls from people amplifying the message of an earlier caller: 'Get out while the getting's good.' A man from Strathewen struggles to describe the speed of the fire that tore his town apart twelve hours ago – its ferocity, the intensity of the heat. A woman from Kinglake has made it to the evacuation centre at Whittlesea but is grieving for her husband, who she fears may have perished.

I stand on the veranda with the voices of fire victims and firefighters playing behind me. The sky is the muted blue seen in paintings of seventeenth-century Dutch and Flemish townscapes. The birds have gone, all of them. Helicopters beat their way east. Alerts for residents of forty or more towns are being broadcast, including ours. A presenter announces that he can now confirm that Marysville has suffered the devastating impact of a firestorm. The death toll of a number of fires still raging appears likely to grow, he says, qualifying the message with professional caution: 'Nothing is confirmed at this stage.'

One of the worst things happening anywhere on earth at this time is happening in broad patches of Victoria, and the voices that confirm this make it less likely than ever that I will head for safety. When the radio is playing in the morning I'm usually listening to stylised hyperbole, the patter of gossip, the laments of footballers caught pissing or rooting in public, torrents of complaint, clever lies. But now I'm listening to the terrible beauty of tales in which there is no exaggeration, no sentimentality. When a caller who has escaped the flames says 'horror', it *is* horror; dread is dread; sorrow is sorrow. I'm absorbed by the way in which disaster restores the vigour of language, and by remaining within this horseshoe of fire I'm earning the right to be absorbed. This is the vernacular of Australian catastrophe, the remorseless bushfire, and its stories reveal much more about the wherewithal of the broad community than those of ill-advised young men clambering up cliffs on a Turkish peninsula.

So if Anni and I escape being withered to char by the closing fires, this is what I'll settle for: I stayed because the people in the fires spoke with such spare beauty of what they'd endured, and because a nong in a *Big Brother* T-shirt was shouting in the street, and because our trees would have been compelled to remain where they stood and become flame while I was drinking gin in fire-free Carlton.

SIX WEEKS AFTER that night of enchantment, dread and irrational conviction, Anni and I are driving over the black spur north of Healesville where the highway climbs to Dom Dom Saddle. Mountain ash flourishes here, conscientiously nurtured after the fires of 1939, the slender trunks as straight as pillars. Before the fires of February the forest was a collage of greens, intense at ground level where the ferns thrive, fading to a shimmery borage-coloured shade at the crowns of the ash. The ferns are gone now, leaving the bare earth exposed. The tree trunks are charred but the fawn husks of leaves, emptied of oil, still cling to twigs and boughs. And this is now a forest from which shadows have been banished in all their variety: the dappling of the forest floor; the deep caves of darkness in places where the light can't reach; the criss-crossing of shapes printed on the ground cover below. At first it seems as if the forest has been stripped of all nuance, but before long the austerity of the scene comes to seem less a diminishment of vigour and variety than the creation of a new beauty altogether. It's a cleaner and more disciplined expression that makes the lavish use of green in the remaining unburnt patches of forest seem superficial. It complements perfectly the pared-down narratives of the bushfire survivors, as if the chastened forest had experienced its own conversion to austerity from excess.

Over the weeks following the fires we watched and listened to a number of memorial services for the victims of the fires. All of them struggled to fit response to event. A concatenation of clichés is no less lowering to the spirits just because it purports to honour dead people. The language of tributes and memorials is a language of capitals, and probably cannot be other; heft and emphasis reliably complement gloom, at least. But to my mind, a finer memorial to the suffering of the bushfire victims would be the unrehearsed narratives of those who escaped the holocaust of February: *I ran with the kids. I saw horses sprinting in the paddock. A man stopped his car and helped us in. Thank God for that good man.*

Robert Hillman is a Melbourne author. His most recent publication is *The Rugmaker of Mazar-e-Sharif*, with Najaf Mazari (Insight). His account of his experiences with asylum seekers, 'Beyond Pity', was published in *Griffith REVIEW 15: Divided Nation*.

FICTION

THE REAL THING

CATHERINE HARRIS

OUR family's never been very good at 'family'. When my nephew was conceived my sister and I weren't even speaking, some silly argument about my Northwestern Wildcats T-shirt she'd borrowed when she was sixteen which came back filthy weeks later, torn with a smudge across its logo. At the time she said it was an accident, that I was making too much of it, that the stain would probably come right out if I took it to the drycleaners, their chemicals able to dissolve almost anything (though it never did), besides which, what right did I have to be upset when decades earlier I'd borrowed her copy of *The Snow Queen* without even asking and then lost it and hadn't even apologised? That was the same year that Mum chucked out our Fair Isle jumpers, just after we got back from Chicago, eight months into our eighteen-month stay, departing from the bitter chill of the northern winter into the morass of a scorching summer daze, jetlagged and distraught, the searing heat of a Melbourne February no place for woollen cable knits even if they had been hand-made by our grandmother. Days later Mum said she wished she hadn't done it, that they might have made nice keepsakes she'd realised, but by then Dad was well and truly dead, his lithe body rigormortised into its own semi-rigid phase, and it was too late to change her mind: the rubbish had been collected that morning.

My nephew cries intermittently; it starts as a gentle squeak but rapidly intensifies until my sister puts him on her breast. If her breast isn't available he can be temporarily bought off with a little finger to suck (he hasn't been graduated to dummies yet), but that only lasts so long. If he's really hungry, he'll soon want the real thing. I wash my hands extra thoroughly before inserting my pinkie upside-down into his mouth, not wanting to overwhelm his small newborn-baby senses with the aroma of chopped garlic or to spoil his pristine palate with the flavour of spaghetti bolognese or whatever else I have prepared for dinner that evening, shocked that this can even be allowed to happen: 'Why have they let you out of the hospital?' I ask him as his determined tongue works at my unyielding fingertip. 'You're way too young to be left alone with the likes of us.' His tiny body rallies around my finger, minute fists clenched against my fist, his head cradled in the palm of my other hand, fiercely latched on the way we all fiercely latch on, grasping for nourishment, ever grateful for those hands. And then, even though his stomach is apparently full of gas, his pained writhing attesting to the fact, he pulls his head away as though in complete agreement and projectile vomits right across my shirt.

I think that's what Dad would have called a definite phase transition. For him everything was molecules and combinations of molecules, the ability of matter to shift from gas or liquid to solid form, and then sometimes back again, holding particular fascination. 'In some instances you can't even tell which state is which,' I remember him saying. Glaciers being his favourite example, the way they could slip down a mountainside like slow-moving treacle, looking for all the world as solid as brass.

LIKE DAD, THE baby was touch-and-go for a while. First he took forever to move into the right position and then he got stuck. They waited for him to unstick himself, but he didn't and then his heart-beat faltered. I felt like I was twelve years old again as I watched the heart-rate monitor, staring into the dark, waiting for my father to re-emerge, the sounds of screaming audible off in the distance, then a nurse slamming the emergency button with the flat of her hand, saying *we can't guarantee a good outcome here.*

This is what happens when you're not paying attention, when the desire to please overtakes natural caution and suddenly you're pregnant or fat or skating on thin ice, the cheap satisfaction of immediate gratification outweighing your ability to see straight, to make sensible decisions, because it's all so new or delicious or your daughters are pleading with you *please, one last time*, so that even though it's late in the season you know you won't get a chance to do it again for a while (and besides, you're sick of them always saying you're no fun), the tremendous consequences masked by the urgent flurry of it all like vapour lifting off a roiling sea.

Sometimes I still dream about Chicago: we might be carving pumpkins for Halloween, Dad showing us how to find the grain of the vegetable, using his pocket knife to dissect the eyes and teeth, explaining how everything has a natural direction or tendency (even fifteen-pound jack-o'-lanterns); or it might be evening, the four of us sitting around on the couch sipping hot chocolates with marshmallows, Dad saying *ain't life grand* as candlelight flickers from the jack-o'-lantern, casting great toothy shadows on the living room walls. Other times I might even dream about the duck pond. The snow will have dusted the park fantasy-white and we'll be gliding around in our thick parkas practising skating backwards or performing our newly mastered half turns, laughing about how we'd never be able to do this in Australia, the weather never getting sufficiently cold, and I'll forget all about the softened ice (a freak accident, they said), how it was just waiting to break, that awful cracking sound, and then the sudden hole and Dad falling down in it.

MY SISTER'S HUSBAND left her at twenty-nine weeks. He didn't love her any more, he said. That, and that she looked like she had a giant watermelon stuffed under her jumper. *Have you got a giant water-melon stuffed under there?* he said, laughing. His way of relieving the tension, as though it were funny, being estranged from your body by another body, something you were responsible for but not. Now she looks like a tired version of my sister who barely has the energy to make herself a cup of tea, let alone to argue with me. Mum and I hover around like nursemaids, fetching nappies and baby wipes, trying not to trip over each other as we get in each other's way. At night I coax myself to sleep by systematically not thinking about all the annoying things Mum's done throughout the day. Either that or I recite multi-plication tables. This is called meditation, I've been told, the practice of clocking events in your mind's eye (*your thoughts are a moving stream*) then letting them go through to the keeper.

Dad's nickname for Mum was Firecracker, a well-earned epithet, though he mostly referred to her as Mother, an almost offensively innocuous moniker I realise now, yet when I raise it she gives me her wide-eyed blink as though she doesn't quite understand, the province of Dad and his peccadilloes remaining well and truly off-limits. His pet name for me was Zigzag, the hieroglyphic sign for water, his favourite chemical substance (putatively for its life-giving properties, but also because of its multiphase potential, its transitions between liquid, solid and vapour often visible to the naked eye), though one time when my sister was really angry she said that Dad had only called me that because of my changeability. 'He never knew what mood you'd be in when he got home.'

'At least I had a nickname,' I countered.

'More than one,' she muttered under her breath.

This is how it goes with us, each quietly blaming the other, still. There are times when I think Dad would have appreciated the way his memory constantly plays about our lives and other times when I think he would have found it infuriating, an affront to common sense, as though in his absence we had moved backwards rather than forwards, any advances our family unit might have made towards firmness and solidity being slowly undone by our inability to accept the basic facts.

MUM TIDIES UP the flower arrangements, stripping the dead flowers from the floral foam, then transposing the remaining stems into vases. 'What are you doing?' I ask her, it being perfectly obvious what she's doing, but I don't think it's her place to be doing what she's doing, it being my sister's business to decide about her own flowers, though I know Mum hates flowers. Depressing, she always says (even though these are happy flowers, sent to celebrate the new baby, I remind her), ever since Dad died and the house, musty from our abandonment, overnight filled with a dank mass of floral arrangements, so many they seemed to crowd every surface, fronted by their neat little cards all politely lamenting the tragedy of our loss.

When we left Chicago the snow had turned a dirty grey. As we took off in the taxi you could see the neon-yellow patches where people had urinated on it and other places where they'd tossed their cigarette butts, along with all their other rubbish like Coke cans and beer bottles which were now wedged into the unsightly banks lining the footpaths and the sides of roads, like a cross-section of human detritus captured in frozen form for the length of the season, until the weather warmed and the water washed it away.

I knew that wasn't what Dad would have wanted me to picture when he was explaining to me about 'transitional phase', but in the vacuum of his absence it seemed that all this seasonal warming and melting and converting from one form to another, solid to liquid to gas, matter to spirit to soul, conceived to living to dead, was shaded by a cold miserable grey that refused to be brightened no matter how many pairs of brilliantly coloured gloves I donned or snug, cheerful scarves I wound around my wound-up neck. That's when I started to hate winter.

But we hold onto things. The wrong things.

When my sister told me she was pregnant my first thought was *no, not a winter baby.* I thought of the cold and grey bleak winter Chicago streets, of interminably long plane trips with Mum quietly weeping beside me when she thought we were asleep. How the air hostesses were particularly nice to us, bringing us special drinks and colouring books, and then the sight of Dad's coffin being ferried to the terminal after we'd landed, the heat outside like an oven, rising in shimmers from the tarmac.

It wasn't until after the baby was actually born that, one evening watching *Bewitched* on TV, I found myself thinking again about the magic of snowflakes. Dad's colleagues had been obsessed with them, their hexagonal structure, always marvelling at their evanescent beauty, like shooting stars, unable to be grasped or held onto but spectacular in their flight, their rapid burst from being to nothingness powering the universe, as all beauty invariably does, harnessing cold the way solar panels channel heat.

SCIENTISTS' CHILDREN CAN be a sceptical lot. My sister returned to the chemist three times before she was able to accept what the little pink plus at the end of the plastic wand was telling her that she, a dedicated consumer of the contraceptive pill, was pregnant. 'The pill's only 99 per cent effective,' she reminded her husband. But, as he later repeated to me, they were pretty good odds. Now she's having trouble deciding on the baby's name. Various options have been touted – Franklin, Milo, Jeremy – but as yet none of them has stuck; the idea that you could pluck a child's name out of thin air is ridiculous, she says. Mum is convinced the whole naming dilemma is simply a by-product of my sister's indecisiveness – *a chip off the old block*, she's fond of saying – whereas it's plain as day to everyone else that the issue is completely bound up with my sister's marriage breakdown and her ambivalence about the pregnancy itself. 'You might as well give me your two cents,' she says, after Mum's run through yet another list of what she terms 'suitable appellations', summarily knocking them down one after the other almost faster than I can articulate the sounds.

'Choose your own name, then,' I say, losing my patience, wishing she'd just done that right off the bat, the quandary of babies' names and birth registrations and whether or not one should be having children in the first place lying well beyond my jurisdiction. Plus, she's just giving me the shits.

'Fine, then. I will.'

'Good.'

'Good yourself.'

'Fine. Just don't call him after Dad.'

In *The Snow Queen* an evil troll invents a magic mirror that reflects all beauty as ugliness. After the mirror shatters, the tiny splinters pierce people's bodies, freezing their hearts and blinding their souls to virtue. Even when my sister and I are bickering, the irony is not lost on me that what drives us most apart is the very thing that binds us most together, as though the cold of Dad's passing had entered our hearts preventing us from appreciating anything kind or generous about each other. We are attracted and repelled as magnets are attracted and repelled, our currents drawing and resisting in almost equal force depending on how we are positioned to one another. There's no clarity. It's not as though Dad's accident brought some truth to light. He is dead. That is all. This is what I mean when I say to her that *it is what it is*. No amount of honorary naming can redeem us. Refrozen snowflakes are just ice. Water has no memory. The baby has come to us whole and unique – he is an entire, separate person.

MUM WHISKS THROUGH the house, the tsk-tsk of busywork, washing and cleaning and preparing special meals. Today, for example, she'll bake pumpkin pie, she announces. Her specialty. An unpalatable briny custard concoction she picked up in the Midwest. She walks from room to room asking if there's anything more we need from the shops — milk, apples, bread? — as alarm bells start ringing in my head as loudly as they did fifteen years ago when the dish was first showcased at my cousin's confirmation party. 'Your mother's a lousy cook,' my aunt said behind Mum's back. Except that Mum was behind her back and so heard every word. 'The recipe had no sugar,' Mum later argued in her defence, though she also added that Dad's family had always hated her and blamed her for everything so why shouldn't she speak her mind? 'If it wasn't for you girls they wouldn't bother with me at all,' she wailed. And then, on the recipe again: 'There must have been a mistake.'

I was so embarrassed I hid in the back garden, taking off up the side of the house once the fracas had died down and I was sure everyone had returned to their canapés, the low simmer of small talk now firmly fixed on *poor Henrietta and her unfortunate children*, this being our extended family's default setting. What I've yet to reconcile is why the intensity of the feelings continue to be as blistering today as when I was crouched beneath my aunt's camellia bush, swatting bees, trying not to cry. It makes me wonder if perhaps emotions don't also have phases (though I would have hoped that this one might have passed by now) fixed in stable form like matter until their conditions are changed. Liquid doesn't just transform into vapour and then evaporate away. First it must be exposed to heat. 'You know, Mum, I hate your pumpkin pie,' I tell her as she compiles her shopping list.

She puts down her pen and looks at me, completely aghast. 'Well, stuff you,' she finally says. 'I hate the way you eat your cornflakes dry, without adding any milk.'

AT THE CHRISTENING my nephew snivels and cries — an appropriate response, I think, to all that ruckus. The priest drips water on his head, small droplets rolling into his eyes, which I dab with a tiny embroidered handkerchief, the same one my uncle dabbed at me.

Earlier that morning my sister came to find me as I was minding the baby while she got ready for church. 'There's something I have to tell you,' she said. 'I know in the scheme of things it probably doesn't matter, but you were right when you accused me of taking Dad's Wildcats T-shirt to spite you. I did. You were always so philosophical about everything. I was trying to make you angry.'

I don't know what I'd expected her to say, but in that moment I was so relieved it wasn't something more alarming I would have forgiven her just about anything. 'If it makes you feel any better, I never lost your *Snow Queen* book,' I confessed. 'I kept it because Dad had inscribed it *To my daughter*. I liked pretending he'd written it to me.'

For a second there I thought she might attempt to seize the moral high ground, but she didn't.

'I'm really sorry,' she said.

And I was too.

So this is how it is now, our family. All chips off the old block, but slightly new. Even the baby, who I'll concede actually looks a lot like Dad, or the way I remember Dad to be. He has the same chin and eyes and when he smiles I can see Dad smiling at me, the whole history of our clan distilled down to this one tiny moment, transition after transition, phase after phase, me and my nephew tucked up under a rug on the couch, my finger in his mouth, gently rocking.

Catherine Harris' short stories have been published in Australia, Britain and the US. Her first novel, *The Jane Manifesto*, was shortlisted for both the 2008 HarperCollins Varuna Awards for Manuscript Development and the 2009 Dundee International Book Prize. She is currently working on her next novel with a grant from the Australia Council. This story won the 2009 Ulrick Prize for short fiction.

Made in China

Saving capitalism with socialism?

Michael Wesley

FOR the first time in history, a communist country is in a position to bring down global capitalism. The Chinese Communist Party, if it were to sell the $763 billion in US Treasury bonds it holds, would trigger a massive devaluation in those bonds and the value of the American dollar, thereby bringing the world economy to its knees. This situation occurs only twenty years after sledgehammers broke down the Berlin Wall, supposedly heralding the triumph of liberal democracy; and only a decade after the Asian financial crisis, which supposedly proved the superiority of western models of capitalism.

Of course, China's Communism Version 2.0 will do nothing of the sort. The health of China's economy, and ultimately the ability of the Chinese Communist Party to stay in power, depends on the health of global capitalism. In September 2008, as Japan reduced its exposure to US Treasury bonds by $12 billion, China increased its exposure by $43.6 billion. In the meantime, Chinese leaders have plaintively urged the American government to bolster the US economy and safeguard the value of China's investments. As the American budget deficit rattles towards a trillion dollars, it is China's two trillion dollars in foreign-exchange reserves that are seen as the salvation for the world economy. An often-repeated verse in China these days observes:

In 1921, only socialism could save China.

In 1978, only capitalism could save China.

In 1991, only China could save socialism.

In 2009, only China can save capitalism.

Some suggest that China's self-interest in saving global capitalism represents the ultimate triumph of capitalism, a tumbling of the final domino of communist command economies. A closer look reveals far fewer reasons for confidence. While market reform has advanced in China, the state's control over exchange rates, the capital account, investment and infrastructure, energy pricing and development planning reveals an economy that is a long way from being capitalist. There is much evidence that the new administration of Hu Jintao and Wen Jiabao has halted and even reversed some pro-market reforms. And listening to the thinkers within the Chinese Communist Party inspires even less confidence that the country is rushing headlong into the arms of capitalism. The party is in little doubt that history is on the side of socialism; Marxist thinkers predicted globalisation and their reading of its contradictions and convolutions has been borne out.

WITH NO APPARENT sense of irony or self-consciousness, those who two years ago were urging China to be a 'responsible stakeholder' in world affairs are now proposing it play a leadership role in rescuing and reforming the global economy. Luminaries such as the economist Fred Bergsten and the former US national security adviser Zbigniew Bryzenski have proposed a 'G2' structure of collaboration between China and the US to tackle a range of global issues. Many had expected that China – fresh from a dominating performance in the Beijing Olympics, increasingly comfortable as a Security Council powerbroker, and with a newly authoritative voice on global and regional matters – would transition easily into the elite ranks of powers that have controlled world politics for generations. Many thought that being elevated to parity with the US would be China's dream come true.

But Beijing was quick to reject such notions. At a China–European Union Summit in May, Premier Wen Jiabao said, 'It is impossible for a couple of countries or a group of big powers to resolve all global issues…Some say that world affairs will be managed solely by China and the United States. I think that view is baseless and wrong.'

A handful of democracies – the US, the UK, France, Germany, Japan, Canada – has since the end of World War II constituted an oligarchy that controls world affairs: global institutions, trade, finance. Now an autocratic state is insisting on the 'democratisation' of international relations, the provision of an equal and respected voice to all countries on global affairs, the greater use of multilateral co-operation and the right of all countries to order their affairs as they wish.

China has used its greater prominence during the global economic crisis not to assert global leadership, but to continue to build its relationships with a range of developing and developed countries. China has been finalising collaboration agreements almost non-stop since October 2008, and its dance card doesn't meet most conceptions of the global popularity parade: Pakistan, Singapore, Vietnam, Russia, Indonesia, Kazakhstan, Peru, Malawi, Malaysia, Egypt, Saudi Arabia, Tanzania, Thailand, Argentina, Myanmar, Iran, Turkey, Kuwait, Cuba. It is striking how often, and how earnestly, Chinese leaders continue to stress the same solidarity with developing countries that Mao did in the 1950s.

For all its economic might and international prestige, China still is a developing country. Even now, as its economy steams up the world rankings in terms of overall size, China's per-capita income is in the same league as Egypt's and El Salvador's. If all goes well for China and India, they will become great powers, but they will be the poorest great powers in history. The shift in power position will not be accompanied by a shift in mindset, from have-nots to haves.

THE GULF BETWEEN power and mindset is already apparent. The new developing economic powers – China, India, Brazil – have little incentive or inclination to join the few wealthy economies that attempt to structure world trade and investment to their advantage. In November, Chinese President Hu called for a new world order that is 'fair, just, inclusive and orderly'. Brazilian

President Lula da Silva concurred: 'We need to have other countries and other continents for more democratic, more plural decisions.' The poor powerhouses have opposed the stitching-up of tidy global trade deals. No longer do they need to rely on moral appeals to a New International Economic Order, against the global oligopolists; now all they need is absolute economic clout. And, as always, muscle is proving much more potent than morality.

A major part of China's solidarity with other developing countries is its insistence that there is no one valid or superior path to economic development. Each to its own, depending on its specific national circumstances, the wishes of its people and solidarity with other developing countries. This, of course, is an extension of China's insistence that no other country or organisation has the right to lecture it on its internal affairs. Let the country without a blemish on its human-rights record cast the first vote in Geneva.

Still, the sub-prime crisis presented an opportunity to lecture the Americans that was too good to pass up. During a visit to Mexico in February, Vice-President Xi Jinping hit back at American accusations about the value of the Chinese currency: 'There are some foreigners who have eaten their heart's content and have nothing better to do than point their fingers at our affairs. China does not, first, export revolution; second, export poverty or hunger; or third, cause unnecessary trouble for you. What else is there to say?' The same month, at Davos, Premier Wen blamed the global crisis on the 'inappropriate macroeconomic policies of some economies and their unsustainable model of development, characterised by prolonged low savings and high consumption'.

But beneath the bluster, Beijing is obviously worried about its image abroad. It is trying to reduce recourse to the death penalty, improve energy efficiency and minimise greenhouse emissions, stamp out corruption and reduce the spread of HIV. But in doing so it confronts huge complexities, contradictions and feedback loops. The need to maintain high production confounds environmental targets; the need for affordable energy creates pollution and bottlenecks; the need to contain China's growing drug problem means death sentences continue to be common.

China, and its role in the world around it, defies simple categorisation. To look closely at the country is to realise how little you really comprehend it, in all its complexity and contradictions. It is of a vastness and singularity that defies casual understanding, that repels those who want to fit China into their world view, but don't have time to grapple with its complexities. And China itself makes it hard: it is changing faster than any society ever before; it is deliberately opaque; it is increasingly a society of many, furiously discordant voices. This is why the 'China debate' in the West has been characterised by one observer as 'the sprinkling of a few easily gleaned facts on deeply held prejudices'.

Europeans and North Americans may be able to get away with such economy of effort. But not Australia. The time has come to take China seriously, to learn to listen to what it is really saying and to learn to think about what this means. Because one little-noted Chinese export is complexity and contradiction. And the costs of getting China wrong could be very high.

Michael Wesley is the executive director of the Lowy Institute for International Policy and was until recently the director of the Griffith Asia Institute. His essays have been published in *Griffith REVIEW: The Lure of Fundamentalism, Up North, In the Neighbourhood* and *Hidden Queensland.*

MEMOIR

The story behind sister's new villa

Changing fortunes in Beijing

Frances Guo

STANDING in my red coat, next to my luggage on the shining granite floor, I wait anxiously. Facing Gate 10, my eyes survey the cavernous space around me – the dramatic high ceilings, the bright futurist décor and the endless rows of check-in counters.

So this is it: the new Beijing airport. Like a proud phoenix, it spreads its giant wings to the east of the city. When I first saw its striking shape, in Sydney, my eyes were glued to the television screen. I wished I was at the Olympics: such an intoxicating time, all the excitement, all the pride – for China, for all Chinese faces around the world.

But the glory was soon tainted – by poisoned milk, sick babies and the global recall of food containing Chinese dairy products. Even this new complex was caught up in scandal. Not long after the airport revealed its grandeur to the world's top leaders and athletes, the former head of the Beijing Airport Group faced the death sentence, accused of massive corruption.

A WOMAN IN a red down jacket rushes through Gate 10 and looks around. I wave; she hurries towards me. 'Have you been waiting long?' Second Sister asks, a little embarrassed, reaching for my suitcase.

'Not long – don't worry,' I reassure her, our eyes lock, full of warmth.

As we push the trolley out the gate, the bitter wind strikes my face. I pull up my collar. Second Sister's steps quicken. Her gloved finger presses a button and the boot of a chilli-red car pops open right in front of us.

'Is this yours?' I ask.

'Yes, what do you think?'

'Smart,' I reply, admiring its smooth lines and the shining V-above-W emblem on the grille.

'Hop in.' Second Sister tilts her head. I open the door, slump onto the cream-coloured leather seat. After turning off the main road, we pass some open fields, then slow down to go through a black iron gate. A man in dark

PREVIOUS PAGE: Detail of portrait of Mao Tse Tung on the one yuan banknote, People's Republic of China. Photographer: Jovan Nikolic. *Source: dreamstime.com*

uniform and beige cap raises his right hand solemnly, fingers pointing towards temple, palm facing chin. I recognise the salute of the People's Liberation Army, a gesture my sister and I know well from our childhood in a Chinese army compound.

'But he's only a security guard, not a PLA soldier?' I say, puzzled.

'Many of them were PLA soldiers,' replies Second Sister. 'They say you can judge an estate's value by how tall and handsome its security guards are.'

Passing rows of houses, our car pulls into the carport in front of a two-storey house. 'Here we are,' Second Sister announces, leading the way with my suitcase. Past the picket fence, across a small patch of frozen lawn, we enter the front door and change into slippers.

'Wow,' I exclaim, awed by a huge open-plan space. Facing us, French lounges feature delicate details: curvy frames and classic floral covers. To the right, a long table and eight high-back chairs define the dining area. Beyond that, a kitchen sparkles with appliances, a granite island bench and a small red TV on the wall. Next to the lounge, a large floral painting radiates warmth; across the room is a large flat-screen television.

The screen is huge, at least three times the size of mine in Sydney, which is not small by Australian standards. First Sister's admonition echoes in my mind: 'Even a landlord's home is not as lavish.' I smile and wonder what our landlord grandparents would think of Second Sister's new house. If only they had survived those miserable years almost half a century ago – kicked out of their home, thrown into a mud house in a village, bullied by peasants, sweating on the farm they had leased before it was confiscated by the communists.

Second Sister's voice breaks the silence. 'Come, I'll show you upstairs.' Putting my luggage in the guest room, we cross the expensive timber floor and go upstairs. As we step into the master bedroom, my jaw drops. The room makes my bedroom in Sydney seem like a closet. My eyes wander – taking in the indulgent king-size bed, the vast walk-in wardrobe, the ensuite with sparkling spa bath – and freeze. Standing against a wall, half a room away from the bed, is a screen the size of the one downstairs. The bedroom feels like a small cinema. 'Perhaps the TV is a bit too big,' Second Sister says, sensing my reaction.

I follow her to the next room. Facing a large timber desk, matching bookshelves fill the wall from floor to ceiling. Under a bay window, cushions with delicate covers spread across cream-coloured seats. Braided ropes carefully tie intricate silk curtains to each side. Every detail seems to say, 'We love our new home and, as you can see, no expense has been spared.'

'Chenchen, Little Auntie is here,' my sister calls, passing a wall of built-in wardrobes and knocking on a door.

'Ai, coming,' a voice responds. A slim girl, tall as me, stands in front of us in pyjamas.

'Hey, Chenchen, taller again,' I tease. 'What're you up to?' I check out her new room: circular bed, another TV, cushions strewn around the floor, books piled on a low desk.

'Studying…' She rolls her eyes.

'Well, good luck.' Sensing her time pressures, we withdraw.

'She is preparing to study overseas,' my sister explains as we head downstairs.

'So soon?' I raise my eyebrows. 'Doesn't she want to work for a while first?'

'No. When she finishes university, jobs will be even harder to find. I heard nowadays some graduates even burn joss sticks at temples, pray for jobs.'

'Where is Chenchen going?'

'America.' The word slips off her tongue. 'It's her choice and we encourage her, while we still have some Chairman Mao left in our pocket,' my sister adds. We laugh.

It is good to see she still has her spirit and cheeky sense of humour. I love the new nickname for the red banknotes with Mao's portrait: Chairman Mao. It is also ironic – the man who put so few banknotes into pockets for so long is now on all of them. Today, despite the countless traumas and the weeping ghosts his political campaigns left behind, he still smiles at us from the red wall of Tiananmen. At least now his people have more money in their pockets, and enough freedom to joke about him, their old Great Leader, almost openly, without being condemned, arrested or executed.

While Second Sister makes a pot of green tea, I wander around the vast lounge room. Next to the giant screen, I pick up a small photo: a toddler on a bare cement floor in front of a cheap wardrobe. Under a red hat, a big smile fills her sweet little face. As I gaze at the photo, memories of my sister's first home flood back.

I LOCKED MY bike up among an army of rusty black bicycles below the dark grey building. Climbing the cement stairs, I turned left on the second floor. In the dim light from a greasy bulb, as the smoke and the aroma of stir-fried spring onions rose above the hot woks, I walked between gas bottles and cooking tops along both sides of a narrow corridor.

At the third doorway on the right, I stopped. 'Second Sister?' I called through the half-length door curtain.

'Come in.' My sister flipped the curtain aside, her face and forehead soaked in sweat. Chenchen cried in her father's arms, her tiny face red and moist. The room felt like a sauna. Hot and thick, the air stuck to my skin like a wet blanket lifting slightly for a few seconds as the fan finally turned towards me, before turning away again, buzzing like a swarm of mosquitoes.

This was my sister's first home, a fifteen-square-metre room, one of twelve on the floor and sixty in the building. Chenchen was born there in the middle of summer. She cried day and night, lying on her parents' double bed; cuddled in their sweaty arms.

Holding his baby daughter, my brother-in-law paced the narrow space between the open door and the bed pushed against the window. Behind him, a basic wardrobe against the wall; beside him, a round fold-up table next to the bed, behind the door, narrow low shelves with rice, cooking oil, soy, vinegar, spices; fruit and vegetables.

I put down my handbag and took the water spinach my sister handed me. Walking down the corridor, I passed more curtain-shrouded doorways, each with a hot wok and steaming pot outside. Halfway along, I turned into the communal washing room. Cold-water taps were lined long washing troughs on each side wall. I turned on a tap. Next to me a woman was scrubbing her hot wok, and next to her another was soaping linen on a wash board.

I took the green leaves to my sister and headed back to the washroom. I settled myself above a ceramic squatting base, held my breath and closed the half-length yellow door behind me. When I opened it, a man wearing a singlet and shorts stepped in next to me. I bit my tongue and rushed away from my first experience of a unisex public toilet.

It did not seem to bother anyone – it was early days in China's opening up. When we were Mao's Little Pioneers at primary school, we were told that most of the world was still living in 'deep water and hot fire'. As China began to open up that image seemed less convincing, but to most of us the world outside was still a mystery. Compared with what the peasants had to endure, those with an iron rice bowl in their hands, with everything provided by their 'work unit', felt they had little to whinge about. When someone joined a large state-owned factory they were set for life: free kindergarten, free apartment, access to canteens, public baths, cinemas and pensions. Everyone had to be patient, to be allocated a room such as this, and hope someday to move to something better.

'Wha! Wha!' I heard Chenchen's cry before I reached their room. The humid air sapped her energy; she'd caught the flu at the factory kindergarten and had to stay home. 'Who will look after her?' I asked. 'I've called Mum – she is coming on Sunday,' my sweaty-faced sister said, flicking the door curtain aside as she walked to and fro stir-frying the pork and green leaves.

Like a soldier in the reserves, our retired mother was on standby, ready to jump on the train and attend to her daughter's and granddaughter's needs. It was not unusual for Chinese grandparents to devote their retirement to their precious grandchildren. When they became frail, they would expect their children's attention and devotion: the bargain at the heart of the Chinese family bond. To care for your elders is a cornerstone of Confucian values and tradition.

The following week I returned to the building. It was mid-afternoon. Most of my sister's neighbours were still at work in the factory. As I reached the top of the stairs, my eyes caught an old woman and a girl sitting on a stool in the communal washroom. With the cool breeze blowing from the windows to the stairs and over their bodies, Mum and Chenchen looked peaceful and content.

Life went on and, before long, under a dim bulb, I watched Chenchen toddling along the narrow corridor while finely chopped shallots, ginger and garlic were thrown into smoky woks, white vapour danced above bamboo steamers and hotpots bubbled away.

Soon it was time to celebrate Chenchen's birthday. Sitting on the edge of the bed, we clapped our hands while she danced on the bed, her little face shining joyfully. 'Happy birthday to you,' we sang together, watching her blowing out the three candles on her cake, a luxury my sister and I never dreamed of when growing up. Eating the tasty dishes my sister and her husband cooked in their narrow corridor, I watched their perspiring faces proudly following their precious daughter's every move.

SITTING ON THE French lounge I heard the approaching steps and turned around. My sister put down a tray of goodies – Chinese teapot and cups, roasted chestnuts and tiny sugar mandarins. 'How's Brother-in-law?' I ask, as my sister pours green tea for me.

'He's okay – coming home Friday night.'

'How's his new job down in Wuhan?'

'Well, tough, but he's hanging in there – our whole family's counting on him now.' As my sister bends down to fill the teapot, I notice the deep lines around her eyes, the extra grey in her hair: her face is not as smooth and her smile not as bright as it once was.

With a faint smile, my sister looks away and I lower my eyes, sipping tea from a fine cup. A strong current of emotions surges inside me. I wish I could be more direct, like a real foreigner, looking deep into her eyes: *Sister, it's all right. I know what you've just been through, and I know how you feel*. She is avoiding me. The memory of the dark cloud of events in their previous apartment hangs heavy in the air between us.

'IT'S GETTING LATE. Let's talk about this tomorrow, in my office, shall we?' my brother-in-law appealed.

'No, if you don't give us an answer tonight, we aren't going anywhere,' shouted a man.

'That's right. We're going nowhere. It's your bloody problem – you fix it,' added another, his craggy finger pointing at my bother-in-law's nose, his fiery eyes staring.

Ten men took over my sister's apartment that night, and stayed. For two weeks they ate the food in the fridge, used the only toilet, slept on the couch and the floor, yelled, swore, demanded their jobs back. They had decided not to wrestle the security guards in the company, nor to harass the German 'big boss' in his guarded villa. Instead, they stormed the home of the top Chinese manager.

Desperately trying to get their home back, my sister and her husband called the company's security guards and the local police. No one came to their rescue. The Chinese government had just issued an order urging companies across the land to take extreme caution with retrenched workers, 'in order to protect the stability of China'.

The days dragged on. The family struggled to live with the angry mob in their home. Exhausted, my brother-in-law dragged himself into the bathroom. He lit another cigarette, inhaling long and deep, he ran his fingers through his hair, through the new strip of grey just above his forehead. Glancing in the mirror, he saw a face that looked five years older than it had only a week ago: red dreary eyes, deepening wrinkles in dry skin, dark cracking lips. Instead of his normal smart suit and tie, he was wearing a casual jacket, a rumpled T-shirt underneath.

He wished that this was all just a nightmare, but every morning when he opened his eyes it was all still there – the swearing mob, the messy floor. Above all, he could not bear the anger, the fear, and the pain in his wife's almond eyes. 'This is so unfair. She should have never been drawn into this. As for all of you out there, although I wish I could pick each of you up and throw you out of the door, deep down, I feel sorry for you too. I know how hard it must be for you. Do you think I want to see you losing your job? But what can I do? The German partner has bought the company, and their board has made the decision. To make the company more competitive, it has to cut down the number of low-skilled staff. They are, after all, running a multinational company, not a communist commune...'

BIG ZHOU WAS the man who showed Brother-in-law around when he first joined the factory twenty-five years ago. Having worked in the company all his life, Big Zhou could not believe his eyes when he saw his name on the retrenched workers' list. 'How can they do this to us? Aren't we a socialist country?' he heard his angry mates yelling. 'Why me? What have I done to deserve this? What can I do now? Who'll take care of my family?' he asked himself over and over, wandering the streets aimlessly, lying wide awake in the dark.

Days passed, and he had not broken the news to his parents. He did not know where to start; his parents would worry themselves sick over their only son. At home, his eyes avoided the concerned gaze of his wife and the innocent eyes of his precious daughter. He kept asking the same questions. He felt ashamed. He felt he had let his family down.

Then one of his mates called. 'We're gonna get loaded. Coming?'

'Sure, I could sure use a few drinks,' agreed Big Zhou gloomily.

At a cheap local restaurant outside the factory, over stir-fry dishes spread on a large round table, Big Zhou and his mates swore loudly and drank bottle after bottle of Chinese liquor, the cheapest brand but still 60 per cent alcohol, the real stuff.

'Big Zhou, you coward, why didn't you crash the boss's home with us?' demanded one half-drunk man.

'I...couldn't. He's my...friend, my old neighbour,' replied Big Zhou, red-faced.

'*Cao* (fuck). Your friend? Your old neighbour? Bullshit. Look at you. Did he spare you?'

'Well...shut up!' Big Zhou's tongue stiffened, his eyes turning to the speaker, burning with rage.

'Okay, that's enough. No more bloody work. Drink up,' interjected another, clamping his hand on Zhou's shoulder.

In a karaoke bar, a bunch of young girls in sexy skirts wiggled into a dark room. Among the noisy singers around the television, one of the girls sank into the soft couch next to Big Zhou. He opened his eyes. Her legs looked smooth and tempting, her lips red and shining. Still holding the liquor in his right hand, Big Zhou lifted his other arm. He was just about to put it around the slim shoulder, when suddenly he stopped. Under the blue eye shadow, the girl's pretty eyes looked familiar – so familiar that they turned the girl's face into the one he'd been avoiding at home. Blood surged into Big Zhou's head. His world turned black, and he slumped onto the girl's lap.

As my brother-in-law stood among the mess, confronted by angry faces at home, his mobile rang. He went into the bedroom. My sister followed.

'What…when…how did it happen?' he pressed, his voice tense and anxious. 'Big Zhou just had a stroke, nearly died, and now he's paralysed,' he whispered to my sister, his face ashen. For years the two men had enjoyed their cheap cigarettes at the end of the stairs together, their wives had washed green leaves in the same cement troughs, and their daughters had toddled along the same humble corridor. 'I am sorry Big Zhou. I know your area has just been shut down. I know it would be tough for you, but, please, not like this…'

The news about Big Zhou broke my brother-in-law's spirit, and his body – that night, he too was rushed to hospital. After pacing for hours in the corridor, my sister finally saw a nurse and heard: 'Your husband is all right.'

The retrenched workers got what they wanted – more compensation – and proudly withdrew from their protest base. Returning from the hospital, confronted by the mess the intruders had left behind, my sister sank into her stained couch and sobbed uncontrollably.

'It's over. Things will get better,' I said, trying to comfort her over the phone after the angry mob had finally left and her husband was about to come home from hospital. But things were set to get worse.

NOT LONG AFTER the Germans took over, the company was swallowed by another western shark, a Dutch company. Soon the new senior managers arrived and made it clear who was in charge. My sister and her husband did their best to adjust and co-operate. Watching the division she had built and managed for years dismantled overnight and her files taken away, my sister bit her tongue. She went through one internal interview after another, even for lower-level jobs, swallowing her pride each time; but the answer was always, 'We regret…' Then the announcement came: her service was no longer required.

My sister's world was shattered. She could not make sense of it all. She had devoted twenty-five years to her 'work unit'. She was always the last to turn off the lights in the office, sometimes staying until midnight without dinner. She had an engineering degree from a respected university and an MBA after countless evenings and weekends of study. She had always been loyal to the company – despite the regular calls she had received from head-hunters in the last few years, she and her husband had never considered leaving.

They had devoted themselves to the factory they had been assigned to as fresh university graduates. It had become their life; their colleagues were like extended family. Over a quarter-century, the large factory had been transformed from state-owned to joint venture, to fully foreign company. They worked their way up, step by step.

Their salaries jumped from a few hundred RMB a month to packages comparable to those of western managers. Every day my brother-in-law was taken to and from his office by a personal driver. When he came home, he stood in front of his sparkling cabinet, enjoying the sight of his souvenirs, mementos from board meetings around the world – a small Dutch windmill, a red London double-decker bus, a German beer glass and a miniature Thai temple.

The family had long since moved out of their one-room pigeonhole: first to a two-bedroom apartment, then to a brand-new three-bedroom apartment, the first home of their own. Before long, they had bought an apartment for my parents, and one for my sister's mother-in-law. After the siege in their old apartment, my sister was determined to find a new home and, despite the intimidating price and the demanding management fee, they bought the plush new villa.

Then suddenly it was all over: the company which they had helped build was no longer theirs. The new owner grabbed the keys from their hands and pushed them out. My brother-in-law was told he had two choices – take a menial job under the new Dutch owner, on a fraction of his salary, or move inland, to set up a new company for the Germans. He chose the latter. Although he only sees his family over the weekend, and the demanding job and the tiring early morning and late-night flying have painted more grey above his forehead, he seems content. Despite their achievements, he and my sister are just as humble, and just as determined as the young parents whose sweaty arms held a crying baby in that tiny room, twenty years ago.

BEFORE DRIVING ME to the airport, my sister puts a red envelope in my hand. I open it. Some green Australian banknotes slip out.

'No, I can't,' I protest, pushing the envelope back.

'Take it,' they urge.

'I can't. You just bought this house, and…you need the money.'

'No, we have no debts; you still have a mortgage, and you are all on your own,' my brother-in-law insists. 'Don't worry about us – we can always move back to our old apartment.'

'What about Chenchen? She needs money to study in America,' I say.

'Don't you worry, by then we'll have saved enough for her. We won't need much ourselves,' he adds lightheartedly, trying to sound convincing. 'You know the story – when people asked an American tycoon why, unlike his lavish son, he always stayed in moderate hotels, the old man replied: my father had no money, but his father does.'

Half convinced, I take the red pack hesitantly.

Waving goodbye at the new Beijing airport, I board the plane. The cabin is packed. Sitting among Chinese students, as the plane heads south towards summery Sydney, I watch a woman on the small screen in front of me announcing: 'Wall Street tumbled again, despite another stimulus package from the Obama government.' Where will this lead us? I wonder.

How will it affect China, and all of us?

Frances Guo has lived in Australia since 1990. After graduating from Peking University and the Chinese Academy of Social Sciences she worked as a journalist. She has moved between the two countries working for universities, the Australian Embassy in Beijing and News Corporation. She has published in both Australia and China, and is now a PhD candidate at UTS specialising in Chinese media studies.

Cuba's China syndrome

The old has died and the new has yet to emerge

Jorge Sotirios

'**VIVA** Raul! Viva Cuba! Viva la Revolución!' I awoke abruptly, stumbled over bottles at my feet and leaned over the wrought-iron balcony. A group below had emerged from the Confucius Institute, accompanied by a marching band that hit all the right notes at the wrong time. They marched in single file past the derelict El Pacifico restaurant, took little notice of murals of Dr Fu Manchu and swept past waiters plying their trade in silk pyjamas. China's middle class was a new breed. Tourism and solidarity made for a unique mix.

Bleary-eyed I slumped downstairs, sunk a *guava batida* from a hole-in-the-wall café and exited Barrio Chino. I enjoyed this Caribbean Chinatown, strolling past neo-colonial architecture that wasn't UNESCO-approved.

Tour groups aside, the Chinese in Cuba were declining in number. Arriving in the mid-to-late nineteenth century from Hong Kong, Macau, Taiwan and California, they worked as indentured labourers alongside African slaves in sugar plantations. Possessed of an entrepreneurial spirit that was insufferably bourgeois, they faded once the revolution took power.

In Old Havana, cobblestone alleys led to Plaza de Armas, where I bought the daily papers. A rank smell emanated from *Revolución*, as well it might, given that it was published in 1959. The bookseller had piled a stack up to his waist; archives sold more copies than the official *Granma*. *Revolución* almost crumbled in my hands, but its images preserved authenticity. By all accounts, 1959 was a transitional year. Models with long legs in smooth stockings featured alongside beaches finally opened to the public: *Playas Para Todo el Pueblo*. Matrons at Society Balls incongruously rubbed shoulders with gun-toting rebels; Olivier's *Richard III* was advertised besides Fidel Castro's *Libertad o Muerte*.

With a slanted beret and hair beyond his shoulders, Fidel's brother, Raul, cut a dashing figure. The maligned and underestimated Raul has soft Oriental features with a homoerotic edge. Cuba's new leader is often disparaged as *La China* (a bastard Chinese and closet homosexual), suggesting racism hasn't entirely disappeared, nor has that most Latin of traits, machismo.

PREVIOUS PAGE: Raul Castro and his wife Vilma at their wedding.
Photographer: Joseph Scherschel / Time Life Pictures. *Source: gettyimages.com*

Raul's youth has always been striking. At twenty-seven, he looked fifteen. When Jean-Paul Sartre penned 'No old men in power!' in 1960, he was smitten by revolutionaries in their early thirties. 'Everywhere I look they could be my sons,' the philosopher said, beaming in photos taken by Korda. The same heroes shown in *Granma* are now closer to eighty. Greying, they blend nicely with the dilapidated architecture around them. The passage of time means buildings contain cracks and revolutionaries creases, but others have been renovated (building and revolutionary alike). None more than Raul. 'The delegator' is not yet 'the dictator'. Previously the hard man of the army, Raul steered Cuba to Soviet-style communism. Nowadays he's portrayed as a pragmatist, opening up the economy to private enterprise, easing travel restrictions and access to the internet. Perhaps it was inevitable. When the beards were shorn and the long hair cut, Sartre asserted, the revolution ended and administration began.

For the moment I could further reminisce about 1959 by crossing to the seafront. Car names rolled off my tongue as easily as did the vehicles from the assembly line: Buick, Edsel, Studebaker, De Soto, Plymouth, Cadillac. 1948, '55, '57 and '62 paraded by, as if in a retrospective; chrome grilles were polished like mirrors and bench seats upholstered in white leather complemented tail fins piercing pedestrians in reverse. Marxists would call this admiration a fetish. But who reads Marx? Certainly not Cubans, going by the dusty hardbacks at Plaza de Armas.

Beside American cars and the Russian Lada, a third force hurled into picture. *Viazul* buses ferry tourists in a fleet imported from China. Vehicles chug, rattle or roar along the *malecón*. Cannons poised across the harbour at La Cabana were ready to explode at 9 pm, and I made sure to synchronise my watch. Cuba still manages to echo the past of fifty years ago, timed precisely.

FOREIGN REPORTERS ONCE had their shoes shined at the bar of the Hotel Inglaterra, while downing a gin fizz. This morning they were surfing the net. Signals transmitted via a French satellite made them exceptionally slow, in keeping with Cuba's languid pace. Communism, whatever its faults, was a shield safeguarding the island. A country spared the frenetic pace of consumerism is paradise, or at least a Marxist utopia in the making. But I revised these assumptions once I went online.

I scrolled past bailouts, toxic debts, housing bubbles and sub-prime disasters. Capitalism's fall was on Cuban screens and, unlike Chinese censorship, wasn't stifled. A link to Pope Benedict suggested the Pontiff couldn't bring the c-word to his lips, blaming the crisis on 'greed'. Fidel's warning in the 1980s that the IMF's 'Structurally Adjusted Programs' were a new form of economic colonisation was proving true. Baltic States and Eastern Europe, who eagerly complied, were feeling the pinch. Free trade, no tariff barriers and reduced public expenditure didn't make for resilient economies.

With a command economy, no reckless investments by its financial institutions and no rampant speculation by twenty-five-year-old traders, Cuba has maintained a growth of 8–12 per cent of GDP since 2006. But if Cubans were revelling in capitalism's crisis, they weren't showing it. Raul emphasised 'humility' to commemorate half a century of revolution, in stark contrast to the West's triumphalism at the collapse of the Soviet Bloc. Cuba's fall was imminent, the foreign press had editorialised: 'it was only a matter of time'. Yet Cuba's enforced isolation from capitalism suggested it could sail through the new crisis untouched.

The elephant in the room, though, was the Chinese dragon. Its favoured trading status in South America had a ripple effect through the Caribbean. China's stockpiling of minerals fuelled demand for copper (Chile), soy (Brazil), gas (Bolivia) and oil (Venezuela). It's been said the Chinese plan generations ahead (two hundred years after the French Revolution, Zhou en Lai pondered its success but admitted 'it was too soon to tell'), and its long-term survival involved markets in Latin America. Global capitalism's crisis enveloped China, and failing prices worldwide ensnared Cuba, which exported nickel and leased arable land to secure China's food supply.

Communism wasn't much of a shield to brothers-in-arms. I had to reconsider the purity of ideology when I read that the US Chamber of Commerce had called for an end to the Cuba embargo, denounced China's 'exploitation', attacked its human rights and defended the right to work (for Americans, naturally). But surely it's a sign of the times when the biggest communist nation appears solely in the business pages? Take, for example, the *Sydney Morning Herald* headlines in a single day: 'China in talks over Pilbara push', 'China's money mandarins take the hard line', 'China buys up big'. China's role in the global economy has been heightened by the crisis, with an anxiety uniting Cuba to America, and likewise Australia. What kind of world power will China be in the twenty-first century? If the Dragon sneezes, will we all catch a cold?

FOR YEARS I'VE associated vintage cars with pantyhose. Since the 1962 embargo blocking fanbelts and spare parts, pantyhose were an ingenious substitute. Tied together and stretched on pulleys, the fan, generator and water pump functioned, allowing the Oldsmobile to maintain its youth. This was Cuba at its most creative. Mechanics often grafted the motor of one vehicle to the chassis of another, with the skills of a heart surgeon, to maintain life.

I peered under the hood of a 1950 Chevy. A cast-iron motor incorporated crankshaft and carburettor, as though newly minted. Its six-cylinder engine had polished rockers a hand's distance from a shiny radiator. To my regret, a fanbelt meant there was no pantyhose.

Miguel, a former gynaecologist, was happy to be my driver. Normally he'd sell cakes at a stall on Obispo, but a day away from his extended family was preferred. Cranking gears, the two of us lurched in the direction of 'AUSTRALIA'. The Chevy's shock absorbers were not under us, Miguel declared between puffs, but 'somewhere in the US'. Each pothole on the *autopista* reverberated from wheel to steering wheel, a current rippling through us both.

A warm climate and lush countryside made Columbus and Jack Nicholson agree: Cuba was paradise. Swaying palms, sugar plantations and the *choo-choo* trains that serviced them complemented a landscape free of consumer goods and sexist imagery. Miguel translated propaganda outside half-open windows. *Patria es Humanidad!* Firm Unity is Victory! *Socialismo es Irreversablo!* Keep in Line with Fidel!

With so many slogans it's no wonder graffiti is obsolete: the Cuban state is the radical. To call these billboards propaganda seemed harsh, given revolutionary slogans appeal to one's better angels. With an undisguised idealism aimed at youth, alongside Che's compelling gaze, they're secular versions of romantic poetry (Che Guevara was as much a poet as Byron a revolutionary). Each slogan was tailor-made. Messages bore an ecological theme near the coast, were revolutionary strident in Santiago, and voiced anti-Americanisms near universities. Cuba's government might be schooled by the advertising industry given their reliance on 'niche-marketing'.

'CONSEJO POPULAR AUSTRALIA': we had arrived. The 'Central Australia' sugar mill, constructed in 1916, displayed inactive cogs, dormant vats and timbers stripped away, suggesting it had died only recently. The mill played an important role when Cuba was the sugar bowl of America. Notoriously, even Christmas was banned to get the sugar quota in when Russia paid above market price, reaching a peak of eight million tonnes in 1989.

Just as war is too important to be left to the generals, so the economy is too important to be left to economists. A country relying on a single commodity can easily become its slave. Jamaica and bauxite, Chile and copper, Nigeria and oil.

Cuba's planners were reluctant to dismantle the industry when sugar's price fell to a quarter of its peak. Cuba's communists didn't heed the first lesson taught to every small-time investor: diversify portfolios, spread the risk, don't rely on a single buyer. Five hundred years of cane-cutting tradition was pared back at Fidel Castro's insistence; he was disgusted at sentimental economists persisting with an outdated model. The IMF and communist planners are guided by the same instincts: don't jettison a model, even when it has proved disastrous.

In the midst of the rusty shell housing the refinery, I narrowed the incongruity. Was it named because of the combine harvester that greatly assisted Queensland? Or did a sailor shipwrecked at nearby Bay of Pigs settle in the nineteenth century? As Miguel shifted gears, I remembered a notorious advertising campaign with a memorable jingle, 'Sugar: A Natural Part of Life'.

With sugar imported from abroad, and refined near Mackay, CSR sought to mesh the purity of a healthy lifestyle with the sweetener, even if it was a lie. It made complete sense as we passed Matanzas and noticed posters of Fidel in suit and tie celebrating '50'. 'Propaganda' in Spanish is 'advertising'.

ERNESTO STUMBLED AROUND his flat with a pot in his scorched hands. He was dressed in white, as though returned from Wimbledon. Joined by his wife, Natalia, he was preparing a *santería* ceremony. Carrots, pieces of meat and cobs of corn began boiling on a hotplate. Tall, lean and softly spoken, Ernesto gave instructions to a tough pair under American baseball caps. The Pioneer stereo was disconnected; chairs were moved to an adjacent room. The youths then rolled drums inside: rum kegs made of solid wood, with a steel belt fastened around the portly waist. Natalia created a shrine in the corner of the kitchen: cups with water, others with *Tu-Kola*, and placed a half-lit cigar across the plastic rim. The ceremony would occur tonight. As with most things Cuban, no invitation was necessary.

I borrowed Ernesto's bike and headed for the beach. At one time all Cubans were on bicycles. In 'The Special Period in a time of Peace', during the '90s, the government imported more than a million from China due to oil shortages. Ever keen to lead by example, Fidel hopped astride one for a memorable photo. I peddled to Playa d'Este outside Havana and soaked up the winter sun. Frequented by locals, it made for a musical riot. I was thankful that tour groups were corralled at Varadero, a resort peninsula in the north of the island. This was Cuba's Faustian bargain: Fidel deemed tourism a necessary evil in the '90s, thinking it could be controlled. And for the most part it was, with billions filtered annually into government services such as health, education and the arts.

But a distorted job market was created: waiters, cabbies, guides and *jineteras* (working girls) made more money than surgeons, scientists and cabinet ministers. Varadero has fifty international hotels, one for each year of the revolution, surely a galling thought for hard-liners. Since 2004, Cuba created a second economy beside a local one, by introducing a convertible peso equivalent to the American dollar. But this currency division was highly porous. Cubans in tourism can access 'convertibles' (and make a monthly wage in an hour), while travellers can eat a three-course meal off the streets at local prices, for a dollar.

Whenever the contradictions of capitalism arise, Marxists note, they show themselves in discontinuity or dissonance. I realised then that Cuba, with its incongruities, couldn't be purely communist, and non-revolutionary tourism surely showed it wasn't. It's a post-communist society, if anything, and I trace its birth to 1998, when Fidel Castro exchanged khaki fatigues for a pinstriped suit. By the time the staunch anti-communist Pope John Paul II visited he'd become critical of the West's faith in the free market. In a marriage made for media studies, he praised Castro to the skies and called for an end to Cuban isolation, while Fidel toned down his rhetoric, adjusted his tie and synchronised his Rolex. To indicate changing times Fidel reinstated Christmas, having dispensed with the demanding sugar quotas.

THE SHIFT BEING consolidated under Raul is evident in youth. The generation that benefited from schools, clinics and sports is distanced from the triumphs of the revolution; they're jaded because they had no part in it, unlike their elders. *La generación perdida* is a nod to Hemingway's Lost Generation and is applied to the bright young things with mobile phones who see little threat across the Florida Straits.

The question Fidel asked of students continues to echo. Is the revolution ultimately doomed to fail; is communism merely, as the old joke runs, the transition from capitalism to capitalism? The Soviet Union's seamless shift to primitive capitalism haunts Cuba. Fidel Castro, for his part, was never swayed by Che Guevara's liking for the Chinese system, nor did he believe the Chinese possessed a 'higher socialist morality' than the Soviets. Castro denounced China's betrayal of ideological principle 'for a pot of western gold' under Deng Xiao Ping, and painfully remembers the humiliating sugar-for-rice barter in 1964, and China's propaganda campaign inside Cuba (Fidel fumed: propaganda was *his* business).

A crisis comes when the old has died and the new hasn't emerged. Cuba's is as much economic as ideological. If Cuba follows China's authoritarian model to accommodate the demands of global capitalism, will its achievements go the way of China – disparity of wealth, the decline of rural towns, environmental degradation? Will Cuba trade spontaneity and creativity for rigidity and conformity? I suspect Chinese top brass would regard Cuba under Raul as not pragmatic enough.

China is a capitalist motor powering a communist shell. But the Soviet Lada using an outdated American motor doesn't move. The Chevrolet powered by Lada's engine runs, though sluggishly. Gliding into Havana and glancing at idle vintage cars, I had only one thought: whichever model Cuba chooses, I pray they include pantyhose.

THE GATHERING GREW in number. Youths in white singlets jostled shoulder to sweaty shoulder in tribute to the Marx Bros. More arrived: *jineteras* beside Italians with drunken faces. Everyone squished into the dining room and ultimately spilled into my bedroom. All of us queued at an altar draped with the Cuban flag, festooned with flowers. We were chalked three times before giving thanks. An 'uncle' began whipping himself into a trance. His eyes bulged. A cane connected spirits, coaxing them into Ernesto's second-storey apartment with a thump. A pounding crescendo continued; the drummers numbered six; ancestor spirits were now inside Uncle. Chants circulated in every direction. Women in tight jeans began dancing, and stomped with fury. Ernesto's neighbour led an ecstatic dance. Sweat dripped from her braids in a bundle tied beneath a kerchief. After four hours, the air in the room had changed. Having farewelled spirits over rooftops in Barrio Chino, dissipating into dingily lit streets below, it was time to pause. Soup was handed out, along with sweet bread and rum. An elderly man gave a sermon for a better world, and reminded each of us to fulfil our potential. Cigars were passed around and crumbled in collective hands.

I'd like to join Columbus and Jack Nicholson in declaring Cuba paradise. Swaying palms, blue seas and alluring women construct an illusion of Gauguinesque tranquility. But Cuba is not a paradise, nor its secular equivalent, a Marxist utopia. What Cuba offers in a time of crisis is spontaneity, conversion and reinvention. I tallied contradictions. The Museum of the Revolution is equidistant from Lenin Park and Park John Lennon. The Moncado Barracks, the scene of a bloody uprising, is transformed into a school for juniors. The 'Australia' sugar mill doubled as military headquarters during the Bay of Pigs debacle. Fanbelts were replaced by pantyhose.

If the grafting of Spanish Catholicism to West African beliefs can work its splendour and enchant tourists as well as locals in Chinatown, then it's worth cultivating. I gazed in the direction of La Cabana. Each evening the cannon blast signalled *Habaneros* to synchronise their watch. Tourists like me always did, but I can't recall Cubans doing likewise.

Jorge Sotirios is the author of *Lonesome George, C'est Moi!*, to be published in late 2009. His essay 'Lost city of the Amazon' was published in *Griffith REVIEW 20: Cities on the Edge*.

Chère Colette

Letters to a great-aunt about optimism,
compassion and a global financial crisis

Xavier Hennekinne

At irregular intervals of between twenty and thirty years
came great floods which were afterwards remembered
as one remembers insurrections or wars and were long
used as a date from which to reckon time, to calculate
the ages of citizens or the term of men's lives.

— Ivo Andrić, *The Bridge Over the Drina*

Ferney, France, 14 January 2009

Chère Colette,

The bust of Voltaire greets me when I open the shutters and look down on the little square. To his right, the bakery where I buy my breakfast; to his left, the bistro where I sometimes drink or have my dinner; and, adjacent to the bistro, the bookshop where I have been buying books every day since I arrived in Ferney. What a wonderful bookshop! Yesterday I bought the complete works of Nicolas Bouvier and *Lorsque l'enfant paraît* by Françoise Dolto.

My suitcase will be full of books. These books will be my French reading for the year. I plan today to buy the biography of Saint-John Perse I saw in the window when I left the shop yesterday.

My annual trip to Geneva is much shorter this year and I am leaving this Saturday; I won't have time to come up to Paris. I am sorry.

Some friends, superstitious and optimistic, said, 'It is about time 2009 comes; 2008 was a terrible year!' Of course, on 1 January, everything changed (superstition) and changed for the better (optimism).

Are my optimistic friends as candid as Candide was optimistic – until the end, at least? Why wouldn't 2009 be filled with diseases, disasters, daughters being raped by their fathers in basements, unjust executions, mass displacements, crushing poverty in the streets of Manila, and general, profound ennui towards all these diseases, disasters, rapes?

Now we have Obama, I guess. He will get us out of the financial crisis and stop the wars. He will save us. He is so full of charm and intelligence, isn't he? You and I, though, know that charm and intelligence only save those who have it. But he seems determined to help and work hard; he seems to listen and to understand.

I am trying to think of something Voltaire said about financial crises, wars or Obama, but I can't think of anything…

2008 was for me a normal year, but 2009 frightens me. It will be the other way around for you.

Love,

Xavier

Manila, Philippines, 24 January

Chère Colette,

When I told an Australian diplomat visiting Manila of our friendship, he asked me if you had known Proust. I had told him of your editing job. You and the diplomat are about the same age. I said, had he been born in France, he could have not met Proust. Even as a child. Proust had died a decade or so before he and you were born.

People seem surprised you and I are friends. Cross-generational friendships, within families, are rare animals, think the people I meet. The stuff of novels, some say. (Novels would talk about physical love between the great-aunt and the nephew or at least someone from the family, or some sort of awakening of the nephew and revitalisation of the great-aunt. None of that between you and me. A simple friendship, mostly an epistolary one.)

I told the Australian diplomat that you worked with Emmanuel Berl and Jacques Laurent, but they have not been dead long enough to be known in Australia the way Proust or Gide are.

To answer your question, yes, Filipinos are happy people. That is why the cleaner working in your building and many other Filipinos sing to themselves. I find the singing irritating; like you, I like silence. I also think people should not sing out loud unless they are singers performing.

Some local banks are closing down. Smaller ones. Several colleagues fear losing their savings. Deposits are now insured up to 250,000 Philippine pesos (or about €3,900), so if you have more in the account and the bank collapses, the government will only give you 250,000 pesos.

The owners of local banks are usually the rich Filipino families. The banks are often part of a family-owned conglomerate of companies that can include airline, telecommunication, media, real estate and retail businesses.

Other owners are rich individuals. A colleague recently lost his children's education savings in a rural bank 'going on holidays'. (A bank becoming insolvent 'goes on holidays'.) The owner managed to protect his personal and other businesses' assets, and the government's Philippine Deposit Insurance Corporation is now managing the bank's affairs. It is likely that many small savers will lose their money despite deposit guarantees, as not all savers know about the guarantees and how to make a claim.

The international banks featured in the news see – since the news is bad – their customers lining up early in the morning to withdraw their money. One bank near my office offered the concerned customers in the queue doughnuts and coffee to sweeten them and make them forget why they came to the branch in the first place. On my way to work the other day, I stopped at the bank and joined the queue. I was offered breakfast by the branch manager. I thanked her, left the queue and went to my office with the breakfast. The doughnut was very sweet, as was the coffee. I felt awful not enjoying the breakfast offered by the bank where I didn't have an account.

Still, everyone sings, despite banks going down and the price of fuel and rice going up. The Filipinos' happiness is resilient.

The 'jolly jeeps' are street food stalls. Some of them are covered with advertising posters. The other day, I saw on a jolly jeep a poster depicting a little Filipina girl laughing, her arms in the air. Around her, doughnuts were falling from the sky. The slogan on the poster said, 'One day it will rain donuts'; and below, in smaller letters, like a childish whisper, 'And I'll be there.'

I am glad this man – whose name you won't reveal – calls. I am glad his calls make you happy. You are right not to ask him questions. You listen to him and he listens to you smoking over the phone and your little voice. I imagine you also listen to the silence between you. If you like his calls it is because they are filled with silence. I remember how you once said you dislike people who are afraid of silence.

I am flying to Myanmar tomorrow, then Thailand. Will write.

Love,

Xavier

Yangon, Myanmar, 31 January

Chère Colette,

Have you read *Burmese Days*, by Orwell? I haven't. In the streets near my hotel, a boy is selling second-hand copies of the book.

I wanted to go down south but I am confined to Yangon, where my duties keep me. The south was devastated by Cyclone Nargis in May 2008. Many villages in the delta of the Irrawaddy River were washed away, with their inhabitants, by heavy rains and floods. Now we still see the precarious tarpaulin tents in the guise of houses, my colleagues tell me, which we usually only see for weeks and not months after a cyclone… But I don't want to talk about things I haven't seen.

The pace of poverty reduction is slowing. We don't see this in the field but read it in reports. Sometimes you wish reports didn't exist, so you could continue working in optimism. Reports on poverty have a way of killing the poetry of the humanitarian's work. But reports speak to policymakers.

A recent report says, 'Poverty will decline in 2009, but the World Bank estimates that around fifty-five million more people will live on less than $1.25 a day.' I don't understand how these two things can happen at the same time, how these two trends do not contradict each other.

The point, though, is that the financial crisis is ineluctably affecting poor countries. (1) Developed countries are investing less in developing or low-income countries. (2) As demand in developed countries shrinks, so do exports from developing countries. And I am not talking about how the fluctuation of currencies affects poorer countries – I don't understand its mechanism. But what started and what is happening in developed countries spread to, and is also happening in, developing countries.

There is also fear that foreign aid from developed countries might start decreasing this year, because of the resources being directed towards domestic economies. The Obama Administration, though, will increase the amount of US aid, an American diplomat told me. More than the previous administration, it believes foreign aid to be an effective diplomatic tool to develop new or restore old and sour relationships with certain countries. The US directs its aid to regions concerning its security. (France often directs its aid where it wishes to expand its cultural and commercial influence, mostly in West Africa.)

The lion's share of US foreign aid goes to Iraq – by far – then Afghanistan, Sudan, Colombia, Egypt, Pakistan. Almost half is in education, health and building social infrastructure. The current US administration seems to consider foreign aid as a tool to mitigate the effect of the financial crisis on poorer countries… Its potency will depend on the quality of the recipient country's governance and a minimum level of economic functionality.

I wonder whether the American government, now that it appears to have a bit more of a conscience, feels some sort of guilt. That they have to make up to other countries for their country's financial practices having been the main contributor to the global financial crisis.

Did you follow some of the debates at the US Congress on the stimulus packages? Were they reported in the French press? The Republicans reminded me of Pangloss. Pangloss stops Candide from saving Jacques the Anabaptist from drowning, to demonstrate that the Lisbon harbour was made for the Anabaptist to drown in. Later, when caught in the Lisbon earthquake, Candide is buried under rubble. He asks Pangloss to get him 'a little wine and oil'. Instead of helping Candide, Pangloss responds: 'This concussion of the earth is no new thing...the city of Lima in South America experienced the same last year; the same cause, the same effects; there is certainly a train of sulphur all the way underground from Lima to Lisbon.'

'Nothing is more probable,' Candide says, 'but for the love of God a little oil and wine.'

'Probable!' the philosopher replies. 'I maintain that the thing is demonstrable.'

Candide faints away, and Pangloss fetches him some water from a neighbouring spring.

To me, it is folly not to respond to a crisis. Republicans are arguing for free markets, capitalism against socialism, decreasing the size of government; but such a dialectic is abstract in the face of a crisis. Republicans say, 'This concussion of the economy is no new thing...'

Americans, remembering the 1930s and '70s, say, 'Nothing is more probable, but for the love of God may the government help us keep our homes and our jobs.'

'Probable!' the Republicans reply. 'We maintain that the thing is demonstrable!'

They are focusing on economic arguments rather than positive action.

I was saying all this to the American diplomat passing through Yangon and, oddly, he asked me whether I knew *Candide* by heart. I said that I could never know by heart a text as long as *Candide*. I could probably learn parts of it and remember them for a day or two, but would not be able to recite them if I had not learned them a few hours before. I told him that I was not reciting a passage but recalling what was in a chapter. I added that, as a matter of fact, I didn't remember the place of the chapter in the book, though I recalled that the final chapters had to do with Candide losing his optimism and cultivating his garden.

This evening, I went to the magnificent Shwedagon Temple. I was told that on sunny days the gold layer on the immense bell-shaped pagoda reflects the sunlight to blind pilgrims and tourists. Today was a sunny day. When the sunlight softened at about five or five-thirty, the pagoda took on a warm glow.

François Nourissier has been left in a *mouroir*, you tell me. I have read about his condition in the French papers. Most articles by writers and friends do not talk about the mouroir or Parkinson's. They talk about his writing, his place in French literature. It is strange to me to read about his dying, from someone at his bedside, when I only have been a reader of his literary work. I am now a witness to your friendship with him and a spectator of his dying. He saved you after your divorce, you told me once.

I have just opened the copy of *Burmese Days* I bought from the boy this morning. The pages are very dirty and seem to disintegrate between my fingers, like an old parchment. I don't think I will read the book in bed.

Does this man who called you still call?

X

Mae Hong Son, Thailand, 2 February

Chère Colette,

I am sorry that the man who called you doesn't call anymore. I will not worry, because you have told me it's fine. One cannot call forever. When in high school I would call Karine in the evening, even though we had spent the day sitting together in class. Or she would call. We would spend hours on the phone, before and after dinner. Often we said nothing. Often we would fall asleep. I would wake up in the middle of the night and turn off the light and place the phone back on its hook. We were not romantically involved. At one point she stopped calling and her line was always busy when I called. She had become romantically involved with a boy called Loïc. I guessed that she called him instead. In the evenings, I started to call my friend François again. Though we spent time at school together, he and I had not spoken on the phone for a long time, probably because I had stopped calling him when I started calling Karine and he must have found that my line was always busy when Karine and I were talking.

Before I left for Sri Lanka in December, F and I made love. For the first time, it was to…I am not sure how to say…procreate, I guess. We made love though the calendar said it was pointless. So on Saturday, when I passed the child-granting Celestial in my circular walk around the Shwedagon Pagoda in Yangon, I could not resist whispering something, since F and I have only spent four days together since my trip to Sri Lanka and the timing had never been right. I didn't really ask for anything, since I am not of Buddhist (or any) persuasion, but hoped that we would be together at the right time and eventually have a healthy baby.

This morning F called. She said there were two parallel lines, though it remains to see a doctor and have a blood test to confirm the pregnancy. Are other religions as effective as Buddhism in exhausting timid prayers? The timing must not have been so bad after all. The catch is that now I have to go back to Yangon and thank the Celestial in person.

I have been visiting refugee camps at the border (with Myanmar). Today I was at the Baan Mai Naison Temporary Shelter Area, near the small town of Mae Hong Son.

I noticed that people in camps walk a lot. Adults and children walk from one side of the camp to the other, for whatever reason: to meet humanitarian workers at their camp offices; to get things, such as water, food and small goods, or to gather firewood for cooking and heating. In the morning, when we drove up the long and rutted track, we saw men and women walking towards the camp, carrying wood on their shoulders, and sometimes bundles of wood held by material wrapped around their heads and resting on their backs. When we left the camp and drove down the track, in the afternoon, the same people were slowly advancing. They seemed barely to have progressed. Most of them looked too old to carry such burdens.

We arrived at the camp just after trucks had delivered freshly cut bamboo trunks, which are used for the walls of the huts and fences. An orderly distribution was taking place. I thought of the people who I had seen walking up the track, kilometres away from the camp, some with these three-to-four-metre-long bamboo trunks on their shoulders. I told the person who seemed in charge of the distribution about the people I had seen carrying the same bamboo back to the camp. Should we tell them not to bother, I asked the Thai NGO worker; should we pick them up and have them help themselves to some of the trunks lying here? He responded that these trunks were for residents of a particular block of the camp. He added that the people I saw were probably not from the camp, as people from the camp are usually not allowed to leave unaccompanied – they were probably Thai people from the area.

Most of the people in the camp are Karen and Karenni people. They have come from remote parts of Myanmar. Out of the jungle. Most of them are refugees, meaning that they have been granted refugee status under international law; they are no longer asylum seekers. And most of the refugees in the camp are 'transiting': they have been accepted by the US, Australia, Canada, New Zealand and other countries, and while in the camp they are being medically examined, and assisted if they are unwell. The main diseases checked are tuberculosis and HIV. They also undergo classroom inductions to their new home country and new lifestyle. They are shown pictures of the food, places, landmarks, important people in their new country. They are trained to use the style of toilet used there; they are shown the warm clothes they will need to wear in winter; they are told about customs and politeness. They are presented with pictures of the kinds of faces they will see in their new country – invariably they are surprised to see that some faces look just like theirs.

3 February

After lunch, I quickly visited the Phra That Doi Kong Moo temple with two of my colleagues. The temple is perched on top of a mountain. It is a very small temple compared with Shwedagon. The two small *chedis* are of a bright white which, like the gold of Shwedagon, forces you to squint. Below the temple, at the foot of its mountain, lies Mae Hong Son, in the valley, cut through by an airstrip.

My colleagues – a Bosnian-Austrian working in Bangkok and a Macedonian based in Mae Hong Son – and I sat on a wall overlooking the town. I commented on how Mae Hong Son was pleasant and its infrastructure

– hospital, roads, airport – functional and modern, despite its geographical isolation and small size.

'The King of Thailand,' said our Macedonian colleague, 'is the Development King. He has funded many development projects in rural Thailand. For over sixty years he has helped the poor of Thailand, has built hospitals, roads…'

Many people in Mae Hong Son wear yellow shirts (the King's colour) with the royal cipher on their breast on Mondays (the King was born on a Monday).

Mae Hong Son was beautiful. The valley was – the town, too, almost lost in a valley. We could see a small temple near the small lake near the hospital; the restaurant where we had dinner, the office, our guesthouse. The only thing was the airstrip, like a gash, an amputation. It seemed to have taken out a third of the town. But then, thanks to the airstrip, the modern hospital was provisioned – the town, too. And humanitarian workers could arrive and depart every day of the week: fly to Chiang Mai, then Bangkok, then wherever…

X

Manila, 21 March

Chère Colette,

If only I could put in my letters the sweet smell of the almost-rotten fruit, of the meat that has just been separated from the carcass and the meat that was hung the day before under the blue tarpaulin; the smell of the motor vehicles' exhaust, of human and animal urine on the wall; the smell of open sewers – you would realise the attack on the senses that a stroll downtown can cause.

One gets used to everything. We even come to desire this state of alertness. The never-ending concert of klaxons in narrow streets, the whistles of the ridiculous traffic officers, the *jeepneys* that come out of nowhere. The children who run and scream. People everywhere, lying down, sitting, standing; people walking, people talking to you, people talking to others, who demand, who harangue. We come to want this, to want to be on the *qui vive*. To want the smells and dust and not mind the pollution.

Manila is an uncontrollable city.

You say you get angry when you watch the news. You ask what one can do, believing the answer is nothing. That there is no answer. The atrocities, you say: how can they happen? The poverty! The corruption! You kick your heels and smoke more. (I wonder how your voice managed to stay so soft with all the smoking you have done.)

I have been reading about Orwell in Burma since my trip to Yangon. I have also read some of his texts (Hôpital X in the fifteenth arrondissement of Paris, in 'How the Poor Die', made me think of Nourissier's mouroir). Orwell says that the central problem is how to prevent power from being abused, and that this problem hasn't been solved yet. I think this is why you get angry when you watch the news, and why you smoke more.

One text I particularly connected to is 'Shooting an Elephant'. Humanitarian workers from developed countries based in the field must often feel like Orwell about to shoot the elephant. Like the 'conjurer about to perform a trick'. They often carry the weight of expectations from those they are working with or helping. The obligation not only to solve the problems but to solve them by impressing. In the 1920s, Orwell was a police officer in Burma and saw himself and other white men in Burma as a 'sort of hollow, posing dummy, the conventionalised figure of a *sahib*', spending their lives trying to impress the locals by demonstrating decisiveness and resolution – what the locals had come to expect from the white men. The truth is, the developed countries gave themselves this role of conjurer but cannot live up to it.

One thing you should know is that most humanitarian workers are from developing countries. Any organisation working in any poor country would employ most of its workers from the local workforce. Only a few expatriates (not always from developed countries) would pose as the conventionalised figure of the *sahib*.

I am wondering why you have not seen for a while the singing Filipina cleaner working in your building. Did you ever talk to her? Do you know where she is from?

In the past weeks, I have been opening and closing and opening *Candide*. Because of Voltaire's bust in Ferney, which I seem to have photographed in my mind. His cheeky smile. I think there is something Candidesque about the Filipino overseas worker. The travels, for one thing. The search for a better life. The optimism and excitement when they leave Manila.

Candide becomes immensely rich in El Dorado. With this richness, he thinks that he will no longer face the problems he has been facing (unfair arrest, beating). He thinks he will be happy. Of course, he is not. He worries about how his money is trickling away to rather unsavoury characters, such as the merchant Vanderdendur, who sails away with most of it. His wealth brings him friends with motives. Wealth is one of the things that turned Candide away from optimism.

Money earned in developed countries, and the need to keep earning that money, has kept Filipinos away from their families. The cleaner in your building was probably sending most of her pay back to her family in the Philippines.

The Filipino overseas workers often come across the unsavoury kind of characters you read about in *Candide*. Remind me to one day tell you the story of Flor Contemplacion. Perhaps the cleaner in your building has returned to the Philippines. We have seen many overseas Filipino workers return in the past few months.

Do you remember what Candide says about optimism when he comes across a half-naked slave with no left leg and right hand? He says, 'Alas! It is the obstinacy of maintaining that everything is best when it is worst.' I wonder if the Filipina cleaner working in your building, along with the singing, has maintained her optimism. Or if she now says that everything is for the worst.

I have been reading about the financial crisis. People in government are not often the reflective kind. And I suppose you do not have time to stop and think when you are running a country. You have to react, constantly. But Australia's Prime Minister, Kevin Rudd, has stopped what he was doing for a moment – I assume he had to stop – and in writing an essay thought about the global financial crisis. I do believe that in facing problems of certain magnitude, one sometimes has to analyse and ponder. Sometimes brilliant instinct and swift action are not enough to deal with complex problems.

(The US Republicans are not analysing or pondering the stimulus packages or alternative solutions; they are still arguing for neo-liberalism.) Mr Rudd's essay is not a plan of action but a reflection. Perhaps it helped him (and will help his readers) get to the core of the matter. It outlines a direction – which, frankly, seems to be the right direction. It is also *the* politico-economic direction of the moment, which most democracies seem to now follow: social capitalism. Rudd is rather intellectual; he is an intellectual but also a politician; his essay is unavoidably a political essay. I will translate it into French and send it to you.

You haven't told me yet how you feel about the financial crisis. Did you get angry? Are you optimistic? You tell me about the seasons coming and going. The birds on your balcony. And Nourissier.

Perhaps, after all, it might not be worth my while translating the Rudd essay. You have never mentioned the global financial crisis in your letters, and if I am going to translate something from the English into French, it should be something literary. I will translate some of my friend Frank's stories that have not been translated into French and will send you a summary of the Rudd essay.

X.

Manila, Philippines, 12 April

Ma très chère Colette,

It took me a long time to decide to go Garbage Mountain. I was afraid. I was afraid to catch something, afraid of the smell, afraid of the mountain collapsing on me, as it happened a few years ago on people who scavenged there. But I wanted to meet the people who live there, to see what I thought was the worst that can happen to a human being who doesn't have a job or a home or a family to look after him or her, so I went. It has now been several weeks and I have not visibly caught anything. Perhaps I was never to catch anything. I did not sieve through the rubbish, I did not sleep at the bottom of the mountain; I didn't shake any hands – I think I didn't – I just looked around. I was a simple tourist though without a camera but with a readiness for astonishment.

Garbage Mountain, a mythical mountain in my mind, was many very big piles of garbage – a range of hills, if you like – with humans, insects and animals sieving through the formless mass, a moveable ground, and hundreds of trucks coming and going. It was a buzzing hive of activity. A large chain of sorting and recycling garbage...

I have been thinking and writing about the financial crisis. The world was in an endemic phase of economic crisis; the credit crunch triggered the pandemic. The Philippines and many other countries are, it seems, in a permanent state of economic crisis. They were before the current crisis and will remain so after the 'recovery'. Poor countries are in economic crisis whether the economic trends are positive or negative. 'The world was in an endemic phase of economic crisis; the credit crunch triggered the pandemic' is a cliché, isn't it? I don't think I understand what is happening and what will happen. I can only ask questions.

I am sometimes inhabited by a tremendous and horrifying uncertainty: what is going to happen; what will happen to my child?

I was born during the early '70s oil crisis; my child will be born during the global financial crisis. I remember the year the oil crisis hit France because I was born that year. I will remember the year the global financial crisis hit us all because my child will be born that year – the crises 'used as a date from which to reckon time, to calculate the ages of citizens or the term of men's lives'.

Independently from the crisis, I don't feel *I* am more in a crisis than before, meaning in a world in more trouble than before.

Your last letter said it is unlikely that those who have lost their optimism will find it again. I think I did. I want to ask you if you think those who have children can lose their optimism. Did Candide become a father? I cannot remember. I think he wasn't into Cunégonde in the end. After looking for her all around the world, he was greatly disappointed when he finally met her again...

My friend Frank started his first book with the following line, as if setting out the problem developed in the book's stories: 'The central dilemma is that of giving birth, of creating new life.' You probably have to be an optimist to create new life.

You say people – *beings* is the word you used – don't have a civic spirit; they only think of themselves, they are rotten, they possess too much; it is even so for the blue-collar worker who you can't feel sorry for anymore. Perhaps living in a first-world country numbs our compassion. We have become stoics.

I remember thinking like you when I was twenty and living in Paris. The repetitive demonstrations by teachers, civil servants, truck drivers, public-transport workers made me despise their causes. How dare they prevent others, us, from getting to work, getting on with our lives? How does their cause justify such an inconvenience to us? Why are their problems obstructing our lives? I thought, because I was reading Nietzsche, that the demonstrators were conspiring against those who had no problems to obtain their compassion and support. Those with problems created problems for those who didn't have any. And I resented them for this.

In *On the Genealogy of Morals* Nietzsche warns that the failed and the weak might one day inject their misery into the conscience of those who are happy and strong. One day, he says, because of the failed and the weak, we, the happy and the strong, will feel ashamed of our happiness. This is done through compassion. Compassion spreads suffering; it is a vector of unhappiness.

The first world has a Neitzschean, stoic attitude towards the poor of the third world and their suffering. It sees the third world as the weak that can undermine their happiness, wealth; in the end, their superior value.

I see in France strikers now lock up managers in factories and ransack their employers' offices. You regard the vulnerability of the French blue-collar worker as somewhat 'bourgeois' because a blue collar of the first world is not a poor or a weak being, and therefore not worthy of compassion or pity. The original vulnerability that leads them to strike is not as primal as those of the poor and weak you read about or see in the news, those without the basic resources to live, without what you might think is dignity.

It is also hard to feel sorry for people who exert violence to solve their problems. A group of angry *grévistes*, numerically superior to those who are not angry and those who are managers, storm a factory, strong by their number with blood boiling, use – abuse, to you and me – their power to take over the premises and incarcerate the managers in their offices. What do they achieve? A counter-imbalance of power. They are now too powerful and a period of status quo begins, where no just, meaningful negotiation can take place because a party is now abusing its power to oppress another.

The grévistes I am talking about not only broke criminal laws but also what you or I would consider moral laws. They are *wrong* to have behaved in such a way. We cannot feel compassion for those who do not behave morally. We cannot feel sorry for those who are angry and powerful.

We should; we often do. We feel sorry for poor, sick individuals. For vulnerability. For power that has evaporated into vulnerability. For suffering. For Nourissier.

Suffering doesn't disappear with power, though. Compassion is not something that depends on whom one directs it to; it is something innate. A disposition. One has it, in different quantities; some have more than others. (Because he considered it detrimental to those who have it, Nietzsche didn't want to have compassion; he only had pity.)

We should demonstrate compassion to those who have and are powerful. For one, power takes away freedom. Expectations are placed on the powerful with very little chance that they will meet them. The grévistes didn't keep their jobs, didn't get their indemnities. They became powerful and behaved immorally – I feel sorry for those who will spend time in jail for not appreciating how to use their power wisely.

You tell me about your death. You tell me about Nourissier. He is your powerless friend. He is not the poor stranger in the news. He is someone like you. Nourissier's predicament is soliciting your generosity, your energy, your time. He presses your hand, smiles to you gratefully, asks you to come back. His suffering assails you. And you go back every week. You expose yourself to his suffering, to some extent you share a little of it; you are compassionate. You have compassion for Nourissier and pity for the poor people in the news.

You visit Nourissier to reassure yourself, you say – but to reassure yourself of what? That the injustice of sickness inflicted upon him will not be inflicted upon you? You visit him every week, as if to say that you are not part of the injustice and horror. But you do fear his suffering; you do not desire it. You descend somewhere, I don't know where, but you go down somewhere when you visit your dying friend. Like a walk in the rain, your head is bowed and you are humble.

I went to Garbage Mountain with the thousand arms of compassion, but they were unnecessary. No one there needed compassion. No one was on their deathbed wanting to press my hand. No striker made demands. Certainly no one or nothing needed my pity. All I did by going to the mountain was reassure myself, I hope with humility.

I wish you could see the apocalyptic blackness of the clouds and the relentless force of the rain and wind. They are frightening. Exciting. I want to leave my office and walk in the powerful rain and then go to bed, wet, having been assaulted by the elements.

Will you let me take you to the gardens and temples of Kyoto after Nourissier's passing?

Love,

Xavier

Over the South China Sea, 18 May

I would like to ask you this: can noise, heat bring peace to someone?

You are lying down. You hear motorcycles – in this place there are no cars – and hundreds of other noises. Motorcycles backfire. You hear the cries of daily activities. You are lying down almost naked in a small, dark and humid room. It is very hot. There is a ceiling fan that is shuffling the hot and humid air. You are stuck to your bed by sweat. A book is open on your stomach, like a small tent. In this torpor, you doze off. You are resting. You are at peace. If by whatever magic all the noises were to stop, you would wake up in extreme panic.

X

Xavier Hennekinne lives in Manila where he works for an inter-governmental humanitarian organisation and occasionally lectures on forced migration. His essay 'In the eye of the beholder' was published in *Griffith REVIEW 18: In the Neighbourhood*.

FICTION

WHO'S THAT DANCING WITH MY MOTHER?

LLOYD JONES

WE were living in Napier at the time. My father pulled the keys down from the hook in the kitchen and my mother asked where he was headed.

'Up the coast,' he said, and my mother went on slicing the ends off the beans for the meal she now knew he wouldn't be around to eat.

'Allie,' my father said by the kitchen door. 'I feel like being alone for a while.'

My mother quietly emptied the colander of beans into the sink. She turned around to face us both.

'Just say where it is you are going.'

My father looked at the keys in his hand, and turned down the challenge. He crossed the lawn to the Hunter parked in the driveway. My mother followed as far as the porch. There she stopped, as if the lawn was a slippery area she would rather not cross, and yelled out, 'Why can't you say it, you lousy stinking coward!' My father settled behind the wheel and backed down the driveway. My mother raised her hands to her face. Then she noticed me; and that seemed to be the last straw.

'What are you looking at…goddamnit!'

From being hurt, she wanted to be forgiven. It was a confusing moment. Her face screwed up with anger, and she drew me over and said, 'Hug your mother, Charlie.' I was happy to, of course, but when I looked I noticed she had drawn herself into two parts: one I hugged, and the other – her proud face – had already turned with a thought to something inside the house.

I followed her inside, through to the living room. She walked directly to the bookcase, where she pulled out a thick book on flora. Most of our books were on plants, lichen and mosses. My father worked in the ecology division of the DSIR.

The book fell open, and the photo of my father fell out. It was taken near the snowline. There was no snow in the photo but you could tell from the rocks and the lichen grown over them that snow was not far off. My father had on his hiking boots. His arm was draped around a woman, an Australian. She was a plant illustrator, who had come here for dinner one night, a long time ago.

My mother studied the photo. She seemed to be trying to prise a bit more from it than the contents were prepared to tell. I couldn't say what she found. Perhaps it was because the photo was deliberately vague that she got so angry. She tore the photo into quarters and watched them settle over the carpet. My father's head was now severed, his whiskery smile even more of a mystery.

My mother stepped back and almost fell over. She had forgotten I was there. She swore, then smiled bravely. 'Know what we're going to do, Charlie? No. Second thoughts, I'm not going to tell you. Let's make it a surprise.'

Our town held few surprises, although it was useful to pretend otherwise. I was just as happy not knowing in any case, because we ended up at Chee's.

SOME OF THE pub crowd had wandered across the road and were trying to chat up the Chinese girl behind the counter. The girl blushed and smiled out of politeness, but you could see she didn't know what the men were on about, and I thought it just as well.

We took the table by the window. Cars were leaving spaces outside the hotel. One of the men at the counter came over and sat at our table. 'Hello, beautiful,' he said.

My mother turned and looked straight into his face the way it is said to be cruel to do with dogs. The man said 'Jeeesus,' and got up as quickly as he had sat down. Our meals arrived. My mother hardly touched her fillet.

She counted out the money on the table. She had enough, clearly more than she had thought, because she appeared to be relieved.

'Now is the real surprise,' she said, and we started toward the beach.

The sea breeze was on the way out and the leaves in the trees along the esplanade had stopped rustling. It was growing dark, and sure enough the storm clouds were bunched inland over the ranges.

'I feel like dancing,' my mother announced. She looked at me, then burst out laughing. We walked briskly. The music from the roller-skating rink grew louder, and my mother pulled the sides of her cardigan to cover her chest. We could hear Cadillac Jack trying to hustle the crowd onto the rink. He spoke in rhyming couplets, so my mother said, and word had it he was brother of a famous American DJ. My mother always said it was worth believing anything so long as it wasn't harmful. So little happened around here, anyway.

My mother fussed over the skates like they were vegetables from the cheap bin.

She glided out onto the rink. She did a lap. Her lips were pursed, kind of hard-looking without lipstick. She usually wore lipstick when she went out. Her eyes were concentrated, as if trying to find a way back to some partially lost feeling. She came down off the high shoulder at the beach end and overtook a bunch of kids from the high school. You could easily be fooled, but if you forgot the rest of her and watched the skates you saw she was in complete control.

The third or fourth lap she came soaring down and picked me off the rail. 'Push off your toes, Charlie. Push. Push. You're much too stiff.'

She glided out ahead, and started to do a goose-step, holding one skate out front about knee height and alternating with the other. She came past the crowd and turned the heads on half a dozen cowboys. Her face glowed. She knew what she had done. She took off her white cardigan and tied it about her waist. Some of the slower skaters moved out of her way and found the sides as she barrelled down the straight past the hotdog stand. Cadillac, inside his glass dome, let go a ginormous *hoooeeee*. My mother went into a speed crouch and shot up high on the end bend.

Just short of the cowboys, a guy in black jeans and a bush shirt tied at the throat with a length of string pushed off the wall. There were twenty metres in which to decide whether she would go around him. He held his hand out like a ballroom dancer. My mother dug in the toe of her back skate. The stranger's hand collected her around the waist; she spun around once, then again, this time under her own steam to show she enjoyed it.

They pushed off together. The cowboy holding her hand, and my mother bothered by a strand of damp hair that kept falling across her face.

I had stopped trying to skate. I leant against the rail in front of some spectators. I was wondering where my father was right at this moment. What he was doing. And what kind of person the Australian woman might be getting to know. I suppose I had taken over my mother's thoughts for the time being – caretaking while she skated.

My mother and her partner seemed none the wiser that a lot of attention was on them. The people behind me had begun to mutter. Something about the 'prison escaper'. Cadillac had gone quiet.

At the town end of the rink they rose together up the shoulder; the escaper hoisted my mother into the air. She threw her head back and used one leg to clamp his shoulder; the other leg she clasped behind the knee and held it straight out in front. In this formation they swept down off the bend. By the hotdog stand some of the pub crowd began to clap. I caught a glimpse of the escaper's face: it appeared caught halfway between a big loony grin and serious concern.

'I thought he had gone bush forever and a day,' a voice said behind me.

Somebody else said he had slipped out of the bush this morning. 'Robbie Hale seen him sniffing on the edge of town at daybreak.'

This time, as the skaters came barrelling down the straight before the crowd, my mother threw her head all the way back until her skates were over the escaper's head, which brought a gasp from the crowd. Then she brought her skates overtop, as if she were doing a backward roll. Over she went until her skates touched the rink. The escaper reached between his legs and drew her through until my mother was the lead skater. She turned to face him now, and he lifted her so she had her legs splayed either side of him and they were joined at the waist. People had stopped talking and were just staring. My mother's head was tossed back and she held onto the escaper's shoulders. She started to move up and down with her hips. Neither of them seemed concerned for skate speed. The escaper managed to steer them both up the end shoulder to see them down the straight. On the far side of the rink they moved through the pool of light from the overhead lamps, into shadows, then light again. My mother's face turned a fluorescent colour; now the escaper's head fell back. They were locked together in another movement that had nothing to do with skating.

I heard Cadillac come on over the PA to get more skaters onto the rink. But no one was listening. And there was no heart in the message, because Cadillac did not repeat it.

What happened next had nothing to do with Cadillac, or the crowd looking on. From the esplanade a police siren could be heard. The escaper's head turned a fraction. I believe it was the only intervention he would have heeded. He and my mother had come almost to a standstill in a shadow at the end of the rink. Some of the crowd had moved there to get a better look. The sirens were close now. My mother was lowered onto her skates. She and the escaper stood straight and near to each other, like lovers in a park.

He kissed her once – on the cheek. Then he split. He pushed off and was nearly in a speed crouch when he passed me.

I heard someone bitch that the escaper hadn't returned his skates. 'Typical,' from someone else.

He leapt the turnstile for the esplanade and skated through the first set of lights. One violation after another, cast behind like discarded clothing.

My mother was buttoning her cardigan, as if it was the most important thing in the world. Her cheeks were still flushed. She knew I was nearby, but she looked up in her own good time. She said, 'You enjoying yourself, Charlie? Not too much, I hope, because I feel like going home now.'

The drunks near the hotdog stand called out things, but she took no notice. 'Look at that, Charlie,' she said, and very deliberately she pointed over the heads of the cowboys, to a fairly ordinary sunset.

While we were getting out of our skates Cadillac came out of his glass dome. I had never actually seen him. He had a pointed beard – like the famous record-spinner – but he only just cleared the top of my head. He looked frightened, and in a quiet voice I never imagined

267

might be his he said the police had sent through word that they wished to speak with my mother.

He mentioned the man being an escaper, and my mother, still cool as a cucumber, said, 'What, you mean that nice young man?'

Two blocks away from the skating rink she permitted herself to say something, and I realised she was shaking like a leaf.

'I feel like singing,' she said to the trees. Then she stole a quick look at me. 'Charlie, you're not angry with me. Are you, Charlie? Don't be. I haven't skated like that for years.'

We came to our street and from here we should have been able to see the house lights. The car wasn't in the driveway, and I worried that it would have some effect. But she didn't appear to notice. Or, if she did, she didn't care. At the door she said she thought she might have a bath. As it happened we pushed through to the living room, where her eyes went straight to the torn quarters of the photograph. She crossed her arms, and thought.

'Charlie,' she said. 'Go get that glue from the top of the fridge. Let's not disappoint your father.'

Lloyd Jones is a Wellington-based writer with several novels to his name: *Mister Pip* (Text, 2008), which won the 2007 Commonwealth Writers' Prize and was shortlisted for the 2007 Man Booker Prize; *The Book of Fame* (Penguin, 2000); and *Here at the End of the World We Learn to Dance* (Penguin, 2000), among others. 'Who's that dancing with my mother?' is from *The Man in the Shed*, a selection of stories due to be published by Text in September.

Julie Catt

has raised 6 kids on 2 continents with 2 husbands,
1 boyfriend and a pretty hot girlfriend.
Along the way, there's been the usual stuff:

grand romance, long-lost families, feral lesbians,
misspent youth, obsession, jealousy, break-up,
grave parenting errors, feminist politics, enduring friendship,
love, laughter, tears, cosmetic surgery…

This is Julie's story: the true story of an everyday family.
A little complicated maybe, but otherwise completely

The best, funniest, queerest real-life adventure
since *Running with Scissors.*

AVAILABLE
NOW IN
ALL GOOD
BOOKSHOPS

Text Publishing, Melbourne Australia
WWW.TEXTPUBLISHING.COM.AU

The long-awaited history that will change the way
Australians think about their country

'Both rollicking yarn and scholarly essay, this
wonderful book offers an archaeology of our national
psyche. With vivid imagery, irreverent wit and
penetrating insight, Michael Cathcart exposes the
cultural forces that still powerfully shape our plans
for this land. *The Water Dreamers* is exhilarating to
read—intelligent, wry and compelling.'
TOM GRIFFITHS

AVAILABLE
NOW IN
ALL GOOD
BOOKSHOPS

Text Publishing, Melbourne Australia
WWW.TEXTPUBLISHING.COM.AU

Save 20% with a 1 or 2 Year Subscription plus receive a FREE copy of a past edition of your choice*

☐ I would like to subscribe   ☐ I wish to give a subscription to: (please tick ✓ one)

Name: _____

Address: _____

_____ Postcode: _____

Email:_____ Telephone: _____

Please choose your subscription package (please tick ✓ one below)

☐ 1 year within Australia: $80.00 (inc gst)   ☐ 2 years within Australia: $150.00 (inc gst)

☐ 1 year outside Australia: $130.00 AUD   ☐ 2 years outside Australia: $250.00 AUD

I wish the subscription to begin with (please tick ✓ one below)

☐ CURRENT EDITION†   ☐ NEXT EDITION

For my FREE copy, please send it to ☐ me   ☐ my gift recipient (please tick ✓ one)

EDITION TITLE* _____

Select from past editions at www.griffithreview.com *While past edition copies remain in stock.

PAYMENT DETAILS

Purchaser's Address (if not the subscription recipient):

_____ Postcode: _____

Email:_____ Telephone: _____

☐ I have enclosed a cheque/money order for $_____ made payable
to **Griffith REVIEW** (Payable in Australian Dollars only)

☐ **Card Type (please circle one):** Bankcard / Mastercard / Visa / Amex

Card Number: ☐☐☐☐ ☐☐☐☐ ☐☐☐☐ ☐☐☐☐

Expiry Date: __ __ / __ __

Cardholder name: _____

Cardholder Signature:_____

▶ **MAIL TO:**
Business Manager - Griffith REVIEW
REPLY PAID 61015
NATHAN QLD 4111 Australia

▶ **FAX TO:**
Business Manager - Griffith REVIEW
07 3735 3272 (*within Australia*)
+61 7 3735 3272 (*International*)

● The details given above will only be used for the subscription collection and distribution of Griffith REVIEW and will not be passed to a third party for other uses. For further information consult Griffith University's Privacy Plan at www.griffith.edu.au/ua/aa/vc/pp ● † Current Edition only available for subscriptions received up until 2 weeks before Next Edition release date. See www.griffithreview.com for release dates.